Revolutionary Currents

18. 99

Revolutionary Currents

Nation Building in the Transatlantic World

Edited by
Michael A. Morrison and
Melinda Zook

A Madison House Book

ROWMAN & LITTLEFIELD PUBLISHERS, INC.
Lanham • *Boulder* • *New York* • *Toronto* • *Oxford*

ROWMAN & LITTLEFIELD PUBLISHERS, INC.

Published in the United States of America
by Rowman & Littlefield Publishers, Inc.
A wholly owned subsidary of The Rowman & Littlefield Publishing Group, Inc.
4501 Forbes Boulevard, Suite 200, Lanham, Maryland 20706
www.rowmanlittlefield.com

PO Box 317
Oxford
OX2 9RU, UK

British Library Cataloguing in Publication Information Available

Library of Congress Cataloging-in-Publication Data

Revolutionary currents : nation building in the transatlantic world / edited by Michael
Morrison and Melinda Zook.
    p. cm.
    Chiefly revisions of papers from a symposium on transatlantic revolutionary traditions
sponsored by the Dept. of History at Purdue University.
    Includes bibliographical references.
    ISBN 0-7425-2164-8 (alk. paper)—ISBN 0-7425-2165-6 (pbk. : alk. paper)
    1. Revolutions—History—18th century—Congresses. 2. Revolutions—History—19th
century—Congresses. 3. History, Modern—18th century—Congresses. 4. History, Modern—
19th century—Congresses. I. Morrison, Michael A., 1948– II. Zook, Melinda S. III. Purdue
University. Dept. of History.
    D295.R48 2004
    303.6'4'09034—dc22   2003020291

Printed in the United States of America

♾™ The paper used in this publication meets the minimum requirements of American
National Standard for Information Sciences—Permanence of Paper for Printed Library
Materials, ANSI/NISO Z39.48-1992.

CONTENTS

PREFACE

The chapters in this volume originated in and developed from a symposium on "Transatlantic Revolutionary Traditions," sponsored by the Department of History and Purdue University. Four distinguished scholars were invited to speak on the national traditions, global crosscurrents, and ideologies that inspired modern revolutions on both sides of the Atlantic in the eighteenth and nineteenth centuries. Lois G. Schwoerer analyzes the formation and substance of the English "jury ideology," its importance preceding and during the Glorious Revolution of 1688–1689, and ultimately its transition to the British North American colonies. John M. Murrin, taking note of this and other political traditions inherited from England, examines the series of imperial conflicts that issued in the American Revolution, which itself ran against all the integrative tendencies of the eighteenth century. In stark contrast to what Murrin calls the "countercyclical" nature of the American Revolution, William H. Sewell Jr. stresses the profound influence of the French Revolution on the history of the nation-state. Though like the American Revolution it produced a republican political regime, upheaval in France and the revolutionary French government that emerged from it was more unitary and integrated under a central state than was the United States. Eric Van Young's analysis of the Mexican War of Independence demonstrates how the motives of the revolutionary Creole elite and its indigenous followers both complemented one another but also diverged in very significant ways. Issues of race and class problematized the revolutions in Mexico and attenuated those movements from the broader Atlantic revolutionary tradition.

This one-day transatlantic symposium generated so much intellectual excitement that the Department of History subsequently invited Jack P. Greene to contextualize, expound, and expand on the specific arguments and broad integrative themes raised in the original papers. His contribution to this volume focuses on the structures and tensions within early modern states and empires and the emergence of revolutionary movements in the Atlantic world from the sixteenth to the early nineteenth centuries. Broad in scope and inclusive of the original essays, it forms the introduction to this volume. Peter Onuf has the final word. His concluding chapter discusses the idea of the "nation" and how in our postmodern world we have come to envision it as a historical contingency. He too assesses the chapters on their own merits and, more critically, evaluates how each contributes to contemporary debates about nationhood and the future of world governmental structures.

Separately and together, the chapters in this volume respond to three historiographical trends: an older, venerable interest in revolutionary ideology; a newer concern with transatlantic cross-fertilization of ideas, models, and traditions; and a very recent focus on state formation, nation building, and nationalism. *Revolutionary Currents* is unique in that it addresses and contributes to all three of these areas of interest. As Peter Onuf reminds us, scholars are only beginning to offer a suggestive array of explanations for the emergence of the nation and nationalism. We now speak of the patriotic founders of new nations in the Age of Democratic Revolution as having "invented traditions" and "imagined communities." The nation, we now understand, is a social construction imagined historically in the same way that concepts such as class or gender are invented. But such inventions never broke wholly with past traditions. They were often inspired by long-cherished foundation mythologies, such as France's Gallic constitution or England's inheritance of Saxon liberties, as well as by influences outside national boundaries. In the Age of Democratic Revolution, countries on both sides of the Atlantic were linked together in a common revolutionary dynamic that oscillated back and forth. What this volume begins to answer is how each nation reshaped these revolutionary traditions, making them their own, and in what form they were exported once again.

Each of the original contributors was asked to revise her or his essay in light of the others. Thus, readers will discover that there is an internal exchange among the four scholars that is at times explicitly undertaken in the text and at other points continued within the notes to it. The volume, therefore, works at two levels. The first and most basic is to provide readers with the central impetus and intellectual dynamics of four similar yet disparate revolutions that spanned the late seventeenth to the early nineteenth centuries as well as the Atlantic world. They also invite readers to engage, reflect on, and contribute their own thoughts to the dialogue among the chapter authors. Scholars and students in history, political science, and literature interested in the emergence of nations, nationalism, and national identity will have much to ponder and profit from this volume.

Although time has passed from the first symposium to the publication of these chapters, our gratitude for the efforts of others has not flagged. The editors would like to acknowledge those who gave guidance and assistance along the way. In particular, we would like to thank our colleagues in the Department of History at Purdue University who helped recruit the contributors and host the symposia. We are especially grateful to Charles R. Cutter, Ariel E. de la Fuente, Frank Lambert, John L. Larson, James R. Farr, Michael G. Smith, and A. Whitney Walton. Thanks go as well to Professors John J. Contreni and Gordon Mork, who, as successive heads of the Department of History, encouraged and supported this effort.

STATE FORMATION, F
THE CREATION OF F
TRADITIONS IN THE EARLY MODERN ERA

Jack P. Greene

I

The chapters in *Revolutionary Currents* seem to have been a response to two historiographical trends: an older interest in revolutionary ideology and a newer interest in the transoceanic context of historical developments around the Atlantic rim. Particularly evident in the English-speaking world and stimulated by the pioneering works of Bernard Bailyn, Gordon S. Wood, J. G. A. Pocock, and many students of early modern and Enlightenment political thought, the interest in revolutionary ideology has, over the past thirty years, generated a vast, if relatively narrowly focused, literature on the conflicting ideologies used to sustain—or explain—the revolutionary and nation-building projects from the late seventeenth through the early nineteenth centuries. Dating back at least as far as R. R. Palmer's seminal transatlantic comparative studies in the 1950s and 1960s of late eighteenth-century revolutions in North America and Europe, the rising interest in Atlantic studies calls attention to the possibilities for comparative studies and the interconnectedness of developments within the larger Atlantic world.

But there is still a third historiography that is relevant to understanding the emergence and character of revolutionary traditions in the early modern world: the historiography growing out of the new literature on state formation and, to a lesser extent, nation building that began to appear in the early 1990s and continues to proliferate. By showing that the unitary nation-state was principally a development of the nineteenth and twentieth centuries, this historiography has called attention to the *premodern* character of early modern states and empires, to the structural tensions inherent in them, and to the relationship between those tensions and the emergence of "revolutionary" movements in the Atlantic world between the mid-sixteenth and the early nineteenth centuries and to the traditions that both informed and grew out of them. This chapter focuses principally on these subjects. What the nature of state and empire should be, it suggests, was the principal underlying issue that linked together all early modern "revolutions" and the traditions associated with them.

II

That early modern polities differed radically from modern states is perhaps the central conclusion of the recent literature on state formation. As Charles Tilly and other contributors to this literature have shown, the organization of Europe into "a small number of unitary and integrated nations states" is relatively recent. "It took a long time," Tilly writes, "for national states—relatively centralized, differentiated, and autonomous organizations successfully claiming priority in the use of force within large, contiguous, and clearly defined territories—to dominate the European map."[1] In 1490, on the eve of Europe's expansion across the Atlantic, "Europe's political structure," as Mark Greengrass notes, was still "dominated by a multiplicity of regional political entities," just under 500 in all, with "a rich variety of [political and constitutional] traditions." These included "large old-established states, new principalities, dynastic empires, city states, confederations"; the Holy Roman Empire, representing "the ideal of universal world monarchy"; and the papacy, claiming worldwide spiritual and temporal jurisdiction.[2]

The process of state building during the early modern era resulted in the creation of the first large nation-states in Portugal, England, Spain, France, Sweden, and the Netherlands. It proceeded in two ways—either through *voluntary agreements*, such as dynastic marriages or defensive confederations or, much more rarely, through *conquest*; and it took two principal forms—either *amalgamation*, as happened with Spain, or *incorporation*, as was the case in England (with regard to Cornwall and Wales) and France (with regard to Toulouse, Champagne, Brittany, Gascony, Burgundy, and Flanders). As yet, monarchs lacked the fiscal resources necessary to achieve centralized and integrated polities through either coercive or administrative means. For this reason, coalescence, however it happened and whatever its form, invariably involved negotiation, or what Tilly has

2

called bargaining "between the crown and the ruling class[es] of their different provinces." As J. H. Elliott explains, the arrangements worked out through these negotiations almost always, even in cases of conquest, ensured the survival of provincial "customary laws and institutions," permitted "a high degree of continuing local self-government," and left considerable authority in the hands of local magnates.[3] "The effectiveness of any pre-modern regime," John Miller observes, "depended as much on the subject's acceptance as on the monarch's power of coercion."[4] The result was a system of "composite monarchies" or "multinational states" in which, notes H. G. Koenigsberger, the "constituent parts . . . always antedated their union" and "therefore had different laws, rights, privileges, and traditions." "With this multiplicity of jurisdictions," writes Miller, "went a multiplicity of laws, especially in those areas, mainly in the northern half of Europe, where law was based on custom." By this system, observes Koenigsberger, "a prince could add province after province, kingdom after kingdom to his realm and rule each as its own prince under different laws, and with varying powers."[5]

These new national entities involved some concentration of power in agencies of the central state but also left considerable authority with the principal holders of power in the peripheries. "Peaceful coexistence," notes Koenigsberger, "depended on the king, who resided in the bigger kingdom, governing [each] . . . smaller one in the way it had been used to, that is respecting the rights of its ruling elite, especially in the matter of religion, and, in the absence of an effective civil service," acknowledging the country's privilege of *jus indigenatus*, by which only natives of the province could be appointed to public office, and "running the country with that elite's advice and cooperation."[6] To paraphrase Elliott, these composite states were thus founded on mutual compacts between the prince and the ruling class of each of his (or her) different provinces, compacts that displayed "a profound respect for [existing] corporate structure[s] and for traditional [provincial] rights, privileges and customs."[7]

Nor did this "dispersal of authority" stop at the provincial level. Within the several components of most early modern colonies, the principal magnates also had to negotiate the terms of their governance with various local jurisdictions and corporate groups—with regions, towns, communities, and other organized social, economic, and religious groups and institutions. In such negotiations, these corporate and territorial bodies effectively traded allegiance and resources for corporate privileges that guaranteed them extensive rights of self-government within their respective spheres.[8]

By thus ensuring that each province enjoyed its "existing privileges" and a large "measure of self-government," this widespread distribution of authority, Elliot writes, left local power holders "without any urgent need to challenge the status quo" and thereby "gave even the most arbitrary and artificial unions a certain stability and resilience."[9] In the absence of a well-developed conception of unitary sovereignty before the middle of the seventeenth century, composite monarchies were thus characterized by indirect rule, consultation, and, at least initially, fragmented sovereignty.

Especially in the conditions that obtained throughout most of the early modern era, this type of polity contained a fundamental structural weakness. This weakness lay in a built-in tension between centripetal impulses toward centralization and centrifugal tendencies toward localism. For princes confronted with major challenges to their regimes, including war and religious dissent, the loose and decentralized character of early modern polities posed a major problem. Whether they were offensive in pursuit of dynastic, territorial, or religious ambitions or defensive, wars were ubiquitous from the late fifteenth century through the early nineteenth century, and the steady increase in the cost and scale of warfare required vast fiscal resources for which princes had to seek the consent of statewide or provincial representative bodies. If the emerging nation-states of Europe "were still marginal to their domestic social [and political] environments," the Dutch historian Marjolein C. t'Hart writes, they were nevertheless centralized when it came to making wars.[10]

Confronted with the need to mobilize more and more men, ships, and other war materials, princes became increasingly impatient with the local-mindedness and the provincialism of local magistrates and provincial estates and scornful of the various systems of local law, privileges, rights, and constitutions that required the consent of local bodies for all taxes. They responded to this situation by endeavoring to find ways to enhance royal authority and to subordinate or bypass the hodgepodge of local and representative institutions that prevented their efficient acquisition of needed resources. Moving powerfully in the direction of trying to achieve "a more unitary state structure, with union conceived [of] primarily in terms of uniformity of religion, laws and taxation," writes Miller, they came more and more to regard the "institutional and legal diversity" that was characteristic of early modern composite states as "an intolerable impediment" to their "plans to maximize resources and ensure the military co-operation" of all the constituent parts of their polities.[11]

As an ideological justification for these efforts, princes and their spokesmen elaborated an ideology of what would later be called "absolutism." This emerging ideology stressed the superiority of the monarch or prince. Drawing on an analogy between state and family, it emphasized the monarch's or prince's role as patriarch and his duties as defender of the polities over which he reigned, duties that required him to override the particular privileges and interests of the several component parts and representative institutions of the state, in favor of the security and welfare of the state as a whole. This ideology further stressed the religious dimensions of kingship, elaborating the old concept of the divine right of kings and the godly origins of monarchical power to provide the prince with an authority transcending that of the customary constitutions and local privileges that were the essence of the early modern composite state.[12]

"Hampered," in the words of Miller, "by poor communication, insufficient financial resources," a "personnel limited in numbers and proficiency," a "view of office as private property," and a "well-entrenched habit of putting local interests first," advocates of "a more unitary state structure" everywhere encountered considerable resistance and made little headway in their projects, and, as the centralizing activities of the state provoked widespread fear for the loss of national, provincial, and local liberties, local authorities became increasingly proficient in the "techniques of evasion, obstruction, and manipulation." Subordinate kingdoms and provinces and, where they existed, statewide representative institutions alike regarded any steps toward the enhancement of central authority as *innovations* and, as Elliott writes, "scrutinized every move by royal officials which might be interpreted as a violation of their laws" and sought to amplify and fortify "their constitutional defenses whenever possible."[13]

In an effort to provide protection against such intrusions of central power, jurists and other representatives of "the dominant social and vocational groups" in states and provinces—"nobles and gentry, urban patriciates, the lawyers, the clergy, the educated"—threw themselves into projects for "rediscovering or inventing customary laws and constitutions." In turn, these projects stimulated an enormous "enthusiasm" for "legal and historical research" and gave rise to a substantial increase "of interest in the customary law," an interest symbolized by the works of van Wesembeeke in the Netherlands, Bodin and Hotman in France, and Coke in England. Such works "not only provided new defences against arbitrary power . . . but also helped to establish the idea that each nation [or each subordinate kingdom or province] had a distinct historical and constitutional identity," an identity "founded on history, law[,] and achievement, on the sharing of certain common experiences and certain common patterns of life and behaviour." The result of this linking of ancient privilege with national and provincial identity was "a new sophistication and a new awareness" of the constitutional foundations of the community, an enhanced emphasis on the "constitutional and contractual character" of the polity, and a far more determined insistence on the importance of retaining those communal rights and liberties that, embodied in statutes, customary laws, charters, and written and unwritten constitutions and "kept alive in the corporate memory," everywhere provided the essence of the distinctive identities of states and provinces.[14]

As Elliott points out, the "corporate or national constitutionalism" on which these identities were based could "provide both a program for action and theoretical justification for movements of [resistance and] revolt." In several instances during the sixteenth and seventeenth centuries, in the 1560s and 1570s in the Netherlands and in the 1630s and 1640s in Spain, France, and England, exponents of this ideology of constitutionalism, anxious over repeated infringements of their rights and liberties, believing the historical identities of their corporate or national communities to be in jeopardy and expressing their discontent through their representative institutions, eventually, in response to the monarch's efforts to override their liberties, whether through the suppression of religious dissent or through new and "illegal" fiscal exactions or both, withdrew their allegiance and led large-scale revolts or revolutions.[15]

In these events, opponents of centralization were not much concerned with either structural innovations in the state or explicit projects of nation building. Anxiety about the preservation of the old constitutional order sometimes stretched downward into the lower social orders, and these early modern revolts occasionally generated popular movements demanding abolition of existing aristocratic or corporate privileges, but they mostly remained firmly under the direction of the dominant power holders in the state. Similarly, although these power holders almost always spoke in terms of the defense of the ancient rights, liberties, and constitutions of their *patrias*, or fatherlands, they were relatively little concerned with creating or consolidating the nation, defined as those who shared a broad sense of commonality and patriotism as members of the same territorial, linguistic, or political entity. Students of the emergence of early modern states are careful to distinguish between *state formation* and *nation building*, insisting that while these two processes may coincide, they are separate and analytically distinct, the latter often being the unintended consequence of conflicts over the former. In any case, as Elliott noted almost thirty years ago, the "concept of *patria* was hesitant and uncertain in sixteenth- and seventeenth-century Europe. The word was probably more often used" to refer to "a local than a national community; and, insofar as it betokened a national community, its command over loyalties was insecure." A focus on the *patria* was most prominent in those separatist revolts that occurred in polities—Scotland, Catalonia, and Portugal—with long and relatively recent experiences as "historical, national, and legal entities" that had always been suspicious of the intentions of the dominant partner in the composite monarchies to which they belonged.[16]

Leaders of early modern revolts were, rather, in Elliott's words, "obsessed by *renovation*—by the desire to return to old customs and privileges, and to an old order of society." Their principal objective was the preservation of a constitutional heritage against the demands of the central state as represented by the monarch and his ministers. This heritage was sometimes closely tied to religious, linguistic, or ethnic commonalities, but, Elliot insists, it invariably "outweighed every other cause, including that of religion, in its appeal to the majority of the ruling nation." In early modern Europe, revolts "originally sparked by religious protest, or sectional discontents" usually coalesced around an ideology of "the constitutionalism of the privileged classes."[17]

III

This general pattern can be seen in all the great revolts and revolutions of sixteenth- and seventeenth-century Europe. The Netherland Revolt in the 1560s and 1570s, arguably the first of the great revolutions, provides a case in point. The Netherlands consisted of seventeen distinct provinces that, though under the jurisdiction of the Habsburg monarchy, had no formal union until 1548–1549, when they began to meet together in a common

Estates General. Each province was essentially self-governing, and most had their own provincial representative assemblies. Many town and local corporations enjoyed further self-governing privileges founded on "a diversity of charters acquired or extorted by cities, guilds, crafts, clergy and nobility from [the] imperial princes, vassals, dukes and counts, who had ruled the Netherlands during the late medieval period." As Martin van Gelderen writes, these privileges—provincial, local, and corporate—both "restricted central power" and supported "claims to participation in the decision-making process" on the part of the "provinces, towns and inhabitants of the low countries."[18]

When King Philip II of Spain became monarch of these provinces in the 1560s, he was appalled by their fissiparous autonomy as well as their religious heterodoxy and regarded the Estates General and the provincial estates as serious threats to royal power. In the 1560s, he and his military governor, the Duke of Alba, provoked "a spirit of opposition in the provinces by pursuing to their logical conclusion" his "fiercely orthodox religious" policies, which he endeavored to enforce with a special inquisition. Considering "the growing activities of the inquisitors an important threat to their autonomy and privileges," especially to the individual's "right to be put on trial only by the Court of Aldermen in one's own town," many Low Country provinces and localities vigorously opposed these measures. In the 1570s, Philip II and his representatives further inflamed local notables and representative bodies by proposing a series of new taxes, and the Estates General and provincial estates, knowing that he could levy no taxes without their consent and fully "conscious of their fiscal and institutional strength, rallied behind the great nobles of the realm in a national campaign against" these measures. During the succeeding struggle, the large provinces of Holland and Zeeland, in 1572, "launched a Revolt that gained the support of five other northern provinces and eventually culminated in" the abjuration of the king in 1581, the achievement of de facto independence from Spain in the 1590s, and, by the Treaty of Westphalia in 1648, Spain's eventual "recognition of the United Provinces, or Dutch Republic, as an independent nation."[19]

The "defence of local privilege against the encroachments of the new central power" was thus, in Geoffrey Parker's words, "the mainspring" of the Dutch Revolt. The "threat to their corporate 'liberties' posed by the 'novelties' introduced by Philip II and his ministers"—the "Spanish garrisons, the control of policy" by the king's minions, the "rigorous persecution of heretics by a special inquisition," and the threat of new taxes—drew together the "various provinces, and the different social groups within them." The same threats produced a rich literature of protest. In pamphlet after pamphlet, van Gelderen explains, opponents of Philip II elaborated a complex ideology of resistance. Arguing that "the Dutch people . . . had esteemed . . . and cherished liberty throughout the centuries," they contended that the Dutch political order "had originally been created with the deliberate aim of protecting liberty," an objective that had been achieved "by means of a constitutional framework consisting of a set of fundamental laws[;] the privileges, rights, freedoms and old customs" of the provinces, towns, and other corporate bodies; "and a number of institutions, in particular the States," that served as guardians of this ancient constitutional inheritance. In their view, the Dutch "value *par excellence*" was liberty, "the 'daughter of the Netherlands,' the source of prosperity and justice," and they over and over again emphasized "the intrinsic connection between the liberty of the country and the personal liberty and welfare of the inhabitants."[20]

This ideology of revolt stressed the common constitutional traditions of the Dutch provinces and the virtues of uniting against the centralizing ambitions of Philip II, and it appealed to the "instinctive antipathy to outsiders" that animated other provincial revolts against the center in early modern Europe. The Dutch Revolt led to the establishment of a national republic with a national parliamentary regime centered on the Estates General in The Hague; nevertheless, it did little to stimulate a sense of national consciousness. "The Dutch Republic was only weakly integrated," and national feeling remained "quite problematic." Because all the "'privileges' or 'liberties' of each town and province" pre-dated the state, "local loyalties were . . . tenaciously defended," and "particularism was more potent than patriotism." Indeed, in the Low Countries, the revolt seems actually to have "reinforced centrifugal tendencies, reviving the powers and privileges of former communities" and thus "intensifying borders and boundaries that made it extremely difficult to 'think' of the Dutch as a nation." Nor did this situation of "cultural fragmentation" change quickly. "Despite many long and expensive wars, despite a hegemonic position in the world of the seventeenth century, and despite advanced methods in military organisation and finance," t'Hart writes, The Hague imposed "no powerful structures" on the provinces, and until the French Revolution the Netherlands remained a loosely organized federal republican state.[21]

The abortive revolts known as the Fronde in mid-seventeenth-century France followed a similar trajectory and generated a similar ideology.

Although France may have been the most successfully absolutist state in seventeenth-century Europe, it remained a composite monarchy in which the crown shared power widely with "princely and ducal families at court and in the provinces," with "representative estates on the *pay d'états*," with "municipal councils and guilds in the towns," with "*seigneurs* in the countryside," with "the church throughout the kingdom," and with the "financiers who kept the monarchy solvent." When, on the assumption that France was a unified state, Cardinal Mazarin acted "arbitrarily" and "illegally" without consultation, local power holders charged the ministers with "illegal [constitutional] innovations." Citing law, "privilege, tradition and numerous precedents to justify their" resistance, they insisted that, if ministers would "return to traditional ways of governing, all would be well."[22]

IV

The great revolutions that occurred in England during the seventeenth century, the revolution associated with the English Civil War and Interregnum in the 1640s and 1650s, and the Glorious Revolution of 1688–1689 represent a significant variation on the pattern exhibited in the Dutch Revolt, the Fronde, and several revolts that occurred in the Spanish monarchy in Catalonia, Portugal, Sicily, and Naples in the 1640s, of which only the Portuguese was successful. In contrast to the Netherlands, France, and Spain, England had already under the Tudors developed many of the political, administrative, social, and cultural institutions characteristic of a unified national state. As John Morrill observes, "Thomas Cromwell's work in the 1530s created the 'unitary realm' of England, with the incorporation of the Palatinates, the extinction of [many local provincial] liberties, the establishment of the ubiquitous royal writs, the establishment both of a veritable conciliar argus at the centre of government and of the characteristic institutions that replaced the noble household by the county courts and administrative offices where government business was effected. The reforms of 1536–1543 both systematized and standardized the legal and social institutions of Cambrian Englishries and Welshries alike and also made Wales part of England for all purposes of government."[23] Through these measures, Morrill notes, Tudor monarchs had been able to expand "the crown's functions and powers" and to achieve "many of the aims of absolutism—

above all the mobilisation and resources for war—without recourse to authoritarian methods and [without] sacrifice of traditional liberties of local self-government."[24]

But the Stuarts, who succeeded to the English throne in 1603, had a much more "authoritarian view of monarchy." Drawing on and contributing to the emerging body of absolutist thought, they and their ministers emphasized the divinity of kingship, the superiority of the royal prerogative over constitutional privileges and liberties, and the preeminence of necessities of state in the conduct of the state. They made much more extensive use of prerogative courts, including especially the Court of Star Chamber, than had their predecessors and imprisoned people without due process of law. Endeavoring to "break out of the financial straightjacket imposed by the need to seek Parliamentary consent to taxation," they "exacted money without Parliament's consent." While their use of prerogative courts "seemed to threaten personal liberty," writes Miller, their efforts to raise money appeared "to threaten the future of Parliament."[25]

As Stuart spokesmen sought to justify such expansions of royal power, English jurists and other political leaders and writers appealed, like their Dutch counterparts some decades earlier, to "ancient" political and constitutional traditions. In the process, they elaborated what scholars have since labeled the English jurisprudential tradition of political thought, which emphasized the role of law as a restraint on the power of the Crown. By law, the exponents of this tradition meant not only the statutory law enacted by Parliament but also, more particularly, the common law, that complex bundle of customs and judicial decisions that was the product of centuries of the English legal system at work. Presumably embodying the collective wisdom of the ages, the common law was, in their view, the chief guarantor of the Englishman's celebrated right to security of life, liberty, and property through such devices as trial by jury, habeas corpus, due process of law, and representative government.

This tradition considerably antedated the English Reformation. Rooted in such older writings as Sir John Fortescue, *De Laudibus Legum Angliae* (written about 1470 and known to the English law community, though not published until 1616), it was fully elaborated during the early seventeenth century in a series of works by several of the most prominent judges and legal thinkers of the era. Most prominent among these was Chief Justice Sir Edward Coke, whose *Institutes of the Laws of England*, published in four parts in London between 1628 and 1644 and frequently reissued thereafter, became the principal foundation for the English jurisprudential tradition during the early modern era.

In an effort to erect legal and constitutional restraints that would ensure security of life, liberty, and property against extensions of royal power, these experts invented the tradition of an "ancient" English constitution, antecedent to the common law itself and finding expression through that law to which public leaders could appeal to justify an expanded governmental role by Parliament as protector of the rights of the people and guarantor of their security against arbitrary government by the Crown.[26] Despite the fact that monarchs had frequently ignored or violated it since the Norman conquest, this ancient constitution, Coke and his colleagues contended, provided the context for *legal* government in England. Composed of a variety of maxims, precedents, and principles that these writers traced back through Magna Charta to the ancient Saxon era, this ancient constitution, English jurisprudential writers said, at once served as the foundation for all governmental authority in England; confined the scope of the discretion, or "will," of the Crown within limits specified by the higher, fundamental, or natural laws it expressed; and, in particular, prevented the Crown from governing without Parliaments.

From the perspective supplied by this tradition, Charles I's entire reign seemed by 1640 to have involved "a systematic assault on English liberties and religion,"[27] and confrontations between Parliament and the king over the latter's efforts to raise taxes without Parliament's consent produced a major constitutional crisis in the English state, followed by civil war, the execution of Charles I in 1649, and the adoption of a republican regime under Oliver Cromwell. "Having taken up arms to defend the traditional order against arbitrary taxation and religious innovation," Miller writes, England's parliamentary champions eventually found "that Parliament's radical supporters (in the streets of London, in the New Model Army, among the Levellers and separatist sects)," with their proposals for electoral reform and frequent elections and their claims for popular sovereignty, also posed a formidable threat to the traditional order they claimed to be defending, a threat that, in the eyes of some, "raised the spectre of the total expropriation of the propertied by the propertyless."[28]

Fears of such a development lay behind the rapprochement with the Stuart family and the restoration of the monarchy in 1660. But reimposition of monarchy was accompanied by a renewed commitment to the consensual mode of governance for which England had long been famous. To a greater extent than the first two Stuarts, Charles II accepted the fact that his regime depended on consent, not just in Parliament but also in the localities. Not professional magistrates but "leading members of the local community, country gentlemen or urban bigwigs: much the same sort of people as sat in the Commons," enforced the laws and handled administration in the localities. With "very few professional officials in the provinces" and not many more at the center, the king had little choice but to rely on such unpaid officials to uphold the royal writ in the peripheries.[29]

When James II, a professed Catholic, succeeded to the throne in 1685 after Whigs and Dissenters had failed in a bitter campaign to exclude him from the succession in 1679–1680, his "conduct created fears of a sweeping extension of royal power and of the emasculation of the Commons." In response to their efforts, Charles II and his Tory supporters had already undertaken a variety of authoritarian measures in the early 1680s, including direct attacks on the rights of various corporations dominated by Whigs and Dissenters, including the city of London, many provincial towns, and the colonies in New England, instituting quo warranto proceedings against their charters in the court of common pleas. James II not only continued these measures but also, as Lois G. Schwoerer explains in chapter 1, intensified his brother's recent efforts to turn the courts into an instrument of the royal will by packing them with judges he could control, confining judicial tenure to the king's pleasure, and influencing jury selection. He also dispensed with laws on religion that discriminated against Catholics and Dissenters. A "much more sweeping and radical assault on the old constitution than" any of his Stuart predecessors had undertaken, James II's "misuse of law raised unpleasant echoes of the 1630s." Invoking and expanding on the still vibrant ideas of Coke and other early seventeenth-century jurisprudential thinkers, a new generation of advocates for England's ancient constitution depicted the Crown's efforts "as part of a wicked design . . . to establish absolutism" by rendering the laws uncertain and Parliament subordinate to the royal prerogative. As Schwoerer suggests, this ideology provided the justification for James's displacement during the Glorious Revolution of 1688–1689 and dictated the principal statement of revolutionary ideology, the Declaration of Rights of 1688.[30]

The Glorious Revolution thus became what Miller has called "England's definitive escape from [royal] absolutism." It put a stop to executive interference with the judiciary and the rule of law, seriously limited the Crown in its use of prerogative powers within Britain itself, and, by raising Parliament to an equivalency with the Crown, ensured that the English or, after 1707, British state would never be under the "unfettered control of the monarch." In the wholesale expansion of the fiscal–military state after 1689, Crown and Parliament would be equal partners. With "Parliament's active support, the armed forces and revenues—above all the excise—became," Miller writes, "the most technically proficient (and closely supervised) in Europe."[31]

Notwithstanding this expansion of state power, Britons yet held on to their "'negative liberties' against the state, as protected by law." Indeed, as Lawrence Stone points out, the Glorious Revolution and its aftermath in the 1690s and early 1700s effectively put a stop to most central encroachments on local authority. Both Parliament and local government remained where they had long been, "in the hands of independent-minded squires and aristocrats, most of whom were deeply suspicious of armies, resented taxation and insisted on their own control of all aspects of local government, including the mobilization of manpower and the assessing and raising of taxes. Moreover, a powerful private corporation like the East India Company acted almost like a ministate, with its own large army. "Power certainly flowed from the centre, but," Stone writes, "the flow had to pass through local, independent, channels in order to reach the population at large." In Stone's words, the eighteenth-century British state was "a uniquely decentralized political system in which local government, law enforcement, tax collection, supervision of the militia, drafts into the armed forces and so on were largely left to the discretion and loyalty of amateur local landed gentlemen and clergy, acting in their capacities as Justices of the Peace, Collectors of Taxes, Colonels of local Militia, and so on." And recent research has shown that this devolution of authority and power "increased as the century wore on, as" Parliament, by statute, shifted "more and more responsibilities . . . to local volunteer authorities." Thus did Britain manage to increase taxes and its naval and military capacities without losing "its parliamentary control of finances, its decentralized government[,] and its ideology of liberty and property." The rule of law and the traditions of legislative consent and decentralized government had survived Stuart efforts to transform the English state into a unitary state with power centered in the royal monarch.[32]

Like the Dutch Revolt of the sixteenth century, the English revolutions of the seventeenth century were thus revolutions in behalf of ancient privileges and expressive of an ideology of local corporate as well as personal rights. They reaffirmed the integrity—and even extended the jurisdictions—of the ancient localities that composed the national state and thereby produced a national political regime marked by the wide dispersal of authority that was characteristic of the early modern European state. Although they appealed to and manifested the strong sense of English national distinctiveness that, fully articulated in the generations just before the revolutions,[33] emphasized the uniqueness of the English system of law and liberty with its consensual institutions of juries and parliaments, its traditions of the subordination of the monarch to the law, and its commitment to due process of law, the English revolutions did not extend to the broader population the full rights of civic participation, and the postrevolutionary English/British state continued to be dominated by the propertied independent class. For this reason, the English revolution, again like the Dutch, did not facilitate the development of an inclusive idea of the nation as the repository of sovereignty and the foundations of a unitary state.

V

If the Glorious Revolution saved Britain itself from the centralizing aggrandizement of absolutism, its implications for the British colonies turned out to be less salutary. The American Revolution occurred in a minority of the colonies that composed the early modern empire, and that empire, like the state to which it was attached and, incidentally, like all early modern European American empires, was characterized by indirect governance, dispersed authority, an inchoate theory of imperial sovereignty, and limited fiscal, administrative, and coercive resources on the part of the metropolitan center. The new extended transatlantic polity that would come to be called the British Empire was not characterized by a devolution of authority outward from an imperial center to American peripheries. Rather, authority in that empire was constructed from the peripheries inward, in two phases. The first involved the creation in

America, through the activities of participants in the colonizing impulse, of new arenas of local and individual power. The second involved the actual creation of authority through negotiation between these new arenas of settler power and the metropolitan representatives of the center that aspired to bring them under its jurisdiction and to which they desired to be attached.

Throughout early modern English/British America, independent individual participants in the colonizing process, English and other Europeans, were thus engaged in what can be only described as a deep and widespread process of individual self-empowerment, and this development gave rise to strong demands on the part of the large empowered settler populations for the extension to the colonies of the same rights to security of property and civic participation that appertained to the empowered, high-status, and independent property holders in the polities from which they came. In their view, colonial government, like metropolitan government, should guarantee that men of their standing not be governed without consultation or in ways that were patently against their interests.

Combined with the scarcity of fiscal and coercive resources and the reluctance of the metropolitan government to spend money for imperial purposes, settler expectations inevitably meant that authority in the early modern British Empire would not be concentrated at the center but, instead, distributed between the center and the peripheries. More specifically, these conditions meant that the metropolitan government would lack the means unilaterally to enforce its will and authority in distant peripheries, that central direction in the British Empire would be minimal, that metropolitan authority in the colonies would be consensual and heavily dependent on provincial opinion, and that effective power in distant colonial polities would be firmly situated in provincial and local governments that were widely participatory and solidly under the control of large, broadly based, and resident property-owning settler classes. The early modern British Empire was thus a consensual empire composed of a loose association of essentially self-governing polities in which authority and effective power were distributed between the center and the peripheries. What was legal, what was constitutional, was determined not by fiat but by negotiation. Predominantly reflecting a respect for the extensive empowerment and high degree of corporate and individual liberty of property-owning classes, British imperial governance, like British internal

16

governance, functioned in the colonies to preserve that empowerment and the liberty and the property on which they were founded.[34]

From the perspective of the political revolutions that preceded it, the American Revolution that occurred in this particular empire on the part of these particular societies was not distinctive.[35] Like those revolutions, it was not the result of internal social, religious, or political tensions. Although the southern and middle colonies were wealthier than New England and although high military expenditures during the Seven Years' War created short-term economic problems for some colonies, all of them were broadly prosperous on the eve of the American Revolution. Throughout the 1760s and 1770s the colonies continued to exhibit the territorial expansion, the economic and demographic growth, and the social elaboration that had long characterized them. Like earlier revolutions, it was principally a consequence of the consolidating efforts of the central state to which the colonies were attached. As metropolitan officials increasingly began to appreciate the growing economic and strategic importance of the colonies to British prosperity and national power in the 1740s and 1750s, they more and more began to worry lest the weakness of metropolitan authority and the extensive autonomy enjoyed by the colonies might somehow lead to their loss.

Moved by such fears and by the developing sense of imperial order that would reach full flower only in the nineteenth century, metropolitan officials undertook a series of measures designed to convert the British Empire from the loose federal polity it had long been into a more unitary polity with authority more clearly fixed at the center. Such measures directly challenged the autonomy of colonies over their local affairs. By subjecting the colonies to legislation and other directives to which the settler populations of those colonies had not given their consent, those measures further called into question the claims of colonial settlers to a British identity and their capacity to enjoy the traditional rights of Britons. Not surprisingly, these measures immediately became what H. G. Koenigsberger has called "a flashpoint for rebellion, repression, and war."[36] Interpreted by the broadly empowered settler populations as an effort to subject them to a far more intrusive imperial order, they elicited a powerful settler defense of the local corporate rights of the colonies and a rising settler demand for explicit metropolitan recognition of the British liberties and identity associated with those rights.

Of course, this quarrel was complicated by changes in the internal governance of Great Britain following the Glorious Revolution. Koenigsberger has recently analyzed the composite monarchies of early modern Europe in terms of a distinction he borrowed from the medieval English legal theorist Sir John Fortescue between *dominium regale*, a condition in which "the ruler could legislate and tax his subjects without their consent," and *dominium politicum et regale*, a situation in which "the ruler needed such consent and" in which that "consent usually had to be given by the representative assembly." Before 1688, the English had had a regime of *dominium politicum et regale*. But the Glorious Revolution and its attendant developments changed that regime "into something quite different, parliamentary government . . . in which there" was "no longer a balance between the monarchy and parliament as two basically independent authorities." As the repository of sovereign authority within Britain, the King-in-Parliament now became, Koenigsberger persuasively suggests, "an absolutist parliamentary regime," while the colonies and Ireland retained *dominium politicum et regale* regimes. Parliament's efforts to tax the colonies for revenue directly in the 1760s and 1770s and the colonists' refusal to accede to such taxation pointedly raised the fundamental theoretical problem of how to reconcile the sovereignty of the King-in-Parliament with the colonial demand for limitations on metropolitan political authority in accordance with their long "experience of *dominium politicum et regale* and . . . their mythology of liberty*" arising out of their by then ancient claims to identities as *British* peoples who enjoyed *British* forms of governance. In this situation, as Koenigsberger points out, the colonists were inevitably "driven back to the traditional solution of the composite monarchy made up of states with equal rights and held together only by a common allegiance to the crown."[37]

Along with the intense settler resistance to these new measures, the stridency of settler demands in turn wounded metropolitan pride and provoked counter and highly condescending assertions of metropolitan superiority that suggested that colonists were, so far from being true Britons, a kind of other whose low characters, rude surroundings, and barbarous cruelty to their African slaves rendered them, on the scale of civilization, only slightly above the native Amerindians they had displaced or the Africans among whom they lived. Such attitudes powerfully informed the measures that elicited the broad-based and extensive settler resentment and resistance of 1774–1775 and the decision for independence in 1776. The American Revolution can thus best be understood as a settler revolt that was a direct response to centralizing metropolitan measures that seemed both to challenge settler control over local affairs and to deny settler claims to a British identity. As such, it fits comfortably within the pattern of early modern revolutions earlier exhibited in the Netherlands and England.

In rejecting monarchy and the British connection and adopting republicanism, the leaders of these settler revolts did not have to preside over a wholesale, much less a violent, transformation of the radical political societies that colonial British Americans had constructed between 1607 and 1776.[38] In every colony/state, peculiar social, religious, economic, and political tensions shaped the course of revolutionary development. Indeed, these local tensions primarily account for the substantial differences in the revolutionary experiences from one colony/state to another. Wherever during the late colonial era there had been abuses of executive authority, judicial or civil corruption, unequal representation, opposition to an established church, or other political problems, the new republican state constitutions or later legislation endeavored to address those problems. Against the background of the deepening political consciousness generated by the extensive political debates over the nature of British imperial constitution after 1764, the creators of those constitutions also experimented, in limited ways, with improvements to their existing political systems. The widespread political mobilization that had occurred after 1764 and especially in 1775–1776 also resulted, in many states, in an expansion of legislative seats and public offices and a downward shift in political leadership that brought more settlers of somewhat less, though still substantial, property into active roles in the public realm. With astonishingly few exceptions, however, leaders of late colonial regimes retained authority through the transition to republicanism, and the republican regimes they created in 1776 and afterward bore a striking resemblance to the regimes they replaced.

Everywhere, political authority remained in the hands of the predominant groups among the existing settler population. As during the colonial period, the central government, an unintended consequence of the union of colonies that had come together to resist metropolitan aggression, was weak. Effective power remained in the states, even, for a century or more, after the strengthening of the national government with the Federal Constitution in the late 1780s. The election of Thomas Jefferson in the

so-called revolution of 1800 effectively brought to an end whatever nationalizing and centralizing tendencies Federalist leaders had brought to
the project of creating a more unitary national state during the 1790s. For
at least another century, provincial or state identities remained more powerful than the continental, or American, identity constructed during the
1760s and 1770s. At the state and local levels, government remained an
instrument of settler desires. Although it was somewhat more broadly
participatory than it had been during the colonial era, it continued to rest
on limited conceptions of civic competence and civil equality, both of
which extended only to independent people. The exigencies of war stimulated an extraordinary expansion of the public realm, and, at least during
the earliest decades, republican government turned out to be far more intrusive than colonial government had ever been. Yet settler leaders continued to prefer inexpensive and small government. As during the colonial
era, they kept bureaucracies small, refused to pay for permanent peacetime
military and naval establishments, and were cautious in supporting public
works. Like their colonial counterparts, these republican polities everywhere continued to be instruments of the predominant settler classes, concerned principally with the maintenance of orderly social relations, the
dispensing of justice, and, most important of all, the protection of private
property.

Nor did the new republican regimes preside over a large-scale social
reconstruction. The pursuit of individual domestic happiness in the private realm remained the central cultural imperative. The social order continued to be open, social relations continued to be fundamentally
egalitarian, wealth remained the primary criterion for social standing, and
aspiring elites continued to decry the absence of deference from those of
less wealth. With no restraints on the accumulation of private wealth, social differentiation continued unabated. Despite their own frequent, albeit
often unintentional, transgressions against private property, republican
state settler regimes continued to reaffirm the sanctity of private property.
Land titles remained secure, except for those who opposed the Revolution, some of whose land was confiscated and sold to pay public expenses.
Next to land, slaves were the most valuable form of property in the states
as a whole, and notwithstanding the emergence of a powerful antislavery
movement after 1760, the institution of slavery persisted in every state in
which it retained its economic viability and represented a substantial in-

vestment. In effect, the decision to retain or abolish slavery was, like so much else in the new American state, a matter for local option.

So intent have some scholars been on assimilating the American Revolution to the great European revolutions that followed it, on emphasizing its revolutionary character and radical discontinuity with the American past, that they have by and large neglected to explore the bearing of earlier American political and social experience on the events and developments of the American Revolution. A comprehension of the important implications of American social experience on contemporary understandings of that experience powerfully suggests that the colonial and revolutionary eras were much of a piece. The most radical result of the Revolution was the profound reconception of political and social relations that occurred over the following half century and the emergence and endorsement of the idea of popular sovereignty, an idea that, as John M. Murrin says in chapter 2, "took hold as the underlying myth that still organizes public life in the United States."[39] In my view, however, this conceptual discontinuity needs to be understood for what it was: an elaborate working out of the logic of some of the tendencies long characteristic of the loose imperial polity of the early modern British Empire and the radical political societies of colonial British America, societies that, precisely because of their radical character, could make such a profoundly conservative revolution.

During the early modern era, in America as in Europe, no movement toward the consolidation of power in the central state failed to generate resistance, and in the cases examined here such movements led to revolt and revolution. Before 1789, the direction of state development was thus toward not the centralization of state power but rather its dispersal. To the considerable extent that the American Revolution was a response to the centralizing efforts of the metropolis, was animated by an ideology obsessed with the protection of personal and corporate rights, produced a highly decentralized political regime characterized by the dispersal of authority, and, notwithstanding the emergence of the concept of popular sovereignty as the foundation for the state, developed only a rudimentary conception of the people as a nation, it was emphatically not, as Murrin asserts, a "countercyclical event,"[40] at least not within the history of early modern revolutions. Rather, it represented yet another example of the decentralizing revolutions that had earlier occurred in the Netherlands and England.

VI

Indeed, as William H. Sewell Jr. suggests in his excellent chapter, the countercyclical event in the history of early modern revolutions was not the American but the French Revolution. Sewell's chapter demonstrates a clear and thorough command of the new literature on state formation and its relation to our understanding of the various revolutions and revolutionary ideologies with which this volume is concerned.

As he explains, Old Regime France, like the France of the sixteenth and seventeenth centuries, was a composite monarchy divided into provinces of varying size and importance that had come under the king at different times "and had different relationships to the crown. The provinces were of two types: the *Pay d'état* and the *Pays d'élection*," and the former, generally more distant from Paris and more recently joined to the kingdom, usually had "more extensive and advantageous privileges" than the latter. Indeed, the *Pay d'état* "had managed to retain Provincial Estates with significant powers of local government and usually also had provincial Parlements—high courts that governed the administration of laws in the region." Nor were provinces "the only territorial units that possessed privileges. Many cities, towns, and even some rural districts had their exclusive powers, jurisdictions, and forms of government, many of which depended on individual charters or letters patent granted directly by the king." Under the Old Regime, France thus had "not one system of territorial divisions, but several different non-congruent systems": "military divisions called 'governments'; judicial divisions known as 'baillages' or balliwicks; fiscal and administrative divisions known as 'generalities'; and religious divisions, the dioceses."[41]

In addition, Old Regime France, Sewell reports, had a corporate and hierarchical social order "organized as a complex set of relatively bounded units known variously as corps, communautés, ordres, or états. These units were very diverse in scale and function, ranging from the French state, the church universal, or the three estates of the realm at the large end to guilds, academies, bodies of magistrates, village communities, parishes, families, or confraternities at the small end. Such bodies varied greatly in organization and character, but most were largely self-regulating within their particular sphere." This social order, Sewell observes, "assumed differences in quality, precedent, rank, and honor, both between persons and between corporate units."[42]

In this diffuse political and social order, much authority rested with the provinces, communities, and corps, and in disputes between the center and the provinces about raising taxes and implementing new edicts, provincial états and local magistrates, in Roger Mettam's words, "were often on the side of provincial elites in resisting these innovations of a distant central government" in Paris.[43] For this reason, as Sewell explains, in disputes between the central government and the peripheries, "the more local loyalties [frequently] won out in practice."[44]

When indebtedness, partly owing to the French government's support of the American Revolution, forced Louis XVI in 1789 to call together the Estates General for the first time since the early seventeenth century, various members, following their Dutch, English, and American predecessors, protested the king's recent policies, expressed the local patriotism of their provinces, and called for the restoration and updating of the ancient French constitution. But such impulses, Sewell writes, rapidly gave way to the desire to construct an entirely "new kind of state and society around the key legitimizing concept of "The Nation." Over the previous two centuries, a well-articulated sense had emerged that the French people were bound together not only by a common language and their residence in a distinct territory but also by "a putatively distinctive set of manners and morals," and the term *nation* had come to distinguish the broader population of France from the state or the king. But when the Estates General transformed itself into the National Assembly in June 1789 and began drafting a new constitution for the country, it established "the nation as the principle of sovereignty." By this action, the revolutionaries profoundly changed "the relationship of 'the nation' to the king and to the state or the government."[45]

Indeed, by making the nation, of which it was to be the embodiment, "a kind of sacred center of political life" in the state, the National Assembly effectively expropriated the ideals of absolutism and put them at the service of the nation. The new national state that it constructed, Sewell observes, "proved itself to be immensely more powerful than its old regime predecessor," and the revolutionaries immediately embarked on a course of trying to achieve many of the objectives of absolutism, carrying out "far-reaching" and centralizing and unifying "reforms touching all spheres of life." "In the course of providing the nation with a new constitution," he writes, "the revolutionaries systematically destroyed the old corporate bodies, sweeping away the legal supports of the old regime's highly elaborated hierarchical and corporate system."

With the twin goals of instituting "a society composed of rights-bearing individual citizens who were equal before the law and who were governed by a legislature made up of their elected representatives" and providing all French citizens with an equal share of "'public liberty' regulated by 'a law common to all Frenchmen,'" it created a unified legal system, replacing the "geographically diverse systems of law" that had obtained under the Old Regime with "a single, unified, national legal code."[46]

By abolishing all existing jurisdictions and substituting for them a uniform system of territorial divisions consisting of more or less equal-sized departments divided into communes, the revolutionaries, as Sewell tellingly remarks, were endeavoring to create new kinds of spaces that owed their existence to the national state. The nation was thenceforth "to take primacy over all other solidary bonds." The revolutionaries intended for the new units of provincial government to provide "the framework for all the functions of state: taxation, administration, the army, the church, the courts, and political representation." Although these new territorial units were to be self-governing, they were "emphatically not [to] be privileged corporations, divided from others by their particular immunities, peculiar laws, and private advantages." In the process of making these fundamental changes, the revolutionaries also "abolished all sorts of previously sacrosanct personal, political, and pecuniary privileges"; expanded "the state's administrative personnel"; "reformed its fiscal system"; and "established new, wide-ranging citizenship rights."[47]

Sewell compellingly points out the many ways in which the French Revolution had a profound impact on the history of the nation-state. In redefining the nation form, French revolutionaries elaborated "a new framework of institutions, laws, modes of behavior, and cultural assumptions that would henceforth be the hallmarks of a fully constituted nation." "By striking down all the intermediate forms of identity and mutual recognition," they effectively "absolutize[d] the nation as the supreme site of solidarity" and thereby, it should be added, fostered an absolutism that was infinitely more powerful than that sought by Philip II, the early Stuarts, or even Louis XIV. By self-consciously remaking France "over as a nation," they "tapped into an astounding source of power," stimulating the enormous upsurge of nationalism that during the nineteenth and twenti-eth centuries would, in J. H. Elliott's words, "give a greater impetus to the creation of a unitary state than the royal decrees and the actions of bu-reaucrats had given it over" the previous three centuries.[48]

In all these respects, the French Revolution marked a radical depar-ture from earlier revolutions. Like the American Revolution, it produced a republican political regime. However, in major part because Old Regime France had no active tradition of broadly participatory provincial and lo-cal self-government of the sort that had existed throughout colonial British America, the French republican regime was far more unitary and far more tightly integrated under the aegis of the central state than the loose federal structure established in the United States. Unlike the Dutch Revolt, the English revolutions of the seventeenth century, or the Ameri-can Revolution, it did not, for long, proceed from demands for the preser-vation of local and provincial authority and the restoration of the ancient constitution. Rather, it represented a wholesale assault on the special rights and privileges that had sustained the old constitution, the elimina-tion of existing subordinate political units, and the subordination of the localities to a unitary state representing the nation. Without a substantial number of inhabitants whose status as unfree people seemed to be vital to the economic health of many areas, the French Revolution, in contrast to the American, generated a political and social regime that was much more fully participatory, inclusive, and egalitarian than that implemented in North America. In all these ways, the French Revolution represented both a crucial redirection in the history of earlier political revolutions and rev-olutionary ideologies and a foundational event in the development of the modern nation-state.

VII

Of all the revolutions that occurred in the Americas in the decades fol-lowing the French Revolution, the one that appeared in the rich slave and sugar-producing French colony of St. Domingue in the 1790s, a revolu-tion not elsewhere treated in this volume, was certainly the most radical and in many respects one of the most interesting. Although this Haitian Revolution began, like the American Revolution, as a protest by white set-tlers against the centralizing policies of the Bourbon imperial state and a demand for greater colonial autonomy, it quickly generated a movement by an extensive free colored population for the liberty and equality of all free people in the colony and, as the American Revolution did not, ultimately generated a massive and successful uprising of slaves determined to gain their freedom. The result, as Franklin Knight writes, was "a complete metamorphosis in the social, political, intellectual, and economic life of the colony," as the slaves overturned the existing planting society, established a peasant economy, and created the independent Black republic of Haiti, "the second independent state in the Americas" and "the first independent non-European state to be carved out of universal European empires anywhere." This achievement, Knight adds, provided an alternative "model of state formation [that] drove fear into the hearts of all whites from Boston to Buenos Aires."[49]

The Hispanic–American Wars for Independence, which occurred during the first quarter of the nineteenth century, stretched over a much larger and politically and socially more complex area than the American War for Independence. In his chapter in this volume, Eric Van Young treats only the Mexican War for Independence, but during the years from 1808 to 1826 similar and related movements occurred in all of Spain's vast possessions on the North and South American continents. Like the American Revolution, these movements occurred in political societies that, under the domination of creole Spanish or Amerindian elites, had long enjoyed considerable self-government and were used to being consulted and to participating in negotiations over imperial decisions that affected them. While the vast number of Amerindians that formed a majority of Spanish American populations "enjoyed rights to lands, language, culture, laws, and traditions under" semi-autonomous republics of Indians "popularly known as *repúblicas*," the equivalent republics of Spaniards possessed "countless representative corporate bodies," including, in the words of Jaime Rodríguez O., "municipal councils that governed provinces (*ayuntamientos*), universities, cathedral chapters, convents, confraternities, mining and merchant organizations, and numerous craft guilds," all of which "enjoyed a large measure of self-government." Like the British Empire, the Spanish Empire was thus a consensual empire in which the various American political entities were explicitly not colonies but "kingdoms in the worldwide Spanish Empire."[50]

Although, in contrast to colonial British America, Spanish colonial America had by the late eighteenth century everywhere evolved into "a multiracial society whose members were integrated culturally and economically, to varying degrees, into a hybrid mestizo society that was neither Indian nor Spanish," the Spanish creole leadership that dominated public life in all Spanish American polities, like the American revolutionaries, took pride in its metropolitan heritage and identity and in their polity's status as an integral and component part of the Spanish monarchy.[51]

Like the American Revolution, the Hispanic–American Wars for Independence were rooted in a protest against the centralizing tendencies of an aggressive imperial state. Like Great Britain, Spain tried to "reorganize its empire during the last years of the eighteenth century." In a series of measures known as the Bourbon reforms, it "established a small standing army and a large force of provincial militias, formed new administrative boundaries, introduced a different system of administration—the intendancies—restricted the privileges of the clergy, restructured trade," and drastically curtailed the access of Americans to administrative and clerical office in their patrias. Charging that Spain intended to transform its American possessions from the kingdoms they had always been into mere colonies and convinced "that an unwritten constitution required that royal authorities consult the King's New World subjects" on any major changes in their status or administration, Spanish American leaders vigorously opposed these "innovations," and "massive opposition" flared up all over Spanish America. In the words of Jaime Rodríguez O., "tax increases, the expulsion of the Jesuits, and other changes led to protests and to violent riots in Quito in 1765, in central New Spain the following year, and in Upper Peru during the years 1777 to 1780," and Spain had to employ considerable force to overcome the "most serious upheavals—the Túpac Amaru revolt, which threatened to engulf the entire Viceroyalty of Peru during 1780–1783, and the Communero revolt in New Granada in 1781." Although these protests did lead to the widespread articulation of demands for autonomy *within* the composite worldwide monarchy of Spain, they did not result in a movement for independence from that monarchy.[52]

What did ultimately lead to such a movement was the French Revolution, which, Rodríguez writes, "unleashed twenty years of war in which Spain became an unwilling participant." In particular, the collapse of the

Spanish monarchy in 1808 as a result of the French invasion of Spain and the abdication of its rulers "triggered a series of events that culminated in the establishment of representative government throughout the Spanish World," events that in America encountered serious opposition from metropolitan supporters. Nevertheless, in 1810, the American kingdoms sent delegates to the *Cortes*, the Spanish National Assembly, and American deputies "played a central role" in drafting the Constitution of Cádiz in 1812, a constitution intended for the entire empire. In imitation of the French Revolution, that constitution, Rodríguez explains, "created a unitary state with equal laws for all parts of the Spanish monarchy." It "abolished seigniorial institutions, the Inquisition, Indian tribute, [and] forced labor"; asserted the "state's control over the church"; and "enfranchised all adult men, except those of African ancestry." It also "dramatically increased the scope of representative government" at the imperial, provincial, and municipal levels. By encouraging towns "to form *ayuntamientos*, it transferred [much] political power to the local level and incorporated vast numbers of people into the political process."[53]

Except for Peru, the Spanish American kingdoms "established governing *juntas* in 1809 and in 1810, which assumed authority in the name of the imprisoned King Fernando VII and sought to dominate their regions," but they experienced great difficulties in doing so. Conflict and civil war soon erupted, pitting "supporters of the Spanish national government against the *juntas*, the capitals against the provinces, the elites against one another, and the towns against the countryside." As Van Young makes clear for Mexico, at least two wars were going on, "one anticolonial, the other intestine," with the former involving "a frontal assault against the colonial regime and its predecessors" and the latter constituting an "ethnic confrontation between colonially dominated indigenous peoples and descendants of settler colonists."[54]

When Fernando VII returned from captivity in 1814 and resumed the Spanish monarchy, he abolished the Constitution of Cádiz, restored absolutism, and urged royal authorities in the New World "to crush" all autonomy movements. These actions only served in America to intensify movements for home rule, convincing many Spanish Americans "that it was prudent to establish an autonomous government within the Spanish monarchy." When, however, the Spanish *Cortes* rejected a proposal that "would have granted Spanish Americans the home rule they had been seeking since 1808," Spanish American leaders, Rodríguez notes, operating on an ideology that whenever the compacts, the "*unwritten* colonial constitution[s]," between the individual kingdoms and the monarch were severed ("nothing bound an American kingdom to Spain or to any other New World realm"), opted for independence.[55]

In his case study, Van Young stresses the fissiparous nature of the Mexican War for Independence. In particular, he contrasts the focus of the creole white and mestizo elite on the issues of political autonomy and Mexican nationhood with the orientation of the rural masses toward the "defense of community." Notwithstanding the country population's occasional "attacks on local systems of privilege and property," "localocentrism and the integrity of the community," he reports, "were features of village riot and protest right through the colonial era and into the internal war period of 1810–1821 and beyond." During the popular insurgency in 1820–1821, popular leaders espoused a "communalist view" that "was fragmented, feudalized, [and] localized—often more clan feud and riot than mass mobilization." Thoroughly "in keeping with the deep conservatism of popular rebellion," the ideas they used "to justify the insurgency" were "of a notable traditionalist stamp" that looked "backward to illegitimate conquest" and to "the impious motives of Cortes and his sponsors." Popular leaders were far more interested in carving "out for themselves their own spheres of dominance in the countryside" than in creating an independent state. If "the issue of state building was of considerable importance to the directorate of the independence movement," he concludes, "there is little evidence to indicate that it mattered a fig to their popular following." In these divergent views, Van Young writes, the Mexican War for Independence "encapsulated many of the social contradictions and resultant strains within the Spanish American colonial regime as a whole—of race and class, wealth and poverty, center and periphery, authoritarianism and political opening, tradition and modernity."[56]

As Van Young also suggests, however, the impulse toward building a nation, in the postrevolutionary French sense of that word, was relatively limited, even among the advocates of creole patriotism. Creole leaders certainly used the new representative institutions as a forum for their expression of that patriotism, often evoking the idea that Mexico was an ancient nation "whose rightful monarchs and people had been usurped and subjugated illegitimately," and they called for the recovery "of its usurped sovereignty."

Yet "even while many creole thinkers" were attempting "to appropriate a noble indigenous past for purposes of state making and nation building," they displayed a deep "ambivalence about indigenous Mexicans." Rooted "in the attempt of creole ideologues to distance themselves from the stain of *mestizaje* and the prevailing negative concepts about the nature of man in the New World," this ambivalence betrayed a latent racism concerning the "indigenous peoples of New Spain and their [allegedly] 'degraded' condition at the close of the colonial period" that prevented serious efforts to found, in the manner of French revolutionaries, the Mexican state on the concept of an inclusive nation. In Van Young's view, creole patriotism only "began developing into a genuine nationalism in the decades after independence."[57]

Indeed, like the Dutch Revolt, the English revolutions of the seventeenth century, and the American Revolution, and unlike the French Revolution, at least in the short run, the Hispanic–American wars for Independence and the regimes they produced seem to have been principally oriented toward the preservation of the existing social and political establishment. Certainly in Mexico, at least on the national level, "the 'political nation'" underwent only a modest expansion in numbers, and "the huge majority of Mexicans long remained in a political shadow." In social and political terms as well, Mexico's mostly rural, peasant, and non-white population gained little after 1821 from "the separation of colony from metropolis. Fundamental property relations or the distribution of landed wealth, for example, were not really on the agenda of the creole rebel leadership, who were quite socially conservative for the most part; it would take the Revolution of 1910 and the regimes after 1920 to dismantle the traditional Mexican latifundium." The "critique of the late Bourbon state fashioned by the creole directorate of the independence struggles and the project for a national state experimented with in the decades following independence from Spain," Van Young concludes, "were artifacts of elite, essentially urban culture" with little regard for the vast rural masses.[58]

VIII

So what of a general nature can we conclude about the early modern revolutions and the traditions that animated them? What I have tried to argue is that these revolutions have to be seen as a function of the process of

state formation and of the tensions betweer
that characterized that process. Resistance a
sponse to the centralizing activities of royal
It rallied around the defense of existing (or
liberties and was informed by an ideology or constitutionalism and rights
that by no means extended to the entire population. In all but one case,
revolution led not to a strengthening of the central regime but rather to
the perpetuation and even, in the English, American, and possibly Mexican cases, to an expansion of the dispersed system of governance that
characterized the composite monarchies and extended imperial polities in
which they occurred. The grand exception to this pattern was the French
Revolution. Similar in its origins, it was dramatically different in its impulses and results. By doing away with existing corporate privileges and
provincial rights and creating, in the name of an inclusive nation, a unitary state, it produced an entirely new genre of political revolution, a radically new kind of revolutionary tradition, and a strikingly modern form of
the nation-state. The conventional scholarly definition of political revolution as an event that breaks sharply with the past and produces a wholesale transformation of the political and constitutional order in behalf of a
nation and a unitary state representing that nation seems to fit only one of
the revolutions discussed here, the French Revolution.

Notes

1. Charles Tilly, *Coercion, Capital, and European States, AD 990–1990* (Cambridge, Mass.: Blackwell, 1990), 43–44, 224.

2. Mark Greengrass, ed., *Conquest and Coalescence: The Shaping of the State in
Early Modern Europe* (London: E. Arnold, 1991), vii, 1–2, 3.

3. J. H. Elliott, "A Europe of Composite Monarchies," *Past and Present*, no.
137 (November 1992): 52–53, 57, 69.

4. John Miller, "Introduction," in *Absolutism in Seventeenth-Century Europe*,
ed. John Miller (New York: St. Martin's Press, 1990), 13.

5. H. G. Koenigsberger, "Composite States, Representative Institutions and
the American Revolution," *Historical Research* 62 (June 1989): 135–36; Miller,
"Introduction," 3–4.

6. Koenigsberger, "Composite States," 136, 143, 149–50.

7. Elliott, "A Europe of Composite Monarchies," 57, 68–69.

8. Miller, "Introduction," 3–4.

9. Elliott, "A Europe of Composite Monarchies," 57, 68–69.

10. Marjolein C. t'Hart, *The Making of a Bourgeois State: War, Politiics and Finance during the Dutch Revolt* (Manchester, U.K.: University of Manchester Press, 1993), 6.

11. Miller, "Introduction," 4; Elliot, "A Europe of Composite Monarchies," 62–63.

12. Miller, "Introduction," 5.

13. Miller, "Introduction," 17, 19; Elliott, "A Europe of Composite Monarchies," 62–63.

14. Elliott, "A Europe of Composite Monarchies," 60–61; Elliott, "Revolution and Continuity in Early Modern Europe," *Past and Present*, no. 42 (February 1969): 48–50.

15. Elliott, "Revolution and Continuity," 48–49, 54; J. H. Elliott, "Revolts in the Spanish Monarchy," in *Preconditions of Revolution in Early Modern Europe*, ed. Robert Forster and Jack P. Greene (Baltimore: The Johns Hopkins University Press, 1970), 119, 126.

16. Elliott, "Revolts in the Spanish Monarchy," 114–15; Elliott, "A Europe of Composite Monarchies," 64.

17. Elliott, "Revolution and Continuity," 44, 51–52.

18. Martin Van Gelderen, ed., *The Dutch Revolt* (Cambridge: Cambridge University Press, 1993), xiii–xiv.

19. James D. Tracy, *Holland under Habsburg Rule 1506–1566: The Formation of a Body Politic* (Berkeley and Los Angeles: University of California Press, 1990), 2–3, 8; Van Gelderen, *The Dutch Revolt*, xii.

20. Geoffrey Parker, *The Dutch Revolt* (Ithaca, N.Y.: Cornell University Press, 1977), 13–14; Van Gelderen, *The Dutch Revolt*, xiii, xvii–xviii, xxxii

21. Van Gelderen, *The Dutch Revolt*, xxiii; t'Hart, *The Making of a Bourgeois State*, 5–6; Parker, *The Dutch Revolt*, 13–14; Elliott, "Revolution and Continuity," 48–49.

22. Roger Mettam, "France," in Miller, *Absolutism in Seventeenth-Century Europe*, 43, 51–52. See also Oreste Ranum, *The Fronde: A French Revolution, 1648–1652* (New York: Norton, 1993).

23. John Morrill, "The Fashioning of Britain," in *Conquest and Union: Fashioning a British State 1485-1725*, ed. Steven G. Ellis and Sarah Barber (London: Longman, 1995), 22.

24. John Miller, "Britain," in Miller, *Absolutism in Seventeenth-Century Europe*, 195.

25. Miller, "Britain," 198, 204, 206; Miller, "Introduction," 14.

26. See J. G. A. Pocock, *The Ancient Constitution and the Feudal Law: A Study of English Historical Thought in the Seventeenth Century. A Reissue with a Retrospect* (Cambridge: Cambridge University Press, 1987).

27. Miller, "Britain," 208.

28. Miller, "Britain," 199.

29. Miller, "Britain," 202.

30. Miller, "Britain," 211–14; Lois G. Schwoerer, "Law, Liberty, Juries, and the Bill of Rights, 1689: English Transatlantic Revolutionary Traditions," in this collection, 7–10, 19–20, passim (typescript).

31. Miller, "Britain," 214–16; Miller, "Introduction," 14.

32. Lawrence Stone, "Introduction," in *An Imperial State at War: Britain from 1689 to 1815*, ed. Lawrence Stone (London: Routledge, 1994), 5, 7–9.

33. See Richard Helgerson, *Forms of Nationhood: The Elizabethan Writing of England* (Chicago: University of Chicago Press, 1992); and Liah Greenfeld, *Nationalism: Five Roads to Modernity* (Cambridge, Mass.: Harvard University Press, 1992), 27–87.

34. Jack P. Greene, *Peripheries and Center: Constitutional Development in the Extended Polities of the British Empire and the United States, 1607–1788* (Athens: University of Georgia Press, 1986), deals at greater length with these issues.

35. The interpretation advanced here is developed more fully in Jack P. Greene, "The American Revolution," *American Historical Review* 105 (February 2000): 93–102, and "Empire and Identity from the Glorious Revolution to the American Revolution," in *The Oxford History of the British Empire*, ed. W. Roger Louis (Oxford: Oxford University Press, 1998–1999), 2: 208–30.

36. Koenigsberger, "Composite States," 147, 151.

37. Koenigsberger, "Composite States," 136, 149, 150, 152.

38. For a contrary view, see Gordon S. Wood, *The Radicalism of the American Revolution* (New York: Knopf, 1992).

39. Wood, *The Radicalism of the American Revolution*; John M. Murrin, "1776: The Countercyclical Revolution," in this collection, 21 (typescript).

40. Murrin, "1776," 3.

41. William H. Sewell Jr., chapter 3 in this volume, 104.

42. Sewell, "The French Revolution," 99.

43. Mettam, "France," 57.

44. Sewell, "The French Revolution," 98.

45. Sewell, "The French Revolution," 95, 99. See also J. F. Bosher, *The French Revolution* (New York: Norton, 1988), 51–54.

46. Sewell, "The French Revolution," 95, 101.

47. Sewell, "The French Revolution," 95.

48. Sewell, "The French Revolution," 108; Elliott, "A Europe of Composite Monarchies," 70.

49. Franklin W. Knight, "The Haitian Revolution," *American Historical Review* 105 (February 2000): 105.

50. Jaime E. Rodríguez O., "The Emancipation of America," *American Historical Review* 105 (February 2000): 135–36.

51. Rodríguez, "The Emancipation of America," 138.

52. Rodríguez, "The Emancipation of America," 136, 142–43.

53. Rodríguez, "The Emancipation of America," 143–45.

54. Rodríguez, "The Emancipation of America," 145; Eric Van Young, chapter 4 in this volume, XX.

55. Rodríguez, "The Emancipation of America," 145, 147.

56. Van Young, "To Throw Off a Tyrannical Government," 131.

57. Van Young, "To Throw Off a Tyrannical Government," 139.

58. Van Young, "To Throw Off a Tyrannical Government," 133, 156.

CHAPTER ONE

LAW, LIBERTY, AND JURY "IDEOLOGY": ENGLISH TRANSATLANTIC REVOLUTIONARY TRADITIONS

Lois G. Schwoerer

Figure of Justice. Wearing a helmet. Scales and sword. 1572. John Bossewell, Workes of armorie, devyded into three bookes. *Used by permission of the Folger Shakespeare Library.*

Of all the revolutionary traditions that were transmitted from England (or Great Britain) to its American colonies, none was more important to the form of government that the colonists constructed following the American Revolution or more basic to preserving other rights and liberties that they claimed in their Bill of Rights than the institution of the jury. Trial by jury has been called "the genuinely crucial right." Of all the English documents underlying those traditions and the institution of the jury, none equaled the importance of Magna Charta

(1215), the Petition of Right (1628), and the Bill of Rights (1689): they are said to have been "the models in hand, or at least in mind," when colonists crafted their own government.[1] These documents have been exhaustively studied over many years,[2] and recently the institution of the jury, after some neglect, has also commanded attention.[3] In this chapter, I am concerned with three aspects of the jury.

The first is the celebratory attitude toward the jury in late Stuart England and its transmission, as part of a "revolutionary current" (as in the title of this volume) to the American colonies.[4] This attitude I call a "jury ideology." My focus here connects with two major themes of this volume: revolutionary ideology and the transatlantic fertilization of ideas. It may seem paradoxical to think of the ancient institution of the jury as revolutionary. But, as I contend in this chapter, it is not odd to think of the words "jury ideology" in those terms. What do those words signify? By them I mean a commendatory view of the jury as an institution because it protects subjects and their rights, liberties, and laws from arbitrary and lawless government. Grounded in notions about law, liberty, and rights that played a prominent role in England's political and constitutional crises, this ideology, in effect, politicized the old institution of the jury. Praise for the jury and expressed anxiety about its alleged corruption implicitly dispraised, criticized, and challenged the government. When critics of the government dominated the selection of juries, as they did for a while in London in the early 1680s, friends of the government responded in like measure, but only weakly and not in tracts. Printed tracts celebrating the jury were powerful weapons in contests with the Court; the printed word reached a much wider audience than otherwise would have been the case and thus engaged the attention of persons in and out of elite political circles. Although admiration for the jury was present much earlier, the jury ideology emerged most fully articulated during the troubled Restoration era (1660–1689). Antiestablishment tracts about juries from this era helped the famous documents just mentioned to transmit this jury ideology across the Atlantic, where it became embedded in colonial constitutional and political thinking.

The second aspect of the jury with which I am concerned is its part in the coming of the Revolution of 1688–1689 and its place in the revolutionary settlement. This perspective also amplifies this collection's interest in revolutionary ideology. The high-handed treatment of the jury and the consequent fear and anger contributed to popular disillusionment with the government. Reform of some aspects of jury procedure was included in the document, the Declaration of Rights (better known in its statutory form as the Bill of Rights), that settled the Revolution.

Third, I argue that the jury and the ideology surrounding it helped in a modest but nonetheless important way to shape a sense of England's self-identity and self-consciousness and, thereby, contributed to the formation of the English state, a development that had been long under way.[5]

I

As well known as is the jury, a very brief and selective overview of its origins and early history is desirable.[6] The origins of the jury system lie deep in England's history. The jury was a venerable institution, but not so old in fact as seventeenth-century admirers insisted. Although a remote connection may be found to a prototype of the jury among the Anglo-Saxons, the jury trial in a form recognizable to us did not emerge in England until 1066, when the Normans introduced it. Initially the jury was a body of men local to the area where the crime had been committed who provided royal officials with the facts needed to judge an issue, much as witnesses might do. This meant that jurors could decide a case on the basis of their own knowledge. As masters of the facts of the case, jurors had considerable authority and enjoyed a higher status, vis-à-vis the judge, than was the case later on, as seventeenth-century observers later complained. Procedures became more complicated in the late twelfth and thirteenth centuries with the introduction of the grand jury, a body given the responsibility of deciding whether an issue before it should be sent for trial to another body, known as the petit jury or petty jury. Petty jurors now became largely the judge of facts that were presented in court by witnesses who were called by the prosecution and defense, but their own knowledge was not disallowed. In the thirteenth and fourteenth centuries, juries often went beyond judging facts to judging law. Out of sympathy for the defendant or because of bribery or intimidation, they might nullify the law and acquit the accused.[7] The question of whether juries should judge law as well as fact and be able to nullify the former was the subject of debate in the late seventeenth century and remains so today.

Another development of the thirteenth century, King John I's signing of Magna Charta (1215), was central to the development of the jury as an institution, claims to due process, and the jury ideology. The now famous chapter 29 was especially important. It read,

> No freeman shall be arrested, or detained in prison, or deprived of his freehold, or outlawed, or banished, or in any way molested; and we will not set forth against him nor send against him, unless by the lawful judgment of his peers and by the law of the land.

This language was malleable enough for its meaning to be extended so as to include trial by jury and "due process of law" (which meant certain procedures) and to apply to broad social groups.[8]

Further changes in practice occurred in early modern England. For example, by the sixteenth century, if not before, the requirement that jurors be chosen from the neighborhood had faded; jurors could be, and were, drawn from across England.[9] In the late seventeenth century, a legal opinion regarding the jury was handed down that provided a powerful defense of the institution. The opinion resulted from the trial of the Quakers William Penn and William Mead in September 1670.[10] The two men were charged with "preaching and drawing a tumultuous company"; they admitted the fact of preaching but denied that they had broken the law. Four jurors refused to convict Penn and Mead, and when the judge ordered the entire jury to reconsider, all the jurors returned a verdict of "not guilty." The judge had to accept the verdict, but he fined and imprisoned the jury. The foreman, Edward Bushel, and three other jurors refused to pay the fine; instead, they entered a habeas corpus in the Court of Common Pleas on grounds that the fine and imprisonment were illegal. "Bushel's Case" came before Sir John Vaughan, Lord Chief Justice of the Court of Common Pleas, who ruled that judges did not have the power to fine or imprison jurors for their verdicts. The ground of the ruling was that men of integrity may disagree and that, in the final analysis, jurors must be faithful to their own views in coming to a verdict. Vaughan's ruling, which is still cited today, was sometimes ignored, but in law it ended the practice of punishing jurors for their judicial acts.

Not everyone looked with favor on juries, and criticism and efforts to control it came from many quarters. Members of the peerage and gentry were inclined to resent that their social inferiors sat in judgment on them when serving as jurors; they tended to think of jurors as ill-qualified, susceptible to bribery because poor (the property qualification was only £2), and biased against them.[11] In 1665, Parliament, in which these classes dominated, passed a law that raised the property qualification for jury service to £20 and ordered justices of the peace to strike the names of men who did not qualify and insert the names of those who did.[12] Parliament also passed laws calling for settling certain cases by summary justice without benefit of a proper jury trial.[13] Judicial authorities took steps—such as browbeating, fining, and imprisoning—to ensure a verdict pleasing to their interests.[14] Bushell's case and the Vaughan ruling put a stop to these tactics in 1670, at least according to law.

The monarchy restricted the use of juries; in the sixteenth century, it created new prerogative courts—the Court of Star Chamber and the Court of High Commission. In the early 1680s, it tried to exercise control of juries by influencing the selection of jurors through the use of quo warranto proceedings against towns and cities (especially London, where the important political trials were held). A quo warranto was a legal writ that enabled the government to question some feature of a city's charter and require the remodeling of the charter to meet its political needs, as, for example, in the selection of jurors. Since the tenure of judges was at the pleasure of the king, the government could confidently expect to control the outcome of cases, if it could control who served on juries. Yet the fact that judicial tenure lay with the king was a weakness in the contest with his critics, for the Bench was always vulnerable to charges of Court influence. In fact, as fear of the government deepened because of its use of quo warranto and of the judges because of their tenure and their actions, the feeling grew that a free jury composed of properly qualified men was a bulwark, perhaps the most important of all bulwarks, against an arbitrary government. Thus, juries took on political significance, and one's view of them depended in part on one's legal and political principles.

II

The intellectual foundations of a jury ideology appeared in early seventeenth-century England. Proponents of the jury system at that time and later based their defense of it on assumptions about the common law and the ancient constitution.[15] Veneration of the common law had a long lineage in English legal and political thought. The idea that the common law embodied an ancient constitution representing the immemorial custom of the nation, although fading somewhat by the end of the seventeenth century, was still the "nearly universal belief of Englishmen."[16] It was also widely believed that the common law was the preeminent law in England.[17] Sir Edward Coke, the great lawyer and leader of the House of Commons, directly linked the rights or liberties of the English with the common law; he and others stressed that Magna Charta was an embodiment of it.[18] The words "right," "liberty," or freedom" had carried a restrictive meaning in the Middle Ages, signifying that a person or institution enjoyed a privilege or authority that was often attached to property and that was not allowed to others.[19] For example, a town's charter might endow its residents holding property of a certain value with rights not allowed to non–property holders or to residents in another town. Or members of the House of Commons had certain rights or liberties denied men who were not members. But within the context of disagreements between King Charles I and his critics in Parliament in the 1620s, "right" or "liberty" took on a different meaning. Members of the House of Commons, with Coke in the lead, laid claim to rights that protected them from an arbitrary or lawless Crown. Invoking medieval political and legal theorists such as Bracton and Sir John Fortescue (author of *De Laudibus Angliae*) and citing such medieval laws as Fleta, the *Modus Tenendi Parliamentum*, the apocryphal laws of Edward the Confessor, and, above all, Magna Charta, Coke and others insisted that the liberties or rights of the English were part of an "ancient constitution" that pre-dated the institution of monarchy. There had been no conquest in 1066; in fact, King William had confirmed and promised to observe the nation's rights; thus, those rights existed down through the centuries without a break. Magna Charta, accepted by King John in 1215 and many times confirmed, was a statute[20] that, far from making new law, had simply restated the old common law and reaffirmed medieval laws.[21] In 1628, in debates over the Petition of Right, members of Parliament invoked Magna Charta and, reading into it what they wanted to see, insisted that trial by jury and due process were rights of all English persons.[22] Since these rights were justified by common law and the ancient constitution, the king had no legal authority to withdraw or deny them. By their nature, then, such rights, rooted in custom and the distant past, limited the authority of government and protected subjects against arbitrary and lawless government. As was the case with claims to other liberties or rights,[23] those respecting juries grew out of practical political and legal disputes, not abstract theorizing.

Moreover, in the second part of his influential *Institutes*, Coke gave special attention to chapter 29 of Magna Charta, reinforcing what had been said in parliamentary debates. He described it as a "root" out of which "many fruitful branches of the Law of England have sprung"[24] and glossed it to mean that trial by jury was guaranteed to all freemen, arbitrary imprisonment was prohibited, and swift, free, and equal justice was affirmed.[25] Repeatedly reprinted throughout the late seventeenth century—in 1662, 1664, 1669, 1671, and 1681—Coke's *Institutes* reached many people across the century and deeply influenced generations of lawyers and political and constitutional writers and activists.[26] Coke's arguments became part of received wisdom that trial by jury and due process were rooted in ancient custom, enshrined in Magna Charta, and reinforced by the Petition of Right.

The Levellers, the radical group based in London that penetrated the army in 1647 and flourished for several years before withering away during the Cromwellian interlude, continued to stress the value of the jury system and due process as essential shields against arbitrary government for all individuals, regardless of rank.[27] An interesting example is that of William Walwyn, a Leveller leader, who generally despised the common law[28] but felt so strongly about juries that he turned to it to defend them. Arguing in a tract titled *Juries Justified* (1651) against a proposal (made by Henry Robinson) that Parliament should appoint and pay judges to handle certain cases, Walwyn praised trial by jury as England's "principal liberty," her "fundamental essential liberty," indeed her "most essential Liberty," and commended jurors as the nation's "preservers." Walwyn even modified his previous negative view of William the Conqueror because William had kept the jury system intact. Altering also his view of Magna Charta, Walwyn declared that "true English liberties" were enshrined in the document. In 1628, he continued, those liberties were "culled out . . . and reduced into that excellent Law (as this Parliament stiled it since [Charles's] death) the Petition of Right." Therein "trials per Juries is the principal [among them]."[29] Significantly, Walwyn linked juries and parliaments, saying that so long as parliaments stand, "Juries cannot . . . be in any danger." Leveller tracts were not reprinted or referred to in subsequent discussions of juries, but they reveal how deep-seated was the value placed on the jury. In fact, the same points they advanced appeared after the Restoration.

III

The fullest formulation of a jury ideology, however, emerged in printed polemics from 1679 through the 1680s, years that we now know for a certainty, thanks to recent work by Melinda Zook,[30] were full of verbal and physical violence between the newly formed Tory and Whig parties over the Court's political, religious, and foreign policies. The context was the infamous Popish Plot and the Exclusion Crisis, that is, the effort of the Whigs led from the House of Lords by Anthony Ashley Cooper, first Earl of Shaftesbury, to exclude the Catholic James, Duke of York, from the succession to the throne. A series of events highlighted the dangers to the integrity of juries. One example was the acquittal on July 18, 1679, of Sir George Wakeman, the queen's personal physician, on charges of high treason for having conspired to poison King Charles II.[31] Defamatory tracts trumpeted that not only jurors but also the presiding judge, Sir William Scroggs, Lord Chief Justice of the Court of King's Bench, had accepted bribes from Catholic sources (which made the bribes even more heinous) to ensure the verdict that the king wanted. Or again, the trials of radical printers Benjamin Harris, Francis Smith, and Jane Curtis in February 1680 and Henry Care, the pamphleteer, in July 1680 heightened concern that the Court was violating legal procedures. Then from November 1680 through the Oxford Parliament of March 1681, critics of the Court tried to impeach Scroggs, charging him (among other things) with curtailing the work of the Middlesex grand jury by dismissing it.[32]

On the other hand, friends of the Court found much to criticize in the actions of London juries that were commanded in 1681 by Whigs, who at that time had won control of the city's government. Whig-dominated grand juries returned *Ignoramus*[33] verdicts to the draft indictments or bills brought by the Court against its enemies, notably Stephen College in July 1681[34] and Lord Shaftesbury in November 1681. These legal steps sharpened alarm among the king's friends. Within this troubled context, discussion of both the grand jury and the petit jury became pervasive.

The issue was brought center stage from 1680 through 1682 by tracts written mostly by Whigs, by Tory poetry, and by polemical newsletters representing the viewpoint of both Whig and Tory partisans. Court and Tory sympathizers turned to Sir Roger L'Estrange's *Observator* and to Edward Rawlins's *Heraclitus Ridens*, while the Whigs reveled in Henry Care's *Weekly Pacquet of Advice from Rome* and its attached sheets of humor, *The Popish Courant.* These newsletters were exceedingly popular and reached a wide audience that included the elite and nonelite.[35] Newsletter writers offered brief and necessarily scattered but nonetheless powerful comments about the state of the jury that reinforced alarm over the issue. Care defended the *Ignoramus* juries, insisting that the verdict of a jury was the "essential point of law," that jurors alone must judge the credibility of witnesses, and that if in conscience they did not believe the draft indictment before them, then, according to their oath as jurors, they could not find a true bill. If jurors did otherwise, they imperiled their very soul. He scorned anyone who tried to "Over-Awe" or demean a jury for its verdict as an enemy to the king and "the Constitution of our Government." He lavished praise on trial by jury as an institution our ancestors valued as "one of the most precious badges of English Liberty." Tories L'Estrange and Rawlins ridiculed Care's emphasis on conscience, dismissing it as nothing more than an excuse to violate law and advance Whig partisan interests. Liberty of conscience, L'Estrange sneered, had swallowed up the "Authority of Government" by ignoring law. Rawlins charged that the Whig grand juries would indict a Tory whatever the evidence, whereas if a Whig appeared before them, they would "clear him th'Apostles themselves" swore that he was guilty. In such fashion, the press politicized the functioning of juries, but significantly no writer on either side dismissed the jury as an institution.

Only poetry sympathetic to the Tory/Court side seems to have survived, and it pointedly criticized Whig-dominated juries. *The Ignoramus Ballad. To the Tune of, Let Oliver now be Forgotten*, dated in a contemporary hand August 27, 1681, and in that same hand described as "Popish Libell," contains eight stanzas of malicious attacks on Whig juries and the trial of College.[36] The fifth stanza, for example, condemns the "Jury of Rebels" for refusing to find a bill against College and praises "Honester men" who resolved "so to bring it about /To find the Bill,/ By giving the Rout/ To all *Ignoramus* his Skill." Another Tory-inspired ballad, *IGNORAMUS: An Excellent New Song*, also contained eight spiteful stanzas, these against juries who returned *Ignoramus* verdicts. Each stanza ended with the refrain

They sham us, and flam us/ And ram us, and dam us/
And then, in spight of Law, come off with Ignoramus.

The well-known Aphra Behn and the anonymous author of *The Whigs
Lamentation* seized opportunity to criticize "Arbitrary Juries" and Whig
"Packed Juries."[37] The Tory tract writer John Northleigh advanced the
same points in his *The Parallel: or, the New Specious Association an Old
Rebellious Covenant* (1682), writing, "if we find a factious city, then a factious sheriff; if a factious sheriff, then a factious jury; if a factious jury, then
all the factious fellows are acquitted."[38]

Whig-printed tracts presented expansive statements about juries.
Some of the pamphlets were anonymous,[39] among them *Ignoramus Vindicated, in A Dialogue Between Prejudice and Indifference*. An effective
polemic, it offered crisply expressed opinions on various aspects of a jury's
power: the jury must judge law as well as fact (a controversial opinion),
weigh the evidence it has of its own knowledge, decline to follow the
judge's instructions if they run counter to their conscience, possess a certain freehold, and have no connection with the accused. Dissenters may be
jurors if otherwise qualified. None of these anonymous pamphlets mentions the history of juries or speculates on the political significance of trial
by jury, yet each reinforces the same message that is more comprehensively
expressed in the tracts by the identified authors.

Two of the known authors were distinguished members of the House
of Commons and lawyers appointed to high office, and their tracts stand
out in learning and length. Sir John Hawles (1645–1716), author of *The
English-man's Right. A Dialogue Between A Barrister at Law, and a Jury-
Man*[40] (May 13, 1680)[41] and *The Grand-Jury-Man's Oath and Office Explained: and the Right of English-Men Asserted* (October 26, 1680),[42]
studied at Oxford, took a degree at Lincoln's Inn, served as a Lord Chief
Justice of the Court of Common Pleas, became solicitor general from
1695 to 1702, and ended life as a member of the House of Commons.[43]
In *English-man's Right*, a lengthy forty-page essay written in response to
Harris's trial, Hawles was intent on showing that the jury is a "grand concern, on which . . . the Lives, Liberties and Estates of all Englishmen de-
pend." A firm believer in the ancient constitution, Hawles emphasized the
connection between juries and the common law. The origins of the jury
were contemporaneous with the nation itself, he said; it appeared if not

among Britons, certainly then among the Saxons. William I was no conqueror, and the institution of the jury continued after 1066. Citing Coke, Hawles further explained that "this Priviledg of Tryals by Juries in an especial manner [was] confirmed and establisht" in the fourteenth chapter of Magna Charta and "more fully in that Golden Nine and twentieth chapter." Then, "by constant usage, and common custom of England, which is the common Law, . . . [the jury] is brought down to us as our undoubted Birth-right, and the best inheritance of every English man."[44] He promoted the right of juries to judge law as well as fact.[45] In his other, much shorter essay, *The Grand Jury Man's Oath*, published on October 26, 1680,[46] within weeks of the failure of the Second Exclusion Bill and the opening of an effort to impeach Scroggs, Hawles insisted that "the end of juries" was "preserv[ing] our Liberties from the wily encroachments of oppression."[47] Both essays hardened the politicization of the jury issue.

The second identified writer, Sir John Somers (1651–1716), in 1681 brought out a 150-page defense of the grand jury, specifically aimed at vindicating the grand jury's *Ignoramus* verdict in the indictment of Lord Shaftesbury. Educated at Oxford University and the Middle Temple, Somers became Lord High Chancellor of England in 1697. His tract, titled *The Security of Englishmen's Lives, or the Trust, Power and duty of the Grand Jurys of England*,[48] aimed at answering tracts that had denounced the grand jury because of its verdict in the indictment. Somers's biographer regards it as the most wide ranging and detailed of any tract that Somers wrote.[49] Directed at defending the independence of jurymen from both the judge and the Court, the tract insisted that the law applies equally to all persons and that the king is under oath to ensure fair treatment to everyone, regardless of their standing, and is obliged to abide by the law.[50] Somers stressed the importance of preserving the independence of the grand jury and dismissed the notion that the procedure of a grand jury investigation and indictment followed by a petty jury delayed the law and amounted to a double trial. Time meant nothing when the life of a defendant was at stake. He also praised the English law for it mercifulness, saying that the defendant should always be allowed the benefit of the doubt.

A third author was the London publicist, Henry Care (1646–1688), who was also the author of the *Weekly Pacquet of Advice from Rome* and its attachment, *The Popish Courant*. Care was known as "Ingenious" and admired for his "Golden Pen," which, a contemporary said, had made him "deservedly . . . one of the most Celebrated Writers" of his time.[51] Highly intelligent and well read in religion, history, law, and medicine, Care almost certainly worked for a lawyer or lawyers before he turned to pamphleteering for a living. Obviously Care stands apart from Hawles and Somers by reason of his class (lower middle), formal education (he had none), profession, and intended audience. Addressing himself largely to lower-middle- to lower-class Londoners, persons (as he put it) of "middle or meaner Rank" or of "the meanest capacity," Care developed a lively and witty style. He wrote a lot; he had more in print on the Whig side between 1679 and 1683 and again in 1687–1688 on James II's behalf than any other identified author. To do this successfully, he had to be a quick-study artist and able to digest a lot of material rapidly and replay it in his own words and for his own purposes. Thus, his tract *English Liberties: Or, The Free-Born Subject's inheritance*, a substantial 229-page book that appeared in 1682,[52] was heavily indebted to Hawles's *English-man's Right*, Coke's *Institutes*, and the language of parliamentary debate.[53] Care was also influenced by Somers's book and one of the anonymous pamphlets, *A Guide to English Juries*, both of which he commends.[54] Because of his background and role as a publicist, he is arguably the most interesting of the defenders of juries.

Care intended his *English Liberties* to provide uneducated and inexperienced English persons with documents and information about the law and their rights. He printed and commented expansively on statutes such as Magna Charta, all the laws against Protestants, and the "oath and duty of grand and petty juries."[55] Care's message is like that of other writers on juries, but no other author expressed it so well. He traversed familiar territory, praising England's "fundamental laws [as] coeval with government"[56] and describing Magna Charta as "Declaratory of the principal grounds of the Fundamental Laws and Libertie of England." Celebrating law in another piece as second only to the gospel,[57] he described it in *English Liberties* as "the best Birthright the Subject hath," one that protects all he has; it was an Englishman's "surest Saactuary [*sic*]," "strongest Fortress," and sturdiest "Buckler."[58] Care regarded the essence of this birthright as the "priviledge not to be exempt from the law, but to be freed in Person and Estate from Arbitrary Violence and Oppression." For Care, an Englishman's birthright shines "most conspicuously in Parliaments and juries," a thought that recognizes the value of participating in public affairs. Those persons who elected parliament men and those who served in Parliament had a share in the legislative power; those who were appointed as jurors participated in the executive part of the law. "These two Grand Pillars of English Liberty" have made the nation "more free and happy than any other People in the World." To undermine them, he warned, was to "strike at the very Constitution" of the government; it is worse than "letting in the sea or poisoning the springs," for all posterity will be ruined and enslaved.

Although laws guarded England's liberties, they were no more than "Cyphers, if not Honestly put in Execution." Juries played an important part in executing the law, and therefore the right to trial by jury was, in Care's judgment, one of the "principal bulwarks of England's Liberties." Chapter 29 of Magna Charta was "the Storehouse of all our Liberties" and the foundation stone of juries. As such, Care asserted, it "deserves to be written in Letters of Gold, and . . . Inscribed in Capitals on all our Courts of Judicature, Town-Halls, and most publick Edifices." So central an institution as a jury required men of high caliber to serve it. Care's ideal juror was "honest, substantial, and Impartial," a member of the neighborhood and thus able to judge fact but also knowledgeable about law so as equipped to judge it too. His "worth and repute" shielded him from the temptation of bribery.[59] Religion should not be a criterion; if otherwise qualified, dissenters should be allowed to serve. Jurors should not stand in awe of judges. Judges, who served at the pleasure of the king, were susceptible to outside pressures, whereas jurors, if they met Care's criteria, would be impervious to such pressures. To increase their self-esteem and as a mark of their special standing in the proceedings of the court, Care suggested that jurors wear their hats during a trial.[60] The defense and praise of the jury trial, advanced especially by Care and the two legal experts Hawles and Somers, amounted to a jury ideology that would influence the thinking of politically sensitive English people on the eve of the Revolution of 1688–1689 and the American colonists to whom it was transmitted.

IV

Historians assign multiple reasons why English people became disillusioned with their government and were willing, by and large, to accept the terms of the Revolution of 1688–1689 and welcome William and Mary, the Protestant Prince and Princess of Orange, to the throne that the Catholic King James II had vacated.[61] A reason that deserves highlighting was the continued alarm over the treatment and condition of the jury, an alarm no doubt nourished by the jury ideology circulated in the printed material just reviewed. The anonymous author of a tract dated December 24, 1688, written to explain to his friend in Brussels why the Revolution of 1688–1689 was under way featured this point. Insisting that nothing was so grievous to Englishmen as violations of law, the writer declared that of England's laws, "there's none that we are more fond of, than that of Juries . . . in . . . which an English-man doth of right demand to be free." Stressing that grand juries had been compromised, he noted that Scroggs had discharged the Middlesex grand jury before it had completed its business and, to underline how offensive Scroggs's step was, pointed to the article about that action in the impeachment charges leveled against the chief justice. The author further noted that "Base solicitations of Grand-Juries" had occurred, as exampled in the story of an attorney-general "shuffling" into a jury room to persuade the jurors to breach their oaths by accepting a "false presentment . . . which lacked sufficient, credible and consistent Evidence to support it." The writer also lamented that juries had been packed with "Men of dependence" who were "managed" to return a verdict for the government. Self-righteously, he declared that jurors cannot "excuse themselves for they are on their oaths, and their own Souls are at stake upon't." Neither can they blame the judge for their own illegal acts, for a judge cannot fine them. With a flourish, he trumpeted, "More families have been ruined within these ten years past by unjust Judges and unrighteous Jurors, than have been benefitted by the contrary in twice that time." In focusing on the resentment of English people over the corruption of the jury system, the author provides a different perspective on the breakdown of trust in the 1680s.[62]

A desire to reform aspects of jury procedure animated men who crafted the Declaration of Rights. Their handling of the issue illustrates that Englishmen had a propensity for declaring as ancient law what they wanted to be law and for interpreting it in ways to suit their needs. We observed this habit earlier with regard to interpretations of Magna Charta, and Janelle Greenberg has offered many other examples, most recently that of the story of "Sharnborn's Case."[63] Englishmen, however, were not alone in this propensity. As J. H. Elliott noticed, men in sixteenth-century Europe were intent on "rediscovering or inventing customary laws and constitutions" to use against the Crown "in a defence of [their] just (but not always justly interpreted) . . . liberties."[64]

The Revolution of 1688–1689 in seventeenth-century England is a further illustration of Elliott's point. Using the language of the ancient constitution, the committee drafting the claim of rights under the chairmanship of John Somers declared that in laying claim to their "ancient and undoubted rights and liberties," they were doing no more than their ancestors had done before them. So emphatic and consistent was this assertion that historians have taken them at their word and for years have regarded the document as a conservative restatement of existing rights. Historians did not take into account that old law could serve change or consider that an appeal to the past was a disarming way to cloak change in the mantle of tradition. They have failed to consider that a deep form of radicalism promotes change while pretending to preserve the past.

As I have argued in *The Declaration of Rights*, eight rights (including the jury clause) were not, as the committee claimed, "undisputed" and "ancient."[65] Article XI of the Bill of Rights reflected determination to preserve the integrity of the jury, as the drafting committee saw it. It read, "That jurors ought to be duly impaneled and returned, and jurors which pass upon men in trials for high treason ought to be freeholders." I have discussed Article XI in detail in another place;[66] here it is enough to underscore that it implicitly condemned the government's quo warranto proceedings that had resulted in sheriffs impaneling juries who could be counted on to give verdicts pleasing to the crown. It was reported that members of the drafting committee complained that in "every county" men who were "not for the turne of the court had crosses set against their names" to signal that the sheriff should not choose them for jury duty.[67]

The drafting committee was responding to the trial of William Lord Russell, a leader of the Whigs in the House of Commons, a Whig hero and martyr, who was charged with treason for conspiring the death of the king, tried in London at the Old Bailey in July 1683, found guilty, and condemned to die.[68] Memory of the trial and the arguments advanced was freshened by tracts printed at the time of the Revolution.[69] Lawyers for Russell had claimed that jurors in treason trials held in a city must be freeholders but, under questioning, admitted that the laws they cited did not apply to treason trials held in a city. The court properly rejected the claim, a move in keeping with the law at that time. In 1689 the drafting committee contended that the court corrupted the choice of jurors by bringing on nonfreeholders who would do their bidding to find Russell guilty. Their solution was to claim that jurors in trials for high treason ought to be freeholders—a claim that denied current law but one they regarded as important enough to warrant altering it. The reason law did not require freeholders on juries in treason trials held in cities, especially London, was the paucity of freeholders in the city; estates there belonged mostly to the nobility, the upper gentry, or the corporation. The drafting committee was aware of the uncertainty of their position, for in an early draft they placed their claim both in a category of old law and in a category of things that required new law. In the final draft, however, they simply said that it was an "undoubted and ancient right" that juries in trials for high treason ought to be composed of freeholders.

V

The institution of the jury and the jury ideology both reflected and contributed to England's deepening sense of self-identity and to the formation of the state of England. Recently, questions about "nationalism," the meaning of the very word "nation," and how nation-states were formed in Europe have attracted much attention, as the other chapters in this volume illustrate. The concept of "nation" did not exist in early modern England, but an "imagined community," to use Benedict Anderson's pregnant words, did exist, even as did the foundations of a state that functioned in highly complex ways.[70] The nature of the political state in early modern England is foreign to basic assumptions of the early twenty-first century, requires diligent study to understand, and for me must await another occasion for extended comment. For now, I want simply to adopt and illustrate Jonathan Clark's insightful hypothesis that "early-modern national identity" was based in "two systems of ideas: law and religion."[71]

Certainly, the most prominent and important factor in the Restoration period that encouraged a sense of Englishness was anti-Catholicism and its obverse, a feeling of beleaguered Protestantism. This sentiment was, of course, not new—one may see it at the time of the Reformation and more particularly during the reign of Queen Elizabeth I—but it took on new life in the 1680s with the Popish Plot and Exclusion Crisis and

with the writings of such rabid anti-Catholics as Henry Care. And it continued, as Linda Colley insists, writing, "Protestantism was the foundation
that made the invention of Great Britain possible." "Protestantism lay at
the core of British national identity."[72]

Another factor that inspired the feeling that England was set apart
from other states—not just physically as a "precious stone set in the silver
sea," a "blessed plot," as Shakespeare put it[73]—was the common law tradition, which was regarded as unique to England. The jury was a part of
that ancient constitution. If a jury ideology was most fully articulated, as
I have argued, in the Restoration, admiration for the jury was not new. For
example, William Cecil, Lord Burghley, Elizabeth I's Lord Treasurer, ex-
travagantly eulogized the procedure of indictment by grand jury in England, saying that "it was the liberty of the subject of England more than
of all other nations that he cannot be molested or imprisoned without indictment." Other nations have an accusation, which process imperils the
liberty of the subject.[74]

In the 1680s, advocates of the jury also contended that it was unique
to England. Care, who was borrowing words from Hawles without ac-
knowledgment, was emphatic on the point: "Look abroad in France,
Spain, Italy, or indeed (almost) where you will, and observe the miserable
Condition of the Inhabitants" whose "Lives, Liberties and Estates" are ex-
posed to the "Arbitrary Lusts of Tyrants" because they are unprotected by
laws and procedures like those in England.[75] In *English-man's Right*,
Hawles chastised his companion for his lack of knowledge about legal
conditions abroad, concluding with an expression of ardent pride in England. "Isn't it an inestimable happiness to be born and live under such a
mild and righteous Constitution [as England's] wherein all these mis-
chiefs [found abroad] (as far as human prudence can provide) are prevented."[76]

Admirers of the jury also insisted on the antiquity of the jury and its
long, continuous history, declaring, as did Hawles, that although "our best
Historians cannot date the Original of the Institution," its origins were
contemporaneous with the nation itself. William I confirmed Edward the
Confessor's Laws, of which juries were "an essential and most material
part," so that the institution of the jury continued after 1066 and "has time
out of mind been . . . carefully preserved by our Ancestors." Then, "by constant usage, and common custom of England, which is the common Law,

... [the jury] is brought down to us as our undoubted Birth-right, and the best inheritance of every English man."[77] The anonymous author of *A Guide to English Juries*, a tract praised by Care, concurred with these sentiments, writing that grand and petit juries are "so naturally the Rights of Englishmen" that they cannot be laid aside. He compared the importance of grand juries to Magna Charta, saying that they were wisely and rightly called "Grand" as "Magna Charta is called the Great Charter, from its great and weighty Contents." Grand juries, he argued, were a "great and good out-guard of . . . [English] Liberty and Property."[78] These sentiments helped engender a love of the community of England and a feeling of belonging to a people set apart from others and fortunate in their legal processes that defended their rights and liberties so effectively, it was said, from arbitrary government.

VI

The institution of the jury and jury ideology were transmitted to England's North American colonies. Magna Charta, the Petition of Right, and the Bill of Rights were the major vehicles carrying these traditions across the Atlantic. In addition, undervalued agents—printed tracts, especially those by Care, Hawles, and Somers—were responsible for highlighting and underscoring the institution and the ideology in both England and the colonies. The reprint history of each shows that their tracts met with favor: Somers's *Security of Englishmen's Lives* enjoyed eight editions in England between 1681 and 1771 and was published in Boston in 1720 and in London and New York in 1773. The Massachusetts Historical Society had a copy by 1792. Hawles's *The English-man's Right* had ten editions in England between 1681 and 1793 and was published in Philadelphia in 1798, 1894, and 1844 and in Boston in 1883. Care's *English Liberties* was equally well received: the essay, or portions of it or with deletions and/or additions, appeared eight times in England to serve various purposes and had two new editions in the colonies: in 1721 in Boston and in 1774 in Providence, Rhode Island. Indeed, the essential message of *English Liberties* was available throughout the colonial era: William Penn silently lifted a sizable portion—pages 2 to 40—into his *The Excellent Priviledge of Liberty and Property Being The Birth-Right Of the Free-born Subjects of England*, which was printed in 1687 in Philadelphia.[79] A testament to its popularity in America is that *English Liberties* was in private and public colonial libraries[80]: the Library Company of Philadelphia, founded in 1731 by Benjamin Franklin, acquired the 1719 edition in 1764 and another edition by 1770; other copies were known to be in Philadelphia in the colonial period.[81] Thomas Jefferson added two copies of *English Liberties* to his library and arranged for it to be included in the library of the University of Virginia.[82] The Burlington, New Jersey, Library Company held a copy, as did Daniel Dulany, a well-to-do, well-read, well-educated Marylander.[83] Further, the book was advertised in New York and Williamsburg and in Philadelphia by Benjamin Franklin.[84]

Care's vocabulary and ideas appeared in the writings of the founding thinkers of the United States of America—Samuel Adams, John Adams, John Dickinson, and Alexander Hamilton. In their speeches and writings may be found exactly the same language that Henry Care used in *English Liberties* when he praised the "two main Pillars of the British Constitution," identifying those pillars as parliament and trial by jury.[85] John Adams was expansive on the matter, writing,

> These two popular powers [the participation of the people in the legislative power and in the administration of justice] . . . are the heart and lungs, the mainspring and the centre wheel, and without them the body must die, [. . .] the government must become arbitrary. . . . In these two powers consist wholly the liberty and security of the people. They have no other fortification against wanton, cruel power; . . . no other defence against fines, imprisonments, whipping-posts, gibbets, bastinadoes, and racks.[86]

As colonists did in other areas, Adams, Dickinson, and Hamilton took the original concept and expanded it beyond what had been propounded by their English cousins. Care had written of the "two Grand Pillars of English Liberty" as an *Englishman's* birthright shining "most conspicuously in Parliament and juries." But the colonists reasoned that "since the Constitution was "founded in the Common Rights of Mankind," since the "Rights of Nature" were "happily interwoven" in its "ancient fabrick," the right to parliament and juries were "properly the birthright of free men everywhere."[87] It is worth noting that all the claims to rights made since the eighteenth century include the basic provisions of trial by jury and due process of law that Care and other men in Stuart England eulogized and tried to protect.

Throughout the eighteenth century, colonists found in Care's *English Liberties* support of their views about the Saxons, Magna Charta as a reaffirmation of old laws guaranteeing the rights of all freemen, and ways to protect themselves against oppression.[88] Indeed, one scholar suggested some time ago that *English Liberties* "had more to do with preparing the minds of American colonists for the American Revolution than the larger but less accessible works of Coke, Sidney, and Locke."[89] Recently, Jonathan Clark came independently to that point in his revisionist study of the "Language of Liberty" in the Anglo-American world. Arguing that the Commonwealthmen were not as important as used to be thought in the transmission of ideas to the colonies, he points to other English works, among them Care's *English Liberties*, that "clearly did engage closely with colonial concerns."[90]

VII

The jury ideology that developed in Restoration England in response to a threat to the institution of the jury from the Court and the judiciary is properly seen as a part of a revolutionary tradition. In the course of the struggle between the Crown and its friends—the Tories on the one hand and its critics the Whigs in and out of Parliament on the other—the jury as an institution became politicized; both sides tried to use it for their own ends. Whigs were more successful than Tories in writing and circulating printed tracts that spread eulogies of an ideal jury composed of substantial freeholders who were impervious to influence and bribery. Such juries, both grand and petty, would protect subjects' liberties from an overbearing, arbitrary government. The prelude to the Revolution of 1688–1689 turned in part on popular disillusionment with the government because of its treatment of the jury. The settlement of that Revolution that was embodied in the Declaration of Rights included a provision aimed at reform of one aspect of jury procedure on grounds that the reform was an "ancient and undoubted" right, although it was no such thing. The settlement achieved significant change in law while cloaking that change in a seemingly conservative appeal to England's past. A sense of identity and self-consciousness inhered in the jury ideology. That ideology contributed to the ongoing creation of an "imagined community" of England.

Perhaps most important of all was the transmission of the institution of the jury and the jury ideology to England's North American colonies.

The printed tracts written by two distinguished jurists, Hawles and Somers, and one highly popular publicist, Care, allowed jury ideology to span the Atlantic. Their tracts should be added to the long list of sources for English transatlantic revolutionary traditions. They played an important role in preserving in the United States the institution of the jury and for some time safeguarding a positive attitude toward that institution. We have reason to be grateful to Care, Hawles, and Somers for writing so persuasively and directly about the value of trial by jury to upholding subjects' rights and liberties. Those persons in late twentieth-century America who are inclined to curtail trial by jury when confronted by its failures would do well to contemplate the jury ideology that was developed in the writings of seventeenth-century Englishmen in response to the threat of arbitrary government, transmitted to the colonies, and reflected in the thinking of eighteenth-century American leaders.

Suggested Readings

Baker, J. H.
"Criminal Courts and Procedure at Common Law 1559–1800." In *Crime in England 1550–1800*. Edited by J. S. Cockburn. Princeton, N.J.: Princeton University Press, 1977, 15–48.

Clark, J. C. D.
The Language of Liberty 1660–1832: Political Discourse and Social Dynamics in the Anglo-American World. Cambridge: Cambridge University Press, 1994.

Colley, Linda
Britons Forging the Nation 1707–1837. New Haven, Conn.: Yale University Press, 1992.

Green, Thomas Andrew
Verdict according to Conscience: Perspectives on the English Criminal Trial Jury 1200–1800. Chicago: University of Chicago Press, 1985.

Green, Thomas Andrew, and J. S. Cockburn, eds.
Twelve Good Men and True: The Criminal Trial Jury in England, 1200–1800. Princeton, N.J.: Princeton University Press, 1988.

Levack, Brian
The Formation of the British State: England, Scotland and the Union 1603–1707. Oxford: Oxford University Press, 1987.

Miller, John
> *After the Civil Wars: English Politics and Government in the Reign of Charles II.* London: Longman, 2000.

Murrin, John M.
> "Magistrates, Sinners, and a Precarious Liberty: Trial by Jury in Seventeenth-Century New England." In *Saints and Revolutionaries: Essays on Early American History.* New York: Norton, 1984, 152–206.

Pocock, J. G. A.
> *The Ancient Constitution and the Feudal Law: A Study of English Historical Thought in the Seventeenth Century. A Reissue with a Retrospect.* Cambridge: Cambridge University Press, 1987.

Schwoerer, Lois G.
> "British Lineages: American Choices." In *The Bill of Rights: Government Proscribed.* Edited by Ronald Hoffman and Peter J. Albert. Charlottesville: University Press of Virginia, 1997, 1–41.

———

> *The Declaration of Rights, 1689.* Baltimore: The Johns Hopkins University Press, 1981.

———

> *The Ingenious Mr. Henry Care: Restoration Publicist.* Baltimore: The Johns Hopkins University Press, 2001.

Speck, William A.
> *Reluctant Revolutionaries: Englishmen and the Revolution of 1688.* Oxford: Oxford University Press, 1988.

Stern, Simon
> "Between Local Knowledge and National Politics: Debating Rationales for Jury Nullification after *Bushell's* Case." *Yale Law Journal* 111 (May 2002): 1815–59.

Zook, Melinda S.
> *Radical Whigs and Conspiratorial Politics in Late Stuart England.* University Park: Pennsylvania State University Press, 1999.

Notes

I am grateful to The Johns Hopkins University Press for permission to draw on the ideas and language in my *The Ingenious Mr. Henry Care: Restoration Publicist*

(Baltimore: The Johns Hopkins University Press, 2001). I thank Jean-Robert Durbin, Henry E. Huntington Library, for his prompt attention to requests for copies of material. As before, I am grateful to the staff at the Folger Shakespeare Library for their unfailingly cheerful assistance.

The place of publication is London if not otherwise noted.

1. Forrest McDonald, *Novus Ordo Seclorum: The Intellectual Origins of the Constitution* (Lawrence: University Press of Kansas, 1985), 40; Eric Schnapper, "The Parliament of Wonders," *Columbia University Law Review* 84 (fall 1984): 1665.

2. For example, J. C. Holt, *Magna Charta* (Cambridge: Cambridge University Press, 1965); Anne Pallister, *Magna Carta: The Heritage of Liberty* (Oxford: Clarendon Press, 1971); Frances H. Relf, *The Petition of Right* (Minneapolis: University of Minnesota Press, 1917); Elizabeth Read Foster, "Petitions and the Petition of Right," *Journal of British Studies* 14 (November 1974): 21–45; Lois G. Schwoerer, *The Declaration of Rights, 1689* (Baltimore: The Johns Hopkins University Press, 1981); William A. Speck, *Reluctant Revolutionaries: Englishmen and the Revolution of 1688* (Oxford: Oxford University Press, 1988).

3. Akhil Reed Amar, "The Bill of Rights as a Constitution," in *The Bill of Rights: Government Proscribed*, ed. Ronald Hoffman and Peter J. Albert (Charlottesville: University Press of Virginia, 1997), 346–76, for discussion of the jury in the Bill of Rights of the United States; J. H. Baker, "Criminal Courts and Procedure at Common Law 1559–1800," in *Crime in England 1550–1800*, ed. J. S. Cockburn (Princeton, N.J.: Princeton University Press, 1977), 15–48; Thomas Andrew Green, *Verdict according to Conscience: Perspectives on the English Criminal Trial Jury 1200–1800* (Chicago: University of Chicago Press, 1985). See also J. S. Cockburn and Thomas A. Green, eds., *Twelve Good Men and True: The Criminal Trial Jury in England, 1200–1800* (Princeton, N.J.: Princeton University Press, 1988), and John M. Murrin, "Magistrates, Sinners, and a Precarious Liberty: Trial by Jury in Seventeenth-Century New England," in *Saints and Revolutionaries: Essays on Early American History*, ed. David D. Hall, John M. Murrin, and Thad W. Tate (New York: Norton, 1984), 152–206.

4. These venerable topics have recently enjoyed renewed interest. See J. C. D. Clark, *The Language of Liberty 1660–1832: Political Discourse and Social Dynamics in the Anglo-American World* (Cambridge: Cambridge University Press, 1994); Lois G. Schwoerer, "British Lineages and American Choices," in Hoffman and Albert, *The Bill of Rights*, 1–41.

5. The subject of juries is of enduring interest to historians of early modern England and to historians and citizens of the early twenty-first century. Truth to tell, I was drawn to it because of discussions that erupted in the press and on the *Lehrer News Hour* in the wake of the O. J. Simpson trial in 1995. The trial provoked conversation and debate across the United States about the value, efficacy,

and "fairness" of jury trials. Their remarks brought home to me how timeless are the criticisms of juries, whether expressed in seventeenth-century England or twentieth-century America. In both eras, concern was voiced over the alleged fact that persons chosen to serve were not well educated or well informed enough in the law to bring in fair verdicts, that they performed their jury service unwillingly or in a perfunctory manner, and that they were subject to corruption or intimidation because of race (in twentieth-century America) and class (in seventeenth-century England and perhaps as a subtext in twentieth-century America). For example, All Things Considered, National Public Radio, July 8, 1995, and October 3, 1995; Julie Gannon Shoop, "'After O. J.' Panel Looks at Race and the Jury," *Trial* 31 (December 1995): 63–65; Albert W. Alschuler, "Our Faltering Jury," *Public Interest* (winter 1996): 28–38.

6. Sir William S. Holdsworth, Arthur L. Goodhard, Harold Hanbury, and John M. Burke, eds., *A History of English Law*, 13 vols. (London: Metheun, 1922–1972), 1:312–13; Green, *Verdict according to Conscience*, chaps. 1, 3, 4, offers a detailed account of the early jury, as do selected chapters from different perspectives in Cockburn and Green, *Twelve Good Men and True*.

7. Green, *Verdict according to Conscience*, chap. 2; Simon Stern, "Between Local Knowledge and National Politics: Debating Rationales for Jury Nullification after *Bushell's* Case," *Yale Law Journal* 3 (May 2002): 1815–59.

8. Holt, *Magna Charta*, 9–10. I thank Janelle Greenberg for calling my attention to these pages.

9. Stern, "Between Local Knowledge and National Politics," 1816 n. 5.

10. For this paragraph, see Green, *Verdict according to Conscience*, chap. 6; Stern, "Between Local Knowledge and National Politics," 1822–27.

11. John Miller, *After the Civil War: English Politics and Government in the Reign of Charles II* (London: Longman, 2000), 15–16, 115–16.

12. Miller, *After the Civil War*, 114.

13. Murrin, "Magistrates, Sinners, and a Precarious Liberty," 155–56 n.

14. Holdsworth, *A History of English Law*, 1: 339–47.

15. J. G. A. Pocock, *The Ancient Constitution and the Feudal Law: A Study of English Historical Thought in the Seventeenth Century. A Reissue with a Retrospect* (Cambridge: Cambridge University Press, 1987), is the well-known classic study.

16. Pocock, *The Ancient Constitution and the Feudal Law*, 50–54 (quotation at 54). For the weakening of the concept, see Howard Nenner, *By Colour of Law: Legal Culture and Constitutional Politics in England, 1660–1689* (Chicago: University of Chicago Press, 1977), 110 and passim.

17. In 1628, a member of the House of Commons remarked that common law was "the" law of England, whereas other laws, like chancery law or maritime law or admiralty law, were only "a" law of England. Mary Frear Keeler, Maija Jansson

Cole, and William B. Bidwell, eds., *Proceedings in Parliament 1628*, 6 vols. (New Haven, Conn.: Yale Center for Parliamentary History, 1977–1983), 2: 530.

18. Chapters 2 and 3 in Stephen D. White, *Sir Edward Coke and "The Grievances of the Commonwealth," 1621–1628* (Chapel Hill: University of North Carolina Press, 1979), are useful for these points.

19. Donald S. Lutz, "The Pedigree of the Bill of Rights," in Hoffman and Albert, *The Bill of Rights*, 63–68, briefly describes the English and American concepts of rights.

20. Technically, Magna Charta did not achieve statutory status until 1297.

21. See Pocock, *The Ancient Constitution and the Feudal Law*, 32–38, 44–45, 214–79; Janelle Greenberg, "The Confessor's Laws and the Radical Face of the Ancient Constitution," *English Historical Review* 104 (July 1989): 611–37.

22. Keeler, Cole, and Bidwell, *Proceedings in Parliament 1628*, 2: 150, 158, 161, 164, 335–36, 337, 432, 439, 440, 519. In 1627 in the Five Knights Case, it was said for the first time that Magna Charta prohibited arbitrary imprisonment without due process, a contention that was readily and easily rebutted in law. See William S. McKechnie, *Magna Charta: A Commentary on The Great Charter of King John. With an Historical Introduction* (Glasgow: J. Maclehose and Sons, 1905), 458.

23. Edward Andrew, *Shylock's Rights: A Grammar of Lockian Claims* (Toronto: University of Toronto Press, 1988), 19, quoting Maurice Cranston.

24. Sir Edward Coke, *The Second Part of the Institutes of the Laws of England Containing The Exposition of many ancient, and other Statutes* (1642; 6th ed., London: W. Rawlins, 1681), 46.

25. Coke, *The Second Part of the Institutes*, 50, 52, 56.

26. These views dominated constitutional histories for 300 years until 1905, when McKechnie showed that they were not the original meaning or intention of Magna Charta: McKechnie, *Magna Charta*, 158–63, 436–59.

27. These points appeared in the *Second Agreement of the People* (1647). See also *Puritanism and Liberty Being the Army Debates (1647–9) from the Clarke Manuscripts with Supplementary Documents*, selected and edited with an introduction by A. S. P. Woodhouse with a foreword by A. D. Lindsay (Chicago: University of Chicago Press, 1951), 339, 365, 444. In a tract titled *The Peoples Prerogative and Priviledges*, John Lilburne, a major Leveller spokesman, expressed outrage that due process procedures were not followed in his own arrest. See John Lilburne, *The peoples Prerogative and Priviledges, asserted and vindicated (against all Tyranny whatsoever) By Law and Reason. Being A Collection of the Marrow and Soule of Magna Charta, And all the most principall Statutes made ever since to this present year, 1647. For the preservation of the peoples liberties and properties* (1647).

28. William Walwyn, *Englands Lamentable Slaverie*, in *The Writings of William Walwyn*, ed. Jack R. McMichael and Barbara Taft (Athens: University of Georgia Press, 1989), 147 (at 143 for attribution to Walwyn). Walwyn referred to Magna Charta as a "mess of pottage" and described the rights in it as having been "wrestled out of the pawes of . . . Kings."

29. McMichael and Taft, *The Writings of William Walwyn*, 438.

30. Melinda S. Zook, *Radical Whigs and Conspiratorial Politics in Late Stuart England* (University Park: Pennsylvania State University Press, 1999).

31. For an account of Wakeman's acquittal, see Lois G. Schwoerer, *The Ingenious Mr. Henry Care: Restoration Publicist* (Baltimore: The Johns Hopkins University Press, 2001), 76–83.

32. For Scroggs, see Lois G. Schwoerer, "The Attempted Impeachment of Sir William Scroggs, Lord Chief Justice of the Court of King's Bench," *Historical Journal* 38 (December 1995): 843–73.

33. An *Ignoramus* verdict meant that the grand jury found no case in the draft indictment or bill, and the bill did not proceed. A bill endorsed *Billa Vera* meant that an indictment was presented to the petty jury. See Baker, "Criminal Courts and Procedure at Common Law," 18–21.

34. Stephen College (1635?–1681), known as the "Protestant joiner," was an ardent Protestant and a skilled carpenter. The government accused him in a bill brought before the Westminster grand jury of seditious words and actions at the time of the Oxford Parliament. The *Ignoramus* verdict enraged the Court, and the case was moved to Oxford, where a compliant jury found him guilty as charged.

35. Schwoerer, *The Ingenious Mr. Henry Care*, 166–67, 170–71.

36. This ballad is in the collection at the Huntington Library, call no. 135846.

37. Quoted in Zook, *Radical Whigs and Conspiratorial Politics*, 1, 88.

38. Zook, *Radical Whigs and Conspiratorial Politics*, 15.

39. For example, *A Guide to English Juries: Setting forth their Antiquity, Power, and Duty, From the Common-Law, and Statutes. With a Table. By a Person of Quality. Also A Letter to the Author, upon the same Subject* (London, 1682); *Ignoramus Vindicated, in A Dialogue Between Prejudice and Indifference. Touching the Duty, Power, and Proceedings of Juries: Together, with some material points Relating thereunto, declared for Law by the Right Honourable Sir John Vaughan, Knight, late Lord Chief Justice of the Common Pleas* (London: Printed for Thomas Cockerill, 1682); *The Power and Privilege of Juries Asserted: In Opposition to the Willfully Blind, and Uncharitable men. Published for the Information of Herclytus Riden and the Doting Observator* (London: Printed for Richard Janeway, 1681); *Twenty Four Sober Quaeries Humbly Offered to be Seriously Considered by all Juries in City and Countrey* (London: Printed for Benjamin Harris at the Stationers Arms in the Piazza under the Royal Exchange in Cornhill, London, 1680).

40. The title continued: *Plainly setting forth, I. The Antiquity II. The excellent designed use. III. The Office and just Priviledges of Juries, By the law of England.*

41. For the date, see Stephen Parks, assisted by Earle Havens, *The Luttrell File: Narcissus Luttrell's Dates on Contemporary Pamphlets 1678–1730* (Beinecke Rare Book and Manuscript Library, Yale University), 77. Also noted in Stern, "Between Local Knowledge and National Politics," 1831.

42. The title continued: *A Dialogue Between A Barrister at Law, And A Grand-Jury-Man.*

43. *Dictionary of National Biography.* An up-to-date biography is badly needed.

44. Hawles, *The English-man's Right*, 1–5.

45. Green, *Verdict according to Conscience*, 255–58.

46. For the date, see Parks, *The Luttrell File*, 77.

47. Sir John Hawles, *The Grand Jury Man's Oath and Office Explained, and the Rights of English-men asserted a dialogue between a barrister at law and a grand-jury man* (London: Printed for Langley Curtis, 1680), 21.

48. The title continued: *Explained according to the Fundamentals of the En-glish Government, and the Declaration of the same made in parliament by many Statutes.*

49. See William L. Sachse, *Lord Somers: A Political Portrait* (Manchester, U.K., and Madison, Wis.: Manchester University Press and University of Wisconsin Press, 1975), 18.

50. John Somers, *Security of Englishmen's Lives* (London: published for T. Mitchel, 1681), 12, 56.

51. *Public Occurrences*, no. 26 (August 1688). See also Schwoerer, *The Ingenious Mr. Henry Care.*

52. The date of publication is 1682, not 1680, as used to be thought.

53. Green, *Verdict according to Conscience*, 258, notices that Care lifted "whole passages" from Hawles. See remark by Henry Powle on November 23, 1680, quoted in *State Trials*, VIII, col. 183.

54. Care, *English Liberties, or The Free-born Subjects Inheritance* (London: G. Larkin, 1682), 228.

55. The contents are revealed in the lengthy title *containing I. Magna Charta, The Petition of Right, the Habeas Corpus Act; and divers other . . . statutes. . . II. The Proceedings in Appeals of Murther; The Work and Power of Parliaments. The Qual-ifications necessary for . . . that great Trust. Plain Directions for all Persons concerned in Ecclesiastical Courts; and how to prevent or take off the Writ De Excommunicato Capiendo. . . . the Oath and Duty of Grand and Petty Juries. III. All the laws against Conventicles and Protestant Dissenters, with . . . Directions . . . to Constables . . . And an Abstract of all the Laws against Papists.*

56. Care, *English Liberties*, 4.

57. Henry Care, *Weekly Pacquet of Advice from Rome: Or, The History of Popery* (London: Langley Curtis, 1682), vol. 5, no. 4, 32: Friday, September 15, 1682, in *The Courant* (attached).

58. Care, *English Liberties*, 29, 4, 30, 5, 105, 136, 22, for quoted material in sequence.

59. Care, *English Liberties*, 207, 210. Care's suggestion that jurors should be resident in the neighborhood where the crime was committed was an anachronism.

60. Care, *English Liberties*, 211.

61. George Hilton Jones, *Convergent Forces Immediate Causes of the Revolution of 1688 in England* (Ames: Iowa State University Press, 1990); J. R. Jones, *The Revolution of 1688 in England* (London: Weidenfeld and Nicolson, 1972); Schwoerer, *The Declaration of Rights*; William Speck, *Reluctant Revolutionaries Englishmen and the Revolution of 1688* (Oxford: Oxford University Press, 1988).

62. *A Letter To a Gentleman at Brussels, Containing An Account of the Causes of The Peoples Revolt From The Crown* (December 24, 1689) (London: n.p.), 3, 6, 10–11 (quotations).

63. See Janelle Greenberg and Laura Marin, "Politics and Memory: Sharnborn's Case and the Role of the Norman Conquest in Stuart Political Thought," in *Politics and the Political Imagination in Later Stuart Britain: Essays Presented to Lois Green Schwoerer*, ed. Howard Nenner (Rochester, N.Y.: University of Rochester Press, 1998), 121–42. See also Janelle Greenberg, "The Confessor's Laws and the Radical Face of the Ancient Constitution," *English Historical Review* 104 (July 1989): 611–37.

64. J. H. Elliott, "A Europe of Composite Monarchies," *Past and Present*, no. 137 (November 1992): 60. The specific reference is to the Aragonese Revolt of 1591. See also Donald R. Kelley, *Foundations of Modern Historical Scholarship: Language, Law and History in the French Renaissance* (New York: Columbia University Press, 1970).

65. Schwoerer, *The Declaration of Rights*, chap. 4 and conclusion.

66. Schwoerer, *The Declaration of Rights*, 96–98.

67. British Library, Add. MSS 51, 590, fol. 12v.

68. Lois G. Schwoerer, "The Trial of Lord William Russell (1683): Judicial Murder?" *Journal of Legal History* 9 (September 1988): 142–68.

69. *A Letter To a Gentleman at Brussels*; Henry Booth, Lord Delamere, *The late Lord Russell's Case with Observations upon it*. This tract was found in the Public Record Office, S32/16, fols. 14–23.

70. Benedict Anderson, *Imagined Communities Reflection on the Origin and Spread of Nationalism* (London: Verso, 1983); Clark, *The Language of Liberty 1660–1832*, 19, 46, 55; Linda Colley, *Britons Forging the Nation 1707–1837* (New Haven, Conn.: Yale University Press, 1992), for the creation of Great Britain;

Brian Levack, *The Formation of the British State: England, Scotland and the Union 1603–1707* (Oxford: Oxford University Press, 1987).

71. Clark, *The Language of Liberty 1660-1832*, 47. At greater leisure I would argue that the bases of early modern national identity included other things, such as new forms of the press, ceremonies and processions, monarchical display and myth, literature (especially Shakespeare's history plays), and even the relatively new urban living. I would also dissent from Clark's emphatic distancing of national identity in the "old society" from its later forms (46).

72. Colley, *Britons Forging the Nation 1707–1837*, 54, 369, and chap. l.

73. *Richard II*, act 2, sc. 1.

74. Quoted in Baker, "Criminal Courts and Procedure at Common Law," 18.

75. Care, *English Liberties*, 206; see also 1, 2, 5.

76. Hawles, *English-man's Right*, 7.

77. Hawles, *English-man's Right*, 3, 4, 22.

78. *A Guide To English Juries*, 156, 157, 162.

79. The title continued: *Containing I. Magna Charta, with a learned Comment upon it. . .V. And Lastly, The Charter of Liberties granted by the said William Penn to the Free-men and Inhabitants of the Province of Pennsilvania and Territories thereunto annexed, in America.* A facsimile was reprinted in 1897. Winthrop S. Hudson, in "William Penn's *English Liberties*: Tract for Several Times," *William and Mary Quarterly* 26 (October 1969): 578–85, was the first to notice Penn's indebtedness to Care's tract. He hypothesized that Penn was the true author. Penn scholars and others reject this suggestion, however: see Edwin B. Bronner, ed., *William Penn's Published Writings, 1660-1726: An Interpretive Bibliography*, vol. 5 of *The Papers of William Penn*, ed. Mary Maples Dunn and Richard Dunn, 5 vols. (Philadelphia: University of Pennsylvania Press, 1981–1987), 5:332–33, 530. See also Richard Ashcraft, *Revolutionary Politics and Locke's Two Treatises of Government* (Princeton, N.J.: Princeton University Press, 1986), 204–5 n. 98.

80. H. Trevor Colbourn, *The Lamp of Experience: Whig History and the Intellectual Origins of the American Revolution* (Chapel Hill: University of North Carolina Press, 1965), 14.

81. See Edwin Wolf, *Book Culture of a Colonial American City: Philadelphia Books, Bookmen, and Booksellers* (Oxford: Clarendon Press, 1988), 119–20. See also Colbourn, *The Lamp of Experience*, 206–8.

82. *Catalogue of the Library of Thomas Jefferson*, compiled with annotation by E. Millicent Sowerby, 5 vols. (Washington, D.C.: Library of Congress, 1952–1959), 3: 118–19; Colbourn, *Lamp of Experience*, 159, 218, 221.

83. Colbourn, *Lamp of Experience*, 135, 205.

84. An advertisement appeared in Franklin's reprint of *Every Man his own Doctor: or, The poor planter's physician. . .* (1673; reprint, Philadelphia, 1734), 55–56.

85. Clinton Laurence Rossiter, *Seedtime of the Republic: The Origin of the American Tradition of Political Liberty* (New York: Harcourt Brace & Company, 1953), 388–89.

86. Quoted in Rossiter, *Seedtime of the Republic*, 388–89.

87. Rossiter, *Seedtime of the Republic*, 388.

88. Colbourn, *Lamp of Experience*, 29, 37.

89. Hudson, "William Penn's *English Liberties*," 585.

90. Clark, *The Language of Liberty 1660–1832*, 27 n. 101.

CHAPTER TWO

1776:
THE COUNTERCYCLICAL REVOLUTION

John M. Murrin

A View of the South Part of Lexington, April 19, 1975, *a painting by Ralph Earl, later engraved by Amos Doolittle. Used by permission of the Chicago Historical Society.*

"I shall burn all my Greek and Latin books," exclaimed the jubilant Horace Walpole in 1762 when he heard of the capture of Martinique; "they are histories of little people. The Romans never conquered the world, till they had conquered three parts of it, and were three hundred years about it; we subdue the globe in three campaigns; and a globe, let me tell you, as big again as it was in their days."[1] In five years beginning in 1758, the British Empire crushed New France, took Guadeloupe and Martinique from France, nearly drove the French out of India, brutally punished the Cherokees for entering the North American war in 1760, and when Spain finally intervened in the struggle in 1762, conquered Havana and Manila before the Peace of Paris ended the fighting in 1763.[2] Nothing in the history of the British people prepared them for so awesome a triumph. And yet, just twelve years later, British soldiers clashed with Massachusetts militia at Lexington and began another world war. Both France and Spain intervened, and by 1783 Britain had to concede the independence of the United States of America.

The irony was overwhelming. It still is. To many contemporaries, including both the duc de Choiseul and the comte de Vergennes (that is, the French foreign minister who negotiated the peace treaty and his successor who gave America the French alliance in 1778), Britain's spectacular triumph over its imperial rivals by 1763 all but guaranteed the revolt of the mainland colonies in the years that followed. With no French or Spanish enemy nearby to threaten them, the colonists would discover, both men predicted, that they no longer needed British protection and would soon throw off British rule.[3]

Choiseul and Vergennes saw the Canada cession as a master stroke of French policy. Many loyalists and historians have agreed with them. Had Canada remained French, lamented Governor Thomas Hutchinson of Massachusetts in 1773, "none of the spirit of opposition to the Mother Country would have yet appeared & I think the effects of [the Canada cession] worse than all we had to fear from the French or Indians."[4]

Yet the argument does not hold up under analysis. The mainland colonies remained vulnerable to assault from the sea, and only Britain could give them naval protection. Although the French army had left Canada, the *habitants* remained behind, and the colonists still feared them. Parliament's Quebec Act of 1774 terrified patriots in the British colonies because they understood its potential. It marked a serious effort to placate the French settlers on their own terms on the eve of conflict between Britain and the thirteen colonies. The First Continental Congress denounced the Quebec Act for encouraging the French settlers "to act with hostility against the free Protestant colonies, whenever a wicked ministry shall chuse so to direct them." Once the fighting began, the Second Continental Congress, fearing that the governor of Quebec "is instigating the people of that province and the Indians to fall upon us," launched its own preemptive invasion of Canada in 1775. The patriots escalated their resistance into armed conflict with Britain not because the Gallic Peril had disappeared but despite their recognition that it had revived.[5]

Britain was unable to convert its gigantic triumph over its imperial rivals into a successful postwar policy for North America. That failure is still, after more than two centuries, the enigma at the core of the American Revolution. Unless we can account for it, we still cannot explain why the Revolution happened at all. In my judgment, the scholarship of the past two or three decades, as wonderful and imaginative as much of it has been, has only deepened this central problem. Old explanations, such as the Canada cession and the rise of a sense of American national identity within the British Empire, have collapsed.[6] Other studies have been giving us an empire that was becoming much more tightly integrated in the three or four decades before independence. We can see similar patterns whether we look at transatlantic migration, the late imperial economy, the rise of evangelical religion, colonial political culture, or the willingness of colonists to embrace a larger British and imperial identity.

The achievement of American independence was a countercyclical event. It ran against the prevailing integrative tendencies of the century. The American Revolution was a crisis of imperial *integration* that the British state could not handle.

I

Beginning around 1730, when the population of the mainland colonies was only about 630,000 settlers and enslaved Africans, transatlantic migration soared to peaks that, in absolute numbers, had never been achieved before. This volume was probably a higher percentage of the existing settler population than any colony had known since its founding generation. About 248,000 enslaved Africans and 284,000 Europeans landed in the thirteen colonies between 1730 and 1775. When the fighting began in 1775, about 10 percent of the residents had arrived in North America since 1760. The British Empire had become a remarkably efficient redistributor of people who took advantage of the demand for labor or the availability of land thousands of miles away. Land in North Carolina, Pennsylvania, New York, or even Nova Scotia could start thousands of people moving across the ocean on quite short notice—close to 10,000 a year by the early 1770s.

But if transatlantic migration was binding ever more people together ever more tightly, the whole process could seem like a disaster to some of those left behind, particularly Irish or Scottish landlords who faced a serious risk of losing most of their tenants and their rental income. Wills Hill, Earl of Hillsborough, owned 100,000 acres of land on his Irish estates and faced constant pressure from emigration. As president of the Board of Trade, he supported the Proclamation of 1763, which created at least a temporary barrier to the settlement of most western lands in North America. He became the first secretary of state for the American colonies in 1768 and again used all his influence to prevent the creation of new colonies in the West. When speculators won over even the king to their Vandalia project, he resigned in frustration in 1772. But the British government did adopt one of his major ideas. It began interviewing emigrants as a way of gauging the seriousness of the problem and, perhaps, as a prelude to a statutory limitation of emigration from the British Isles.[7]

Similar patterns characterized the late imperial economy. It became much more dynamic and efficient after 1730 or 1740, to the great benefit of most colonial consumers and to the pain of some merchants who found that increased competition could seriously reduce their profit margins. The colonial population doubled about every twenty-five years, which meant an automatic increase in demand for British products. But British imports increased even more rapidly than population in the last three to five decades (depending on the colony) before independence and contributed immensely to the growing refinement of life in the half century before independence. And because growing European demand kept the prices of American exports high, while the prices of imports from Britain were falling, partly in response to the first phase of the industrial revolution, the settlers were, in short, getting more for their money. As Glasgow absorbed an ever larger share of the tobacco trade, Scotland also achieved a level of prosperity it had never known before. To a significant degree, Chesapeake tobacco provided the material base for the Scottish Enlightenment, the most exciting intellectual movement of the era.[8]

II

The Great Awakening and internal colonial politics, for very different reasons, have often been invoked to explain why the Revolution happened. On the surface, both seem to provide compelling arguments. Nearly all evangelicals in the thirteen colonies supported the Revolution. Nearly all loyalists, except in Nova Scotia, rejected revivalism. Similarly, the resistance movement after 1764 had strong support within colonial assemblies. It began by affirming the principle of "no taxation without representation," which expanded to "no legislation without consent" by 1774, both of which were strong affirmations of each colony's right to self-government through its elective assembly.

Yet the Great Awakening never pitted North American churches against their British counterparts across the Atlantic. Nothing comparable to the antebellum split of evangelical churches along sectional lines occurred within the British Empire before the Revolution. Instead, the revivals divided communities within themselves and sent both factions looking for allies in other colonies and across the ocean. Beginning with George Whitefield's spectacular tour of the colonies in 1739–1740, the Awakening brought distant peoples into contact with one another who otherwise might never have heard of each other. The College of New Jersey—a Presbyterian institution and the first colonial college founded specifically to propagate vital piety—paid its own homage to the geographical extent of the revivals by taking its first president from Long Island, its second from New Jersey, its third (Jonathan Edwards) from Congregational Massachusetts, its fourth from Virginia, its fifth from Maryland, and its sixth from Scotland. And even though evangelicals gave overwhelming support to the Revolution, antievangelicals were by no means a loyalist phalanx. They can be found all along the political spectrum of the era from Thomas Paine and Thomas Jefferson on the left, to George Washington and James Madison in the center, and to Joseph Galloway and Thomas Hutchinson on the right. Except in Connecticut and New Jersey, evangelicals seldom achieved positions of political leadership. Antirevivalists directed events on both sides of the revolutionary divide.[9]

Underlying trends in colonial public life show similar patterns and ambiguities. In seventeenth-century Virginia, the orthodox colonies of New England, and the Dutch areas of New York, jury trials for noncapital crimes were rare before the Glorious Revolution. Only in the eighteenth century did the colonies fully embrace the jury ideology that had taken shape in England under the later Stuarts, ably described by Lois G. Schwoerer in this volume.[10] In histories of colonial politics, the most misleading assumption has been that of a teeter-totter. If the assembly was rising, royal government must have been declining. Beyond any doubt the assemblies played an increasing role in provincial life throughout the century. They sat longer, passed more laws, and drew on a more elite segment of the population for their membership. But royal government also became measurably stronger in the middle decades of the century. In every colony except New York, the most effective royal governors served sometime between 1720 and the 1760s. In Virginia, South Carolina, and Georgia, they succeeded through a highly ritualized form of persuasion and flattery that the assembly reciprocated. The Virginia House of Burgesses had only one public quarrel with a royal governor in the forty-five years between 1720 and the Stamp Act of 1765. In New Hampshire, Massachusetts, New York, and New Jersey, successful governors used patronage and influence to build majorities in the assembly. And even though all the assemblies helped organize resistance to the Stamp Act and the Townshend Acts, many of them stopped well short of revolution after Parliament passed the Coercive Acts in 1774. In the five colonies from New York through Maryland, no legal assembly ever repudiated the Crown. All of them had to be pushed aside by popularly elected provincial congresses. When the Revolution finally came, much of its thrust was directed at the assemblies, not through them.[11]

Even the language of revolution was a fairly recent British import. Seventeenth-century colonists spoke of their "liberties," not of "rights," much less "natural rights," a phrase that John Locke finally turned into a commonplace expression. The language of natural rights took hold quite late in North America, only during the adult years of the resistance leaders of the 1760s. In the colonies it mixed, sometimes uneasily, with that other heritage from the English Commonwealth tradition, the conviction that public life presents an eternal struggle between power and liberty, that power nearly always wins over time, and that corruption is its most effective weapon. For Bernard Bailyn, this "Country" ideology has become the necessary and sufficient explanation for the Revolution. In the colonies, he argues, formal royal prerogatives were stronger than in Britain, where the Crown, for example, no longer vetoed bills or dismissed judges. But the governors' informal powers, especially their patronage, were never sufficient to manage the assemblies as effectively as Sir Robert Walpole controlled Parliament. This gap between formal and informal constitutions was filled by angry factions who denounced the corruption of royal officials. As early as the 1730s, Bailyn believes, the colonists were primed for revolution. Parliament had only to provide the stimulus to set the process in motion.[12]

The Declaration of Independence did unite the language of natural rights with a formal indictment of George III for a systematic conspiracy to undermine liberty in the colonies, mostly through corruption. Without this pervasive fear, the Revolution of 1776 would not have happened. But for most of the provincial era, the languages of politics had functioned quite differently. Natural rights and English rights were interchangeable terms until the early or mid-1770s. The colonists believed that the English constitution embodied their natural rights.[13]

When the language of corruption was invoked, it often reflected a governor's strength, not, as Bailyn's argument assumes, his weakness. In northern colonies those who attacked corruption were opposition leaders unable to win majority support in the legislature, such as Lewis Morris during the John Peter Zenger affair in New York in the 1730s or the Boston opposition to Governor William Shirley in the late 1740s. In other words, this language replicated its role in British politics in the age of Sir Robert Walpole, who dominated the government between 1721 and 1742. In southern colonies, this "Country" paradigm was not even oppositional after the 1720s. Rather, both governors and planters believed that their colonies had achieved an ideal constitutional balance, and they used the tension between power and liberty to celebrate their own accomplishment, a government without corruption that achieved its goals through mutual trust and cooperation. Maryland's governor, by contrast, had more patronage than any other colonial executive. It never gave him the political effectiveness or stability that Virginia, South Carolina, and Georgia achieved through their stylized politics of harmony.[14]

The Seven Years' War, or what Lawrence Henry Gipson called the Great War for the Empire, brought these integrative tendencies to a culmination. After Britain's very rocky start through 1757, William Pitt took charge of the war effort, sustained about 30,000 redcoats in America, and raised about 20,000 provincial troops for each campaign from 1758 until the fall of Montreal in 1760. The mainland colonies then raised thousands more for the West Indian campaigns of 1761 and 1762. So massive and successful was this overall effort that both Old Lights and New Lights

71

discovered millennial significance in the global triumph of British liberty. The Presbyterian Church, rent by a schism over the revivals in 1741, healed the breach at the height of the war in 1758. When George III succeeded his grandfather as king in 1760, his North American subjects responded warmly to his call for the restoration of virtue and piety to public life. Throughout North America, the colonists gloried in their British identity.[15]

III

We are back where we started. The British Empire by 1763 achieved a level of integration it had never known before, and the result was equally unprecedented—total victory over New France. Yet even though the colonies had been anglicizing their societies for decades, important differences remained between them and the mother country. The most significant involved the household. The English practice of primogeniture had never taken deep hold in America. The head of the household expected to pass his own status down to all his sons and to enable all his daughters to marry men of comparable standing in the community. This pattern dated back to the reforms of the London Company, which made landholding a reasonable ambition for most Virginia settlers after 1618, and Plymouth also made land available to male settlers from the 1620s. Compared with Britain, North America had been a paradise for younger sons for a century and a half. But after about 1750, many households, even if they added a craft to their main occupation of farming, had difficulty sustaining this level of opportunity. Some fathers responded by privileging sons over daughters and older sons over younger ones. In Virginia most tidewater land had been entailed by the 1760s—that is, the owner could not divide the estate for sale in separate parcels or bequeath it to more than one heir, although he could set up other sons on land somewhere else. At this level the basic anglicizing tendencies of the century had to seem like a foreclosure of opportunity to many settlers.[16]

Ceaseless expansion became the American answer to this dilemma, and Indians paid the heaviest price for the ambitions of ordinary settlers. And yet the demand for expansion does not get us very far in trying to explain the onset of the revolution against Britain. The British did slow the process, more for speculators than for actual settlers, and the eagerness of settlers (or squatters) to move west probably helped radicalize great planters who began to despair of the Crown's willingness to grant titles to lands that they claimed. But after Hillsborough's resignation as American secretary in 1772, the British government was also moving toward the settlement of the Ohio Valley. The Revolution erupted because of confrontations along the eastern seaboard, not in the West, although tensions there also contributed to the alienation of affection that fatally undermined British authority.[17]

We are left with the oldest tool available to historians for explaining anything: narrative. We have to tell the story of the three imperial crises that undermined the British Empire despite all the advantages it had won by 1763. The Stamp Act Crisis of 1764–1766 began when George Grenville, the prime minister, tried to address the empire's needs for defense and revenue. In the process he polarized the very real needs of the empire with the traditional rights of the colonists, especially the right to be taxed only through the consent of their assemblies. After Grenville rejected the relevance of this argument, colonial mobs nullified the Stamp Act by compelling the stamp distributors in each colony to resign.

The colonists blamed Grenville's ministry, not Parliament or the Crown, for the crisis, and they rejoiced heartily when George III replaced Grenville with the new ministry of the Marquess of Rockingham in the summer of 1765. Rockingham decided that repeal was the only alternative to a civil war in North America, but he needed a better argument than colonial riots to build a parliamentary majority for repeal. Even before news of colonial nonimportation agreements reached London, he encouraged British merchants and manufacturers to petition for repeal on the grounds that the Grenville program had deranged their trade. This argument then persuaded the colonists that their own nonimportation agreements had been decisive in converting the ministry to repeal, a misconception that would again make nonimportation central to resistance to Britain from 1768 to 1775 as well as from 1806 to 1812. Apparently no one stopped to reflect that the Stamp Act itself, once stamps became unavailable, imposed nonexportation on the colonies for several months. Merchants refused to send ships to sea lest they be confiscated for lack of stamped clearance papers after they reached their destinations. The crisis ended when Parliament repealed the Stamp Act, which had levied taxes on legal documents, pamphlets, and newspapers; but Parliament only amended the Sugar Act of 1764 by lowering the duty on imported molasses from three pence to one penny per gallon while extending the tax to British West Indian as well as foreign molasses. That duty, disguised in the statute's preamble as a regulation of trade, brought in more than £30,000 per year until Lexington.[18]

The colonists believed that they had vindicated their rights as Englishmen. But the resolution of the crisis revealed another gap, this one structural, that hardly anyone but Benjamin Franklin understood. In the debate over the Stamp Act, both sides had rejected the distinction between "internal" taxes, such as excises on the consumption of goods or stamp duties on legal documents, and "external" taxes, or port duties imposed on oceanic commerce. Grenville never doubted that Parliament could lay duties on colonial trade, something that it had been doing since 1673, and he argued that if it possessed that power, it could impose internal taxes as well. Colonial spokesmen denied that Parliament could impose any duties for revenue, either internal or external, but they acknowledged that Parliament could levy port duties for the regulation of trade. Most colonial spokesmen did concede the *power* of Parliament to do all three, but they insisted that Parliament's exercise of the power to tax would deprive them of their rights as Englishmen. The Sons of Liberty, by taking to the streets and nullifying the Stamp Act before it could go into effect, demonstrated—violently but effectively—that whatever Parliament's claim of right, it lacked the power to collect an internal tax. As the Revenue Act of 1766 also demonstrated, it certainly did have that power over American trade, whether or not the colonists conceded the right. Significantly, hardly anybody objected strenuously to the penny duty on molasses. Most merchants saw it as an opportunity to do within the law what they had been doing through smuggling ever since the Molasses Act of 1733.

In short, the Stamp Act crisis was debated along an ideological axis of legislation (the regulation of trade, a power that was conceded to Parliament) versus taxation (which was denied). But the crisis was resolved along the internal–external axis, which both sides claimed was meaningless (see figure 2.1). The Stamp Act was repudiated, but the duty on molasses became more lucrative than ever. Only Benjamin Franklin grasped how the empire had actually been working for the previous century. As he told the House of Commons in 1766, "[T]he sea is yours; you maintain, by your fleets, the safety of navigation in it, and keep it clear of pirates; you may have therefore a natural and equitable right to some toll or duty on merchandizes carried through that part of your dominions, towards defraying the expence you are at in ships to maintain the safety of that carriage." He also thought that elementary prudence would prevent Parliament from

Figure 2.1. Geography and Ideology in the Coming of the Revolution

Internal taxes (1765) Stamp Act	External taxes (1767–1770) Sugar Act (1764) Revenue Act of 1766 Townshend Revenue Act (1767)
Internal legislation (1774) The Massachusetts Government Act showed that this quadrant was the most sacred one to the colonists.	External legislation (1776) The Navigation Acts made this quadrant the most sacred one to the British.

Ideology

Geography

In this figure, the horizontal axis represents ideology, or something in people's minds—for the colonists, the effort to achieve consistency by distinguishing between parliamentary legislation (permissible) and parliamentary taxation (illegitimate). The vertical axis stands for something physical and real, the coastline of North America, which marked the internal–external dichotomy in the debates of the period. To most contemporaries, this dichotomy seemed a matter of expediency, not principle. In fact, it marked the power axis of the empire, the boundary of *effective* parliamentary action. Parliament could exercise power over oceanic commerce. It never succeeded in extending that power to the internal affairs of the colonies.

Note that while the Stamp Act was contested in terms of the taxation–legislation dichotomy, the crisis was resolved along the internal–external axis. The colonists stopped rioting when the Stamp Act was repealed, even though the Sugar Act remained in place and, as amended by the Revenue Act of 1766, became much more blatantly a revenue measure, not a regulation of trade.

Note also that the intersection of the two axes creates four quadrants that can also reveal what the primary issue became in each successive crisis—internal taxation in 1765–1766, external taxation from 1767 to 1770, and internal legislation in 1774–1775. Only with independence did the colonists repudiate the Navigation Acts (external legislation), under which they had lived for more than a century.

abusing this power. Excessive duties would kill trade, not increase revenue. The Townshend Crisis (1767–1770) would change his mind about the underlying decency and wisdom of British imperial policy.[19]

IV

Imperial authority was indeed recovering after repeal of the Stamp Act, but then Charles Townshend launched the second imperial crisis when he persuaded Parliament to pass the Townshend Revenue Act in 1767. It addressed no real problem. It created many new ones. It did not pretend to meet the empire's serious need for revenue to support an army in the West. It took off excises in England that brought in twice as much revenue as Townshend expected to gain from the new duties that he imposed on tea, lead, glass, painters' colors, and paper, to be collected in American ports. That revenue would be used primarily to pay the salaries of colonial governors and judges in northern royal colonies, thus eliminating any dependence they still had on the assemblies. Parliament also created the American Board of Customs Commissioners. In a choice that suggested his desire for a confrontation, Townshend located the headquarters of the new board in Boston, the most violent North American city during the Stamp Act riots, rather than in centrally located Philadelphia, which had been much quieter in 1765.

The colonists reacted much more slowly to the Townshend Revenue Act than they had to the Stamp Act. John Dickinson and other writers realized that whatever Townshend's real objectives had been (he died suddenly in September 1767 before his legislation took effect), it did mark a direct challenge to government by consent in the colonies, but effective resistance to an "external tax" proved difficult to organize. The Massachusetts House of Representatives sent a circular letter to the other assemblies in February 1768 urging a concerted resistance, but not much happened. The southern colonies already paid fixed salaries to their governors and were much less alarmed than Massachusetts by the new use of parliamentary revenue under the Townshend Act. Many merchants balked at the call for another round of nonimportation, and effective agreements did not take hold in the major northern ports until early 1769, more than a year after the Revenue Act went into effect, and then only in response to subsequent British provocations.

If the new measures had been prudently managed, the ministry could probably have gotten through the next few years without creating a serious intercolonial crisis. But in March 1768, raucous (though nonviolent) demonstrations in Boston on the anniversary of the Stamp Act's repeal frightened the Customs Commissioners into a demand for military support, and the violent riot in June that followed the seizure of John Hancock's sloop *Liberty* for smuggling led to a second call for troops. Hillsborough turned these minor incidents into a major crisis. He ordered the Massachusetts House to rescind its circular letter, forbade any other assembly to receive it favorably, and dispatched four regiments of redcoats to Boston. In this way local incidents mushroomed into a confrontation involving all the mainland colonies. Reacting to favorable responses to the circular letter, the governor in every royal province was forced to dissolve his assembly until government by consent really did seem threatened by 1769. The confrontation between the army and Boston led to violence and the deaths of five civilians when soldiers fired in self-defense on an angry crowd on March 5, 1770. As Franklin had warned in 1766 when asked whether soldiers could enforce the Stamp Act, "They will not find a rebellion; they may indeed make one."[20]

Lord North broke up colonial resistance by repealing all the Townshend duties except the one on tea, which had, in fact, provided over 70 percent of the revenue collected under the act. Although British tea continued to be boycotted, the broader nonimportation agreements fell apart by the end of 1770, and colonial spokesmen harshly condemned those colonies, such as Rhode Island and New York, that were first to capitulate. As gratifying as these outbursts must have been to imperial officials, another trend was more significant. Nobody celebrated. The Sons of Liberty knew they had lost a major encounter. The simultaneous failure of the Wilkite reform movement in England, in which about a fourth of the voters signed petitions calling for new parliamentary elections, persuaded many observers that government by consent was indeed under siege throughout the empire.[21]

The real significance of the Townshend Crisis is that it never ended and that it made a conspiracy thesis quite credible to American settlers. Sober colonists now suspected that Parliament itself, not just one particular ministry, was deeply corrupt and still planning to deprive them of their liberties. Why else would it insist on retaining the tea tax? Many colonists were also losing confidence in the integrity of the king, who never responded to any of their petitions. The most significant casualty during the second imperial crisis was the erosion of the mutual confidence, or what colonists called the "affection," that had bound the largely voluntaristic societies of North America together with the hierarchical kingdom of Great Britain into an effective empire. The *Gaspée* affair of 1772, in which Rhode Islanders destroyed a marauding customs vessel, illustrated how far mutual trust had disintegrated by then. When Britain tried to identify the perpetrators and ship them to England to stand trial for their lives, no one in Rhode Island would name them, and even more ominously for imperial harmony, twelve colonies—all but Pennsylvania—created legislative committees of correspondence to keep in touch with one another and *anticipate* the next assault of the British government on colonial liberties. The coming of the Revolution is really a story of growing colonial disaffection, the destruction of the one bond that had held very different societies together despite the inability of nearly all leaders to explain adequately how the imperial system actually worked.[22]

V

In 1773, Lord North revised his colonial policy around a seemingly sensible but disastrously mistaken assumption. Nobody, he reasoned, would start a revolution if the government *lowered* the price of tea in the colonies. In response to a major credit crisis and the possible bankruptcy of the East India Company, Britain's largest corporation, the company, seconded by Franklin, asked North to repeal the Townshend duty in America and thus open the whole continent to British tea. North rejected that suggestion in favor of something more clever. He repealed the remaining import duties on the company's tea within Britain but kept the Townshend duty in America. That change would permit the company to undersell smuggled Dutch tea in both Britain and the colonies. The Tea Act also granted the company and its small number of consignees a monopoly on shipping the tea to America and selling it there to consumers.

These monopolistic features gave the Sons of Liberty the leverage they needed to nullify the act. They did not have to try to police the entire waterfront to enforce nonimportation, as during the Townshend Crisis. They could concentrate their attention on the small number of vessels carrying the tea. They pressured consignees to resign and forced the specially chartered tea ships to depart without landing their cargoes. These tactics worked everywhere but Boston, where Governor Thomas Hutchinson protected the consignees in Castle William in Boston harbor and then refused to grant clearance papers to the tea ships. On the night before the duties would have to be paid, the patriots dumped 342 chests of tea into Boston harbor rather than allow cheap but dutied tea to get loose among Massachusetts consumers and thus establish a precedent for broader parliamentary taxation of the colonies.[23]

Parliament responded with the Coercive Acts. The Boston Port Act, passed in March 1774 and implemented on June 1, closed the port of Boston (including Charlestown) until the town paid for the tea. Britain enforced it ruthlessly and, obviously, the Royal Navy had the power to do so. By the end of June numerous public calls had been issued for a Continental Congress to meet in Philadelphia in September, and it was already clear that any such congress would adopt major trade sanctions against Britain. But then the Massachusetts Government Act, passed in May and implemented in August, transformed the charter government of Massachusetts without the colonists' consent, mostly by making the Council, or upper house, appointive instead of elective and by restricting the powers of town meetings. The result was massive refusal to obey. Jurors would not take oaths under the new arrangements, and county conventions met to close the royal law courts and take charge of local affairs.

Because the new governor, General Sir Thomas Gage, refused to recognize the traditional House of Representatives that had gathered in Salem, the towns elected their own Provincial Congress, which was already convening in Concord, and it created its own Committee of Public Safety as its informal executive body. North's ministry assumed that Gage and his soldiers would be able to intimidate the whole province of Massachusetts Bay. Instead the colonists confined his power to the town of Boston. Taxes went to the Provincial Congress in Concord, not to Gage in Boston. Each county's militia purged itself of untrustworthy officers and accepted leadership from Concord. Stunned, Gage warned North in September that he would need 20,000 redcoats to carry out his mission. He was discovering that the alternative to government by consent was not a more authoritarian and effective structure under the Crown but rather the utter disintegration of British authority in the colony. In January,

North replied by dispatching some reinforcements and by ordering Gage to send an expedition to Concord. The Revolutionary War broke out not over the "external" legislation of the Port Act but in a hopeless attempt to enforce another inland measure, the Massachusetts Government Act.[24]

Once the fighting began and the king rejected even the very moderate Olive Branch Petition of the Second Continental Congress, the conspiracy theses prevalent on both sides of the Atlantic turned into self-fulfilling prophecies. The king believed that the colonists had been plotting independence at least since 1765. The colonists concluded that the 30,000 redcoats and Hessians heading for America proved that the British state was determined to crush their liberties. The last bond of empire to yield was the underlying colonial affection for the British people, who stood condemned in American eyes by their acquiescence in the war and in the king's use of foreign mercenaries. As Thomas Jefferson put it in a passage that did not make the final draft of the Declaration of Independence,

> [T]hese facts have given the last stab to agonizing affection; and manly spirit bids us to renou[n]ce forever these unfeeling brethren. [W]e must endeavor to forget our former love for them, and to hold them, as we hold the rest of mankind, enemies in war, in peace friends. [W]e might have been a free & a great people together; but a communication of grandeur and of freedom, it seems, is below their dignity. [B]e it so, since they will have it. [T]he road to happiness and to glory is open to us too; we will climb it apart from them and acquiesce in the necessity which denounces our eternal separation.[25]

The colonies declared their independence in July, and the British then inflicted on them the bloodiest war in their history to that time. Even two centuries later, the Revolution has been exceeded only by the Civil War in the percentage of casualties suffered by its participants.[26]

VI

The coming of the Revolution is mainly a story of growing popular disaffection. But that pattern does not explain the new political order that arose after independence. To become effective republics, the newly independent states would have to experience internal revolutions that would redefine their public lives in remarkable ways. By 1776 the British made the colonists choose "whether they would be men and not English or whether they would be English and not men," as Edmund S. Morgan has nicely put it.[27] The transition from the rights of Englishmen to the rights of man meant a rejection of the British model of constitutionalism and had truly revolutionary implications. The earliest state constitutions, however, did seem to create something like sovereign legislatures within their borders, even as they groped to find some adequate way to institutionalize what they were beginning to call the separation of powers. At first, in nearly every state, the legislature itself defined the fundamental rights of its citizens, even though, as critics pointed out, any subsequent legislature could then repeal or change them. Rights defined through conventional legislation were not "fundamental" because they could be repealed at any time.

The Massachusetts Constitution of 1780 found an answer to this dilemma. It was drafted by a convention elected only for that purpose, and the constitution was then ratified by the citizens assembled in their town meetings. This procedure drew a sharp distinction between the sovereign people, who alone had the power to make a constitution, and the legislature elected under that constitution. In 1787 the Philadelphia Convention extended that process to the emerging American nation when it insisted that the new Federal Constitution be ratified by state conventions summoned only for that purpose. Popular sovereignty thus took hold as the underlying myth that still organizes public life in the United States.[28]

In France, as William H. Sewell Jr. demonstrates in chapter 3, the Revolution very nearly became the nation, which defined itself as a passionate repudiation of the past. Americans, by contrast, did not reject the Gregorian calendar or the boundaries of their states as they had been laid out under British colonial rule. In Eric Van Young's terms, they launched the most successful creole revolution of the era, an accomplishment made possible because, unlike their Latin American counterparts, they seldom had to listen to the voices of indigenous peoples or of their own enslaved Africans. The muted protests of these "others" enabled the settlers to participate fully in the transatlantic revolution that soon spread from North America to France. But unlike the French, the American public did not even debate the nation or the shape it ought to assume until the ratification struggle that followed the Philadelphia Convention of 1787. In the

United States the Revolution was a military struggle for independence that inspired republican experiments at the state level, but a sense of American national identity emerged only gradually, mostly as a consequence of independence and a recognition, especially among Federalists, that if the Union collapsed, the results could be catastrophic. Americans set about defining their national identity because most of them realized that they were not yet a nation. Why else would some men, two decades after the ratification struggle, have organized an Association of American Patriots for the Purpose of Forming a National Character?[29]

Two aspects of America's countercyclical revolution remain surprising. First, it did remarkably little long-term damage to Great Britain, which soon discovered that it could retain most of the economic benefits of the old imperial system without assuming the costs of defense. Second, although Americans had lived under British rule for a century and a half almost without even contemplating independence, once they repudiated George III, they did not look back. There has never been a serious movement since 1776 to restore monarchy in the United States, and no central government of the United States has ever claimed the powers of a sovereign parliament. From the perspective of most Indians, the new republic was more imperial than the old empire. The Revolution generated irresistible pressure to open the West to settlement and vastly expanded the public role of ordinary householders. But among the victors in the revolutionary struggle, the biggest gainers were middling white householders who won an unprecedented share of public power. The lower houses of the legislature grew much larger and became open to men of modest wealth, the suffrage expanded, and, as the political parties took hold nationally after 1790, voter turnout sometimes reached extraordinary levels.[30]

In the twelve years after ratification, the Federalist Party tried to turn the American republic into a purified version of the British state by funding the national debt at par, chartering the Bank of the United States (modeled on the Bank of England) to handle government finance, and creating a professional army and navy. Their Democratic-Republican opponents denounced them as mad anglophiles who would probably restore monarchy if they could, a charge that all but a few Federalists denied in good conscience. But only after the so-called revolution of 1800, which brought Jefferson and the Democratic-Republicans to power on the national level, did the American Revolutionary Settlement take permanent hold. Jefferson reduced the army and navy to token strength, set about paying off the national debt (without repudiating it), and rejoiced when the charter of the Bank of the United States expired in 1811. The Louisiana Purchase, meanwhile, doubled the land area of the nation.

Jefferson's republic became the embodiment of American exceptionalism. Jeffersonians rejected active participation in Europe's balance of power. They set out to achieve hegemony within North America, not in the conventional European manner of building enormous armies and fleets sustained by a huge burden of taxation but by encouraging American citizens to take physical possession of the continent from the Atlantic to the Pacific, to the terror of its Indian occupants and of the republic's Mexican neighbors. (Canadians fared better because they still had British protection.) The Monroe Doctrine extended these ambitions to the entire Western Hemisphere. No other society has ever tried anything of the kind.[31]

In 1838, young Abraham Lincoln, in his first major public address, spelled out some of the implications of this achievement:

> All the armies of Europe, Asia, and Africa combined, with all the treasure of the earth (our own excepted) in their military chest; with a Buonaparte for a commander, could not by force, take a drink from the Ohio, or make a track on the Blue Ridge, in a trial of a thousand years.
> ... If destruction be our lot, we must ourselves be its author and finisher. As a nation of freemen, we must live through all time, or die by suicide.[32]

The success of the United States made the republic unique and probably gave it the ability to hold the loyalties of its citizens through its most severe crisis, the Civil War. One wonders how often Lincoln recalled these words during that struggle.

But American exceptionalism has also had a price. No other society has ever been able to imitate it. Others can borrow from our constitutions and bills of rights and have often combined them with some version of parliamentary government derived from Britain. But no one else has ever aspired to hegemony over an entire hemisphere, sustained without a serious military establishment only through the everyday economic activities of its citizens. That accomplishment became the most distinctive legacy of 1776 and, for most Americans, defined their national identity until the world wars of the twentieth century forced the United States to create an army, navy, and air force that could match any others on the planet. The long-term consequences of this transformation are still unfolding. Most spokesmen for the revolutionary generation would warn us to be on guard. Global empire and liberty do not easily reinforce one another.

Suggested Readings

Bailyn, Bernard
The Ideological Origins of the American Revolution. Cambridge, Mass.: Harvard University Press, 1967.

Bonwick, Colin
English Radicals and the American Revolution. Chapel Hill: University of North Carolina Press, 1977.

Bushman, Richard L.
The Refinement of America: Persons, Houses, Cities. New York: Knopf, 1992.

Jensen, Merrill
The Founding of a Nation: A History of the American Revolution, 1763–1776. New York: Oxford University Press, 1968.

Landsman, Ned C.
From Colonials to Provincials: American Thought and Culture, 1680–1760. New York: Twayne, 1997.

Maier, Pauline
From Resistance to Revolution: Colonial Radicals and the Development of American Opposition to Britain, 1765–1776. New York: Knopf, 1972.

Morgan, Edmund S., and Helen M. Morgan
The Stamp Act Crisis: Prologue to Revolution. 3rd ed. Chapel Hill: University of North Carolina Press, 1995 [1953].

Palmer, Robert R.
The Age of the Democratic Revolution: A Political History of Europe and America, 1760–1800. 2 vols. Princeton, N.J.: Princeton University Press, 1959–1964.

Pocock, J. G. A., ed.
Three British Revolutions: 1641, 1688, 1776. Princeton, N.J.: Princeton University Press, 1980.

Wood, Gordon S.
The Creation of the American Republic, 1776–1787. Chapel Hill: University of North Carolina Press, 1969.

Notes

1. Horace Walpole to George Montague, March 22, 1762, *The Yale Edition of Horace Walpole's Correspondence*, ed. W. S. Lewis et al., 43 vols. (New Haven, Conn.: Yale University Press, 1937–1983), 10: 22.

2. To regain Havana, Spain ceded Florida to Britain and agreed to pay an enormous ransom for Manila. Britain returned Guadeloupe and Martinique to France.

3. For the prophecies of Choiseul and Vergennes, see Edward Channing, *A History of the United States*, 6 vols. (New York: Macmillan, 1905–1925), 2: 602–3.

4. See especially Lawrence Henry Gipson, "The American Revolution as an Aftermath of the Great War for the Empire, 1754–1763," *Political Science Quarterly* 65 (March 1950): 86–104, esp. 104.

5. For a fuller discussion, see John M. Murrin, "The French and Indian War, the American Revolution, and the Counterfactual Hypothesis: Reflections on Lawrence Henry Gipson and John Shy," *Reviews in American History* 1 (September 1973): 307–18. The quotations are from "The Association" (October 1774) and the "Declaration of the Causes and Necessities of Taking Up Arms" (July 1775), *Journals of the Continental Congress, 1774–1789*, ed. Worthington Chauncey Ford, 34 vols. (Washington, D.C.: U.S. Government Printing Office, 1904–1937), 1: 76; 2: 152.

6. See my "A Roof without Walls: The Dilemma of American National Identity," in *Beyond Confederation: Origins of the Constitution and American National Identity*, ed. Richard Beeman, Stephen Botein, and Edward C. Carter II (Chapel Hill: University of North Carolina Press, 1987), 333–48, and T. H. Breen, "Ideology and Nationalism on the Eve of the American Revolution: More Revisions in Need of Revising," *Journal of American History* 84 (June 1997): 13–39.

7. Aaron Fogleman, "Migrations to the Thirteen North American Colonies, 1700–1775: New Estimates," *Journal of Interdisciplinary History* 22 (spring 1992): 691–709, esp. table 1 on p. 698; Bernard Bailyn, *Voyagers to the West: A Passage in the Peopling of America on the Eve of the Revolution* (New York: Knopf, 1986), esp. 29–36 on Hillsborough; and Bernard Bailyn and Philip D. Morgan, eds., *Strangers within the Realm: Cultural Margins of the First British Empire* (Chapel Hill: University of North Carolina Press, 1991).

8. Some of the most relevant studies, within a huge literature, are James F. Shepherd and Gary M. Walton, *Shipping, Maritime Trade, and the Economic Development of Colonial North America* (Cambridge: Cambridge University Press, 1972); John W. Tyler, *Smugglers and Patriots: Boston Merchants and the Advent of the American Revolution* (Boston: Northeastern University Press, 1986); Thomas M. Doerflinger, *A Vigorous Spirit of Enterprise: Merchants and Economic Development in*

Revolutionary Philadelphia (Chapel Hill: University of North Carolina Press, 1986); T. H. Breen, "'Baubles of Britain': The American and Consumer Revolutions of the Eighteenth Century," *Past and Present* 119 (May 1988): 73–104; Cary Carson, Ronald Hoffman, and Peter J. Albert, eds., *Of Consuming Interests: The Style of Life in the Eighteenth Century* (Charlottesville: University Press of Virginia, 1992); Richard L. Bushman, *The Refinement of America: Persons, Houses, Cities* (New York: Knopf, 1992); Jacob M. Price, "The Rise of Glasgow in the Chesapeake Tobacco Trade, 1707–1775," *William and Mary Quarterly* 11 (April 1954): 179–99; Istvan Hont and Michael Ignatieff, eds., *Wealth and Virtue: The Shaping of Political Economy in the Scottish Enlightenment* (New York: Cambridge University Press, 1983); Richard B. Sher and Jeffrey R. Smitten, eds., *Scotland and America in the Age of Enlightenment* (Princeton, N.J.: Princeton University Press, 1990); and Ned C. Landsman, *From Colonials to Provincials: American Thought and Culture, 1680–1760* (New York: Twayne, 1997).

9. For a fuller discussion, see John M. Murrin, "No Awakening, No Revolution? More Counterfactual Speculations," *Reviews in American History* 11 (June 1983): 161–71.

10. See Lois G. Schwoerer, chapter 1 in this volume. The founders of West New Jersey and Pennsylvania shared the jury ideology described by Schwoerer. William Penn contributed to it in a major way. For the older colonies, see John M. Murrin and A. G. Roeber, "Trial by Jury: The Virginia Paradox," in *The Bill of Rights: A Lively Heritage*, ed. John Kukla (Richmond: Virginia State Library and Archives, 1987), 108–29, and John M. Murrin, "Magistrates, Sinners, and a Precarious Liberty: Trial by Jury in Seventeenth-Century New England," in *Saints and Revolutionaries: Essays on Early American History*, ed. David Hall, John M. Murrin, and Thad W. Tate (New York: Norton, 1984), 152–206, and "English Rights as Ethnic Aggression: The English Conquest, the Charter of Liberties of 1683, and Leisler's Rebellion in New York," in *Authority and Resistance in Early New York*, ed. William Pencak and Conrad Edick Wright (New York: New-York Historical Society, 1988), 56–94. My own research into the court records of nine New England counties for anywhere between three and eight decades after the Glorious Revolution shows that jury trials for noncapital crimes became routine by the early eighteenth century and that acquittal rates rose sharply above what they had been during the Puritan era. For the pattern in eighteenth-century New York, see Julius Goebel Jr. and T. Raymond Naughton, *Law Enforcement in Colonial New York: A Study in Criminal Procedure (1664–1776)* (New York: Commonwealth Fund, 1944).

11. The classic arguments for the rise of the assembly and the decline of royal government were made by Leonard W. Labaree, *Royal Government in America* (New Haven, Conn.: Yale University Press, 1930), and Jack P. Greene, *The Quest for*

Power: The Lower Houses of Assembly in the Southern Royal Colonies, 1689–1776 (Chapel Hill: University of North Carolina Press, 1963). For the growing impact of royal governors, see John M. Murrin, "Political Development," in *Colonial British America: Essays in the New History of the Early Modern Era*, ed. Jack P. Greene and J. R. Pole (Baltimore: The Johns Hopkins University Press, 1984), 408–56.

12. See James H. Hutson, "The Emergence of the Modern Concept of a Right in America: The Contribution of Michel Villey," *American Journal of Jurisprudence* 39 (1994): 185–224; John M. Murrin, "From Liberties to Rights: The Struggle in Colonial Massachusetts," in *The Bill of Rights and the States: The Colonial and Revolutionary Origins of American Liberties*, ed. Patrick Conley and John P. Kaminski (Madison, Wis.: Madison House, 1992), 63–99; T. H. Breen, "The Lockean Moment: The Language of Rights on the Eve of the American Revolution," (lecture, University of Oxford, May 15, 2001); and Bernard Bailyn, *The Ideological Origins of the American Revolution* (Cambridge, Mass.: Belknap Press, 1967), and *The Origins of American Politics* (New York: Knopf, 1968).

13. Jeremy Stern, in a Princeton dissertation (still in progress) on the Townshend Crisis in Massachusetts, is paying close attention to the radicalization of language, including the shift toward an emphasis on John Locke and natural rights.

14. For a fuller discussion of political culture in the colonies, see Jack P. Greene, "Political Mimesis: A Consideration of the Historical and Cultural Roots of Legislative Behavior in the British Colonies in the Eighteenth Century," with a comment by Bernard Bailyn and a reply by Greene, *American Historical Review* 75 (December 1969): 337–67, and Murrin, "Political Development," in Greene and Pole, eds., *Colonial British America*, 408–56. Two excellent studies of northern governors are Jere R. Daniell, "Politics in New Hampshire under Governor Benning Wentworth, 1741–1767," *William and Mary Quarterly* 23 (January 1966): 76–105, and John A. Schutz, *William Shirley, King's Governor of Massachusetts* (Chapel Hill: University of North Carolina Press, 1961). For "Country" politics in southern colonies, see David Alan Williams, "Anglo-Virginia Politics, 1690–1735," in *Anglo-American Political Relations, 1675–1775*, ed. Alison G. Olson and Richard M. Brown (New Brunswick, N.J.: Rutgers University Press, 1970), 76–91; Robert M. Weir, "'The Harmony We Were Famous For': An Interpretation of Pre-revolutionary South Carolina Politics," *William and Mary Quarterly* 26 (October 1969): 473–501; and W. W. Abbot, *The Royal Governors of Georgia, 1754–1775* (Chapel Hill: University of North Carolina Press, 1959). For a spectacular glimpse of the ruthless and dysfunctional tone of Maryland politics, see Cecilius Calvert to Governor Horatio Sharpe, March 17, 1761, *Archives of Maryland*, ed. William Hand Browne et al., 72 vols. (Baltimore: Maryland Historical Society, 1883–1972), 14: 1–13.

15. For a superb study of the conflict, see Fred Anderson, *Crucible of War: The Seven Years' War and the Fate of Empire in British North America, 1754–1766* (New

York: Knopf, 2000). His earlier book, *A People's Army: Massachusetts Soldiers and Society in the Seven Years' War* (Chapel Hill: University of North Carolina Press, 1984), is primarily a study of 1756, when tensions between British officers and provincial soldiers reached their peak. Harold E. Selesky, *War and Society in Colonial Connecticut* (New Haven, Conn.: Yale University Press, 1990), emphasizes the growing professionalism of provincial soldiers as the war progressed, including their willingness to reenlist. For millennialism and imperial patriotism, see Nathan O. Hatch, *The Sacred Cause of Liberty: Republican Thought and the Millennium in Revolutionary New England* (New Haven, Conn.: Yale University Press, 1977). Eleven sermons were published in the colonies to celebrate the accession of George III. Dozens more celebrated the capture of Louisbourg, Quebec, and Montreal and the Peace of Paris of 1763.

16. See especially Toby L. Ditz, "Ownership and Obligation: Inheritance and Patriarchal Households in Connecticut, 1750–1820," *William and Mary Quarterly* 47 (April 1990): 235–65; Gloria L. Main, "Inequality in Early America: The Evidence from Probate Records of Massachusetts and Maryland," *Journal of Interdisciplinary History* 7 (spring 1977): 559–81; Gordon S. Wood, *The Radicalism of the American Revolution* (New York: Knopf, 1992), esp. chap. 3; and Holly Brewer, "Entailing Aristocracy in Colonial Virginia: 'Ancient Feudal Restraints' and Revolutionary Reform," *William and Mary Quarterly* 54 (April 1997): 307–46.

17. Marc Egnal, *A Mighty Empire: The Origins of the American Revolution* (Ithaca, N.Y.: Cornell University Press, 1988), tries to link revolutionaries with expansion and loyalists with opposition to expansion. In my judgment, his argument is too teleological. Eric Hinderaker, *Elusive Empires: Constructing Colonialism in the Ohio Valley, 1673–1800* (New York: Cambridge University Press, 1997), is a brilliant contrast of French, British, and American imperialism in the Ohio Valley. See also Woody Holton, "The Ohio Indians and the Coming of the American Revolution in Virginia," *Journal of Southern History* 60 (August 1994): 453–78, and, more generally, *Forced Founders: Indians, Debtors, Slaves and the Making of the American Revolution in Virginia* (Chapel Hill: University of North Carolina Press, 1999).

18. P. D. G. Thomas, *British Politics and the Stamp Act Crisis: The First Phase of the American Revolution* (Oxford: Clarendon Press, 1975); Paul Langford, *The First Rockingham Administration, 1765–1766* (Oxford: Oxford University Press, 1973); Jean-Yves LeSaux, "Commerce and Consent: Edmund Burke's Imperial Vision and the American Revolution" (Ph.D. diss., Princeton University, 1992). LeSaux shows that, although all British spokesmen accepted parliamentary sovereignty, they could mean very different things when they invoked it.

19. The best study is still Edmund S. Morgan and Helen M. Morgan, *The Stamp Act Crisis: Prologue to Revolution*, 3rd ed. (Chapel Hill: University of North

Carolina Press, 1995). For the Franklin quotation, see Edmund S. Morgan, ed., *Prologue to Revolution: Sources and Documents on the Stamp Act Crisis, 1764–1766* (Chapel Hill: University of North Carolina Press, 1959), 145.

20. Morgan, *Prologue to Revolution*, 144.

21. George Rudé, *Wilkes and Liberty: A Social Study of 1763 to 1774* (Oxford: Clarendon Press, 1962); P. D. G. Thomas, *John Wilkes: A Friend to Liberty* (Oxford: Clarendon Press, 1996).

22. Easily the best narrative history of these events is Merrill Jensen, *The Founding of a Nation: A History of the American Revolution, 1763–1776* (New York: Oxford University Press, 1968), 186–433. Pauline Maier, *From Resistance to Revolution: Colonial Radicals and the Development of American Opposition to Britain, 1765–1776* (New York: Knopf, 1972), is a very perceptive study of the process of disaffection, which was a much stronger word in the eighteenth century than it is today. See also Pauline Maier, "John Wilkes and American Disillusionment with Britain," *William and Mary Quarterly* 20 (July 1963): 373–95, and "Coming to Terms with Samuel Adams," *American Historical Review* 81 (February 1976): 12–30. Richard D. Brown, *Revolutionary Politics in Massachusetts: The Boston Committee of Correspondence and the Towns, 1772–1774* (Cambridge, Mass.: Harvard University Press, 1970), is an essential study of the cumulative process of disaffection.

23. The standard study is Benjamin W. Labaree, *The Boston Tea Party* (New York: Oxford University Press, 1964).

24. David Ammerman, *In the Common Cause: American Response to the Coercive Acts of 1774* (Charlottesville: University Press of Virginia, 1974); David Hackett Fischer, *Paul Revere's Ride* (New York: Oxford University Press, 1994).

25. Pauline Maier, *American Scripture: Making the Declaration of Independence* (New York: Knopf, 1997), 240–41.

26. Howard H. Peckham, *The Toll of Independence: Engagements and Battle Casualties of the American Revolution* (Chicago: University of Chicago Press, 1974), esp. 131–34.

27. Morgan and Morgan, *The Stamp Act Crisis*, 119.

28. Edmund S. Morgan, *Inventing the People: The Rise of Popular Sovereignty in England and America* (New York: Norton, 1988). For a superb, brief account of the development of American constitutionalism in these years, see Robert R. Palmer, *The Age of the Democratic Revolution: A Political History of Europe and America, 1760–1800*, 2 vols. (Princeton, N.J.: Princeton University Press, 1959–1964), 1: 213–35.

29. See William H. Sewell Jr., chapter 3 in this volume, and Eric Van Young, chapter 4 in this volume. See also Isaac Kramnick, "The 'Great National Discussion': The Discourse of National Politics in 1787," *William and Mary Quarterly* 45

(January 1988): 3–32, and, for the Association of American Patriots, Joyce Appleby, *Inheriting the Revolution: The First Generation of Americans* (Cambridge, Mass.: Belknap Press, 2000), 196. For a subtle argument that American leaders understood the importance of the Union but that hardly anybody made its survival his top priority, see James E. Lewis Jr., *The American Union and the Problem of Neighborhood: The United States and the Collapse of the Spanish Empire, 1783–1829* (Chapel Hill: University of North Carolina Press, 1998).

30. Gordon S. Wood, *The Creation of the American Republic, 1776–1787* (Chapel Hill: University of North Carolina Press, 1969); Jackson Turner Main, "Government by the People: The American Revolution and the Democratization of the Legislatures," *William and Mary Quarterly* 23 (July 1966): 354–67; Stanley Elkins and Eric McKitrick, *The Age of Federalism: The Early American Republic* (New York: Oxford University Press 1993).

31. For fuller discussions of the American Revolution Settlement and of American exceptionalism, see John M. Murrin, "The Great Inversion, or, Court versus Country: A Comparison of the Revolution Settlements in England (1688–1721) and America (1776–1816)," in *Three British Revolutions: 1641, 1688, 1776,* ed. J. G. A. Pocock (Princeton, N.J.: Princeton University Press, 1980), 368–453, and "The Jeffersonian Triumph and American Exceptionalism," *Journal of the Early Republic* 20 (spring 2000): 1–25.

32. "Address before the Young Men's Lyceum of Springfield, Illinois, January 27, 1838," In *The Collected Works of Abraham Lincoln,* ed. Roy P. Basler et al., 11 vols. (New Brunswick, N.J.: Rutgers University Press, 1953–1990), 1: 109.

CHAPTER THREE
THE FRENCH REVOLUTION AND THE EMERGENCE OF THE NATION FORM

William H. Sewell Jr.

Unity of the Republic, *painted board. Used by permission of Cliché Bibliothèque nationale de France, Paris.*

The French Revolution has long been regarded as a key episode in the emergence of nationalism. For both Carleton J. H. Hayes and Hans Kohn, who wrote extensively about nationalism between the 1920s and the 1960s, the French Revolution marked a profound intensification of the national principle in European political life and also a point of transition between what Hayes called a "humanitarian nationalism" characteristic of the eighteenth century and of England, France, and America and the more chauvinistic varieties of nationalism that emerged in Germany in response to Napoleonic domination and spread widely in Central and Eastern Europe in the nineteenth and twentieth centuries.[1] But in the more recent round of thinking about nationalism that began in the 1980s, the French Revolution has virtually dropped out of the story. This is most spectacularly true in Benedict Anderson's brilliant and justly influential *Imagined Communities*, surely the most widely read contemporary study of nationalism.[2] One of Anderson's central points about nationalism is that it is "modular." By this he means that there is a reasonably clear and coherent model of what constitutes a nation and that this model can be transported and applied anywhere in the world. In one of his most striking chapters, Anderson argues that this model was initially elaborated and brought to the fore not in the European core but on the American periphery—by what he calls the "creole pioneers," the Anglo-Americans and Spanish Americans who revolted against European colonial powers and established themselves as free and independent republics in the late eighteenth and early nineteenth centuries.

Anderson's stress on the novelty and creativity of the New World revolutions (and more specifically the Spanish American revolutions) is certainly salutary as an exercise in decentering—in counteracting what Anderson quite appropriately terms "European provincialism."[3] But his argument is actually rather clumsy, merely swinging the pendulum back the other way, implausibly leaving Europe out of the story of the emergence of "the nation form"—to use Etienne Balibar's convenient term for the standard model of the nation.[4] Anderson's account belies what seems to me the far more sophisticated form of decentering on which this volume is based, namely, the hypothesis that countries on both sides of the Atlantic were linked together in a common revolutionary dynamic in these years, one whose initiative oscillated back and forth between Europe and the Americas in the "long eighteenth century" between the English "Glorious Revolution" and the Latin American wars of independence. By the early nineteenth century, this transatlantic dynamic certainly had produced a new and portable model of the nation. But I believe that attributing the production of this model solely to the creole pioneers gets the story wrong. My purpose in this chapter is to look more closely at the specific role of the French Revolution in the transatlantic emergence of the modular nation form.

The inadequacy of Anderson's decentering gesture is in fact evident in the rare and contradictory statements he makes about the French Revolution in his text. During his discussion of the Spanish American revolutions, Anderson admits, in passing, the significance of European models:

> There is also no doubt that improving trans-Atlantic communications, and the fact that the various Americas shared languages and cultures with their respective metropoles, meant a relatively rapid and easy transmission of the new economic and political doctrines being produced in Western Europe. The success of the Thirteen Colonies' revolt at the end of the 1770s, and the onset of the French Revolution at the end of the 1780s, did not fail to exert a powerful influence. Nothing confirms this "'cultural revolution'" more than the pervasive *republicanism* of the newly independent communities [in Spanish America].[5]

This, unless I have missed something, is one of only three occurrences of the term "French Revolution" in Anderson's text.[6] And the sentence in which it is tucked away actually casts serious doubt on the claim of American priority since it admits, albeit in double negative, that the French Revolution exerted "a powerful influence" on the Spanish American "pioneers."

Just how powerful this influence was becomes inadvertently clear at the end of the chapter, when Anderson sums up the accomplishments of the creole pioneers:

> [T]he independence movements in the Americas became, as soon as they were printed about, "'concepts,'" "'models,'" and indeed "'blueprints.'" In "'reality,'" Bolívar's fear of Negro insurrections and San Martín's summoning of his indigenes to Peruvianness jostled one another chaotically. But printed words washed away the former almost at once, so that, if recalled at all, it appeared an inconsequential anomaly. Out of the American welter came these imagined realities: nation-states, republican institutions, common citizenships, popular sovereignty, national flags and anthems, etc., and the liquidation of their conceptual opposites: dynastic empires, monarchical institutions, absolutisms, subjecthoods, inherited nobilities, serfdoms, ghettoes, and so forth. . . . In effect, by the second decade of the nineteenth century, if not earlier, a "'model'" of "'the'" independent national state was available for pirating.[7]

The problem is that every one of the elements of the model of the independent national state that Anderson lists here, both the "imagined realities" and "their conceptual opposites," had already been articulated and printed about voluminously—indeed obsessively—during the French Revolution. If this was indeed the model available for pirating, it is hard to escape the conclusion that it had actually been pirated by the Latin Americans from the French—and, to be sure, from the North Americans.

Anderson himself seems to have something of a bad scholarly conscience at this point since he appends a revealing footnote to the final sentence of the passage I have just quoted: "It would be more precise, probably, to say that the model was a complex composite of French and American elements. But the 'observable reality' of France until after 1870 was restored monarchies and the ersatz dynasticism of Napoleon's great-nephew."[8] Here Anderson admits, but only in a footnote, that the French were indeed co-pioneers of the model of the national state. However, he attempts to minimize the significance of the admission by pointing out that for most of the first seven decades of the nineteenth century, the French state was not a republic. This is, of course, true. But earlier in the very passage to which this note is appended, Anderson argues that it is the establishment of models *in print*, not their "observable reality," that matters. If availability of models in print is indeed the appropriate criterion, the French example surely was far more widely available, at least in Europe, than the Spanish American or the North American. Indeed, in a paragraph immediately prior to the one cited previously, Anderson, citing Hobsbawm's *Age of Revolution*, points out that it was in "millions of printed words" written about the French Revolution that the concept or model of revolution became available for pirating. The very same millions of words also made available in print the French model of the nation.[9]

In short, Anderson's argument for the exclusive pioneering status of the Americans is refuted by the contradictions of his own text. The nation form clearly was not entirely a product of the creole pioneers but had a more complicated, transatlantic history. I have neither the space nor the knowledge to trace out that complex history here. But I hope to be able to say something useful about its French phase.

I

Most of the revolutions of modern times have had a significant influence on politics elsewhere in the world. But I would argue that the influence of the French Revolution was particularly profound. Most of the great radical revolutions in the history of the modern world—for example, the American, Spanish American, Russian, Mexican, Chinese, Vietnamese, Cuban, or Iranian revolutions—have taken place on the margins of the world system. But quite the opposite was true of the French Revolution: not only was it by far the most radical revolution that the world had yet seen, but it happened in one of the leading states in Europe, then the politically and economically dominant area of the world. On the eve of the French Revolution, France had Europe's biggest army and the second biggest navy, and although Britain and the Netherlands had somewhat higher per capita incomes, France had the biggest gross domestic product. This was because it was, by the standards of the day, a gargantuan country, with a territory over twice as large as Britain's and a population nearly twice as big. Paris was the intellectual and artistic capital of Europe, and French was the international language of letters, science, diplomacy, and high society. To get a sense of how powerfully the French Revolution affected contemporaries, we might try to imagine how the rest of the world would respond today if an astoundingly radical revolution were to take place in the United States. When Paris rose up in 1789, the world could only watch in rapt attention.

Part of what the world saw when it watched the French Revolution was the construction of a new kind of state and society around the key legitimizing concept of "The Nation." When the delegates of the Third Estate seized legislative power in June 1789, they dubbed themselves the "National Assembly." And when they issued their epoch-making Declaration of the Rights of Man and Citizen in September 1789, its third article stated, "The source of all sovereignty resides essentially in the nation." In the French Revolution, the concept of the nation became a kind of sacred center of political life.

The new "national" state that the French constructed proved itself to be immensely more powerful than its old regime predecessor. It carried out far-reaching reforms touching all spheres of life. It created a new unified legal system; it abolished all sorts of previously sacrosanct personal, political, and pecuniary privileges; it multiplied the state's administrative personnel; it reformed its fiscal system; and it established new, wide-ranging citizenship rights. Moreover, it fielded a new citizen army that—to the amazement and consternation of the European powers—accomplished what Louis XIV at his apogee had never been able to do: it conquered and annexed much of the Low Countries and the Rhineland and, under Napoleon, established a military and political domination over all of Europe except the British Isles and Russia. By self-consciously remaking itself as a nation, France seemed to have tapped into an astounding source of power. It is therefore hardly surprising that the nation form elaborated in the French Revolution came to be widely emulated.

II

On the eve of the French Revolution, "nation" was already a word to conjure with, not only in France but elsewhere in the Western world as well.[10] In the decades before the Revolution, the nation figured in French political discourse, both royal and oppositional, as an active moral person, distinct from the king or the state—as a collective being capable of wishing, acting, judging, and having sentiments.[11] David Bell's recent book argues persuasively that the concepts of *la nation* and *la patrie* had already become absolutely central terms of political debate, imagination, and loyalty in the decades before the Revolution.[12] Appeals to the nation and its interests, judgments, and will certainly were legion in the debates leading up to the French Revolution. But, as Bell points out, the omnipresent invocations of the nation and patrie in the decades before the Revolution had no particular implications for constitutional arrangements in France. Writers in the hire of the royal government were just as likely to extol the nation and patriotic virtue as were philosophes or members of the Parlementaire opposition. To be patriotic and to submit to the sovereign authority of the king were generally understood as perfectly compatible.

Thus, when the National Assembly established the nation as the principle of sovereignty during the summer and early fall of 1789, their action also transformed the semantic character of the concept of the nation. From a highly generalized rhetorical figure that was compatible with all sorts of different political or constitutional orientations and that primarily called up a certain quality of feeling—of devotion to the fatherland and pride in Frenchness—"the nation" came to entail a determinate political position and a distinct set of constitutional relations. The actions of the National Assembly, one might say, redefined the nation from a diffuse sentiment to a specific program for political and constitutional action. Although "the nation" was already a fundamental term in the political discourse of ancien régime France, it is only in the summer of 1789 that one can begin to speak of a nation form.[13]

When the nation was declared sovereign, this revolutionary act fundamentally rearranged the relationship among the nation, the king, and the state or government. The king, who had previously been the sovereign, now became merely a representative of the nation—a particularly august representative to be sure but nonetheless ultimately subordinate to the nation's will. Meanwhile, the National Assembly established itself as the prime representative of the national will and took on itself the task of providing the realm with what it called a "national constitution."[14] It undertook, that is, to reconstitute the state in a new "national" form.

There is a profound semantic ambiguity in the notion of providing France with a "national constitution." On the one hand, it means writing a constitution for the nation—that is, a "fundamental law" that establishes the form of the government, its juridical principles, and the division of powers between various governmental units. But providing the realm with a national constitution also implies the constitution (or the reconstitution) as a nation of the social body to which this fundamental law is applied. In this second sense, the nation, although presumably the sovereign power whose will is represented by the National Assembly, is at the same time to be constituted by the actions of the National Assembly.[15] The paradox embodied in the term "national constitution" was not just a linguistic anomaly: it was also, in effect, the National Assembly's program of government. Writing a constitution for the nation entailed not only drafting a fundamental law but also profoundly recasting the basic relations of French social and political life, a recasting that would bring French society into conformity with the ideal denominated by the term "nation." If the French Revolution created the nation as a form, it did so above all by elaborating a new framework of institutions, laws, modes of behavior, and cultural assumptions that would henceforth be the hallmarks of a fully constituted nation.

III

In order to see what was entailed in constituting France as a nation, we must look briefly at the sociopolitical constitution of France under the old regime—both at its legally based institutional structure and at the forms of solidarity and mutual recognition that this institutional structure both presumed and reinforced.[16] In old regime France—and I think this was true in all European "old regime" societies—the social system was both corporate and hierarchical. It was corporate in the sense that the social order was organized as a complex set of relatively bounded units known variously as corps, communautés, ordres, or états.[17] These units were very diverse in scale and function, ranging from the French state, the church universal, or the three estates of the realm at the large end to guilds, academies, bodies of magistrates, village communities, parishes, families, or confraternities at the small end. Such bodies varied greatly in organization and character, but most were largely self-regulating within their particular sphere, and many held legally enforceable privileges and were recognized as legal persons capable of bringing action in courts. They generally constituted units of solidarity—that is, social units whose members were expected to grant one another mutual respect and recognition, although the extent and character of the recognition varied enormously.

These units were complexly overlapping. Every individual person would as a matter of course be a member (the bodily connotations of this term are intended) of several corps, états, communautés, or ordres. At the very least, everyone was a member of a family, a city or village, a parish, a province, the state, and the church. Some of these units stood in an encompassing/encompassed relation to one another. This was true of the state/province/village set or the church/parish set. In such cases the higher unit would have some degree of authority over the lower, but in practice the relative powers were variable and negotiated, and much was left to local decision. The authority of the higher unit, in other words, did not necessarily trump that of the lower unit. The same was true of solidarity or recognition. Although the king or the church universal had higher claims to loyalty than did the village community or the parish priest, it was frequently the more local loyalties that won out in practice. There were also units that stood in no determinate topological relation to one another, even in theory. There was, for example, no general rule as to whether a person owed more respect to fellow shoemakers, fellow confraternity members, the neighborhood community, or fellow parishioners. People belonged to a whole range of constituted solidary units, sharing communities of recognition in a situationally negotiated fashion with overlapping collections of other persons.

In addition to being corporate, the old regime social system was hierarchical. Far from being built on a notion of the natural or juridical equality of all members, the social order assumed differences in quality, precedent, rank, and honor, both between persons and between corporate units. Indeed, the very term "order," as used under the old regime, implied rank.[18] In this circumstance, recognition was often asymmetrical and graded in character. A given actor recognized some actors as equals but most as either superiors or inferiors. Relations between superiors and inferiors could be genuine relations of mutual recognition in the sense that one's rank or place and consequently one's honor in the social order depended both on whom one treated as a superior or an inferior and on precisely how one treated or was treated by them. Under such a system, recognition was not the opposite of disrespect but was densely interwoven with finely calibrated disrespect, both handed out and received.

France as a "nation" was certainly a marked and named category of solidarity within this system. Attachment to the nation was surely felt most strongly through attachment to the person of the monarch. French men and women recognized one another as French above all by accepting their subjection to the king of France.[19] But France as a national community also had other instantiations: a language, a putatively distinctive set of manners and morals, and a distinct territory. "France" was one of the units of solidarity and mutual recognition that existed in the old regime. However, the boundaries between France and other nations were not especially privileged among the many boundaries that shaped the old regime social system. A boundary between France and other countries was, one might say, relativized by the existence of so many bounded internal units of solidarity. Although certainly far more strongly marked by various military, ideological, fiscal, and administrative means than it had been a few centuries earlier, the national boundary at the end of the eighteenth century was far from being, even in theory, the decisive division between solidarity communities.[20]

IV

When the French revolutionaries reconstituted France as a nation, they attempted to transform radically the old regime social system. The French nation was symbolized and enacted in a whole series of memorable events in the summer and fall of 1789—from the initial proclamation of the National Assembly on June 17, through the tennis court oath later that month, the taking of the Bastille on July 14, the night of August 4 (when the nobility and clergy renounced their privileges), and the October Days (when the king was hauled back from Versailles to Paris, where he would be under the watchful eyes of the people). In these events, the nation was imagined as a supreme unit of solidarity, a sphere of universal and ecstatic mutual recognition. This sense of the supremacy of the nation was perhaps most movingly enacted in the famous *Fête de la fédération*, celebrated on the first anniversary of the taking of the Bastille, in which national guardsmen from all regions of France converged on the capital to celebrate the unity of the nation before throngs of cheering Parisians.[21]

In the course of providing the nation with a new constitution, the revolutionaries systematically destroyed the old corporate bodies, sweeping away the legal supports of the old regime's highly elaborated hierarchical and corporate system. Thus, the preamble of the constitution of 1791 abolished all

> institutions which were injurious to liberty and equality of rights. Neither nobility, nor peerage, nor hereditary distinctions, nor distinctions of orders, nor feudal regime, nor patrimonial courts, nor any titles, denominations, or prerogatives derived therefrom, nor any order of knighthood . . . nor any superiority other than that of public functionaries in the performance of their duties any longer exists. . . . Neither privilege nor exemption to the law common to all Frenchmen any longer exists for any part of the nation or for any individual. Neither the guilds nor corporations of professions, arts, and crafts any longer exist. The law no longer recognizes religious vows or any other obligation contrary to natural rights or the Constitution.[22]

In the place of all the hierarchically ordered corporate bodies, the National Assembly instituted a society composed of rights-bearing individual citizens who were equal before the law and who were governed by a legislature made up of their elected representatives. The welter of intermediary bodies that stood between the individual and the state were swept away. As the deputy Le Chapelier put it in the National Assembly in 1791, "There are no longer corporations in the State; there is no longer anything but the particular interest of each individual and the general interest."[23] The nation, in short, was to take primacy over all other solidary bonds.

This reconstitution of France in the form of a perfected or, as the revolutionaries put it, a regenerated nation meant the transformation of all sorts of institutional arrangements that affected day-to-day social interactions.[24] Marriage was made a civil contract, and divorce was legalized; the lands of the church and of émigré nobles were confiscated, made "national properties," and sold off; the system of weights and measures and the calendar were recast; peasants' seigneurial obligations to lords were abolished, making them either tenants or proprietors in fee simple; forms of address were changed, with the simple *citoyen* and *citoyenne* replacing the old regime's complex and hierarchical system of appelations; geographically diverse systems of law were replaced by a single, unified national legal code; and all the nation's young men were subjected to military conscription. During the radical phase of the Revolution, the revolutionaries went beyond equality before the law to adopt a messianic commitment to political equality as well. In principle, France became, in 1792, a "republic one and indivisible," a nation of equals in which all forms of solidarity intermediate between the nation and the family were henceforth illegitimate. The mutual recognition of citizens was to displace all other forms of social recognition. In short, France as a regenerated nation was very different from France as an old regime monarchy.

In this massive effort of regeneration, both the British Revolution of 1688/1689 and the American Revolution served as important models. During the months before the meeting of the Estates General and right through the summer of 1789, the English constitution served as a ubiquitous, if controversial, point of reference in the raging debates. The group of deputies known as the *monarchiens* favored many of the English constitutional formulas—legislative power shared between a parliament and monarch, a separation and balance of powers, bicameralism, and an absolute royal veto. But over the summer and early fall of 1789, the majority opted for a very different constitutional regime, one based on the concept of a unified general will and featuring a strong unicameral legislature exercising essentially undivided powers—with the king exercising only a suspensive veto. Even before the overthrow of the king in 1792, the French constitutional regime was in reality more a republic than a monarchy.[25]

Nevertheless, both the English and the American models made important contributions to the French constitutional regeneration. For example, the new legal system, even though based on principles very different from Anglo-American common law, adopted jury trials for all criminal cases and for reasons similar to those invoked in the Anglo-American "jury ideology" described by Lois G. Schwoerer in chapter 1.[26] The most important borrowing from the American Revolution was the decision to issue a universal declaration of rights. Here the exemplary character of the Declaration of Independence was unambiguously recognized. It was Lafayette who, drawing on his American experience, introduced the first draft of the declaration to the National Assembly in July 1789. When the debate about the declaration started in earnest the following month, Jean-Paul Rabaut de Saint-Etienne argued that the National Assembly should begin the constitution with a declaration of rights because "like the Americans, we wish to regenerate ourselves." Mathieu duc de Montmorency-Laval, a liberal noble who, like Lafayette, had fought in the American War of Independence, declared in the same debates, "Let us follow the example of the United States. They have given a great example to the new hemisphere: let us give it to the universe."[27]

But as important as the English and American examples were, the basic architecture of the French "national constitution" followed different impulses and was based on different theories from either British or American constitutional practices. Because the French Revolution was directed above all against the hierarchical and corporate character of the old regime sociopolitical system, the model of the British constitution, with its House of Lords and its many lingering privileges, was deemed by the majority insufficient, indeed, downright gothic. The American example, with its insistence that all men are created equal, was much more acceptable, and similarities between the Declaration of Independence and the Declaration of the Rights of Man and Citizen are striking. But the American constitutional architecture, with its strong executive and extensive checks and balances, was hardly suitable in a situation where the problem was to shift sovereignty from the monarch to the nation, as represented by an elected legislature. Finally, as we will see in the following section, American federalism was unthinkable in a situation where the existing provinces were part and parcel of a system of privilege rather than, as in the case of the American states, a band of self-governing republics. The French revolutionaries, largely because they defined their task as the regeneration of a fundamentally vicious sociopolitical order, opted for a highly unified, rationalized, and streamlined national constitution. The solutions worked out by the Americans—who, as the French saw it, were already living in egalitarian republics of rural proprietors before their revolution—were insufficient for the more arduous task of reconstruction facing France.

V

I would like to describe in somewhat more detail one area of institutional reform that I consider particularly important in the emergence of a "modular" nation form: the reform of territorial administration. At first glance, this might seem a tedious and trivial matter, the mere tidying up of assorted boundaries and jurisdictions. But something much more important was going on. The French revolutionaries' reform of territorial administration was intended to produce a new kind of space—a space that was national in character.[28] They regarded the establishment of a new system of territorial divisions as an indispensable step in providing France with a national constitution.[29] This issue seems particularly important for thinking about the emergence of a modular nation form. Benedict Anderson argues that the modern idea of the nation would be impossible without a particular sense of temporality that accompanied the advance of capitalism: a conception of what he, following Walter Benjamin, calls "empty, homogeneous time."[30] In reconstituting the territorial basis of the French nation, the revolutionaries were in effect enacting a new conception of empty, homogeneous space.

Under the old regime, the territory of the French kingdom was divided into provinces of unequal size and importance. These provinces had come under the dominion of the French crown at very different dates and had different relationships to the crown. The provinces were of two types: the *pays d'état* and the *pays d'élection*. The former, generally more distant from Paris and more recently joined to the kingdom, had managed to retain Provincial Estates with significant powers of local government and usually also had provincial Parlements—high courts that governed the administration of laws in the region. Each of the provinces had distinct privileges of one sort or another; the privileges of the pays d'état were simply more extensive and more advantageous than those of the pays d'élection. But provinces were not the only territorial units that possessed privileges. Many cities, towns, and even some rural districts had their exclusive powers, jurisdictions, and forms of government, many of which depended on individual charters or letters patent granted directly by the king.

The territorial organization of the kingdom was, hence, part and parcel of the hierarchical and corporate organization of old regime society. For this reason, the National Assembly made territorial reorganization one of its top priorities. On the night of August 4, 1789, when the privileges of the nobles and the church were abolished by an ecstatic National Assembly, the privileges of the provinces were abolished as well. The wording of the article that did so is particularly telling:

> Since a national constitution and public liberty are more advantageous to the provinces than the privileges which some of them have been enjoying, and which must necessarily be sacrificed for the intimate union of all parts of the realm, it is declared that all the particular privileges of provinces, principalities, regions, cantons, towns, and municipalities, whether financial or of any other kind, are abolished forever, and will be absorbed into the law common to all Frenchmen.[31]

The privileges of all kinds of localities were to be replaced by a "national constitution," which would give them something far more valuable than their particular privileges: "public liberty" regulated by "a law common to all Frenchmen."

But even if the provinces were stripped of their privileges, their continued existence as territorial units could cause difficulties. According to the abbé Sieyès, it was absolutely essential to proceed to a new division of the territory. Otherwise, he argued, the provinces "will maintain eternally their esprit de corps, their pretensions, their jealousies." Moreover, the provinces were of starkly different sizes and would therefore continue to be unequal in fact.[32] There were, moreover, other difficulties: under the old regime there was not one system of territorial division but rather several different and noncongruent systems. There were military divisions called "governments," judicial divisions known as "baillages" or bailliwicks, fiscal and administrative divisions known as "generalities," and religious divisions (the dioceses). The boundaries of these units rarely corresponded; under the old regime territorial system, the national surface was subjected to a complex thicket of overlapping jurisdictions.

Sieyès and his collaborator Thouret, acting on behalf of the Constitutional Committee of the Assembly, proposed a radical simplification of this system, one based on new units—the departments—which were to be strictly equal in size. Sieyès's exposition of the proposed reform began with a geometrical mapping scheme:

Taking Paris as the center, I would form a perfect square . . . of eighteen leagues by eighteen, which would make an area of 324 square leagues; that would be a territorial department. On each side of this first square, I would form another of the same size, continuing in this way until the most distant borders had been reached. . . . There will be 80 departments, because 80 divisions of 324 square leagues is more or less equal to the 26 thousand square leagues that are supposed to make up the total territory of France.[33]

These eighty departments would in turn be divided into nine communes, each of which would be six leagues square, and these would be divided into cantons.[34] These units would become the framework for all functions of the state: taxation, administration, the army, the church, the courts, and political representation.

To an American, this plan for cutting up the national territory into perfect squares immediately brings to mind the Northwest Ordinance of 1785, which decreed the inscription of a rectilinear division of the entire western territory of the United States into quarter sections, sections, and townships and eventually made thinkable the creation of western states such as Colorado, Wyoming, and Utah with entirely rectilinear boundaries.[35] I have found no reference to the American example in the French Revolutionary debates on the subject of territorial division. But the emergence of two such similar plans within four years of each other indicates that politicians on both sides of the Atlantic shared strikingly similar forms of quantitative rational thought in the late eighteenth century.

In the legislation actually submitted to the Assembly, the geometric rigor of Sieyès's sketch was relaxed. The departments remained as equal in area as possible, but the boundaries were not rectilinear. Rather, they followed rivers, mountain ridges, and existing boundaries between villages or municipalities. Indeed, the maps were even drawn in such a way as to follow as closely as possible the former boundaries of provinces, so that the former Alsace was essentially divided up into two departments, the former Brittany into four, and so on. This respect for the boundaries of the former provinces softened the blow for those who still clung to old provincial loyalties. But it did not change the fact that under the new national constitution the provinces became mere geographical expressions rather than units of government. Moreover, the names of the provinces disappeared altogether. The departments were named after rivers, mountains, and other natural features. The two departments that made up the former Alsace were now the Upper Rhine and the Lower Rhine; the former Provence was now the Lower Alps, the Var, and the Mouths of the Rhone; and the former Rousillon was now the Eastern Pyrenees.

In short, the provinces disappeared from the map, and the entire territory of the nation became conceptually and institutionally homogeneous, divided into a well-ordered sequence of progressively larger units—communes, districts, departments, and finally France as a whole. Each of these units would be governed by freely chosen representatives who in turn would choose representatives to the next-higher unit, climaxing in the National Assembly itself. The territorial units, in short, would be self-governing, but they would emphatically not be privileged corporations, divided from others by their particular immunities, peculiar laws, and private advantages. The new units, while spatially distinct from each other, would also mirror each other. They would be integral parts of what the abbé Sieyès called "one great people, regulated by the same laws and the same administration."[36]

The new territorial system would of course create a far more rational administrative system, and its sponsors were certainly aware of this advantage. Yet the real point of the reform was not efficiency but unity and equality, which it was to inscribe on the very soil of France. Thouret, the cosponsor of the legislation, claimed that as a consequence of the new territorial system, "the national spirit" would be "better formed." "[A]ll the French will be united in a single family, having only one law, and a single mode of government. They will abjure all prejudices arising from the spirit of particular and local corporations." "Who," he asked, "will not sense that attachment to the great national union is worth a thousand times more than the partial corporations that are to be disavowed by the Constitution?" Or, as Rabaut de Saint-Etienne put it, eliminating the provinces would mean that "there is no longer a diversity of nations in the kingdom; there are only the French." By instituting the new territorial units, the revolutionaries were creating an empty, homogeneous national space whose units, conceptually and morally identical, combined to form a unified nation.[37]

The redivision of the national territory was one of the most successful and durable reforms of the French Revolution. The new system was retained by the restored monarchy in 1815 and has remained in place through the many changes in the constitutional regime of France right up to the present. Those who designed the reforms may have expected them to succeed above all because of their sublimely rational quality. But the success of the reforms in practice probably had more to do with the way they rearranged the stakes of local politics. While provincial identities—say, as Breton or Provençal—could continue more or less intact, the provinces ceased to be loci of government. If one needed a permit or wished to initiate a lawsuit, one went to the *chef lieu* of the department, which might or might not be the former provincial capital, to carry out one's business. Or if one wished to make a local political career, it was the departmental or arrondissement boundaries that would determine where one should seek influence or make a name for oneself.

Most strikingly, the creation of so many new jurisdictions immediately set off intense local campaigns to retain, improve on, or compensate for whatever powers a town might have had under the old regime. Civic pride immediately got wrapped up in the issue of whether one's town would be a *chef lieu* of a department or at least of a district, whether it would have a court of first instance or an episcopal seat, or whether it would continue to have jurisdiction over surrounding rural territory.[38] As Marie-Vic Ozouf-Marignier remarks, once the National Assembly enacted the new scheme, the constitutional committee received few provincial-level complaints but a "flood tide of local and micro-local reactions."[39] Moreover, the committee took these local reactions into account in making its final decisions about boundaries and jurisdictions; it acted, according to Ozouf-Marignier, more with a spirit of arbitration than of arbitrariness.[40] This intense local engagement in the details of the reform and the generally accommodating response of the Assembly resulted in a rapid acceptance of the new system, which henceforth structured the civic pride and political fortunes of French localities.[41] In short, the new division of the territory succeeded not only because of its superior rationality but also because it effectively transformed the stakes of local political life.

VI

The "National Constitution" was based on the destruction of the corporate and hierarchical institutions that had made up the French monarchy under the old regime. Both on the specific plane of the reconstitution of territorial units and more generally, the logic of the National Assembly's work was to destroy all partial, intermediate, or corporate institutions and to replace them with a homogeneous national institutional system in which all persons and all spatial locations were juridically and morally equal. By striking down all the intermediate forms of identity and mutual recognition, the logic of the "national constitution" was to absolutize the nation as the supreme site of solidarity and hence to absolutize the boundaries that defined the nation's limits. Under the old regime, "the nation" had been merely one unit in a complex system that was populated by numerous other crosscutting units and overlain by a hierarchy of interwoven recognition and disrespect. The disappearance of corporate units of solidarity and the collapse of the finely calibrated hierarchy of deference, disdain, gratitude, and noblesse oblige had the effect of making the nation's boundaries seem unprecedentedly sharp. The Revolution's enactment of a "national constitution" can, therefore, be understood as a crucial moment in the construction of a modular nation form. From the French Revolution on, the idea that the nation must be the supreme object of loyalty was certainly available for import. So were the various institutional means that the French had used to reconstitute the state and society in a national form—including a unified legal code, the establishment of juridical equality between persons, and a uniform system of territorial division based on a conception of empty, homogeneous space.

Yet the French Revolution certainly did not establish the model of the nation for all time. Although there is much that is recognizable in the revolutionary concept of the nation, it is also important to recognize that certain aspects of the French model were not replicated in subsequent iterations of the nation form. I shall discuss three aspects of the French revolutionaries' concept of the nation that differed significantly from the nation form that became standard in the nineteenth century: their attitude toward foreigners, their conception of the national language, and their assumptions about temporality.

It is obvious that the nation form as it developed in the nineteenth and twentieth centuries is built on a powerful, often deadly logic of exclusion: the nation as a bounded community is defined in opposition to foreign peoples—who tend to be denigrated, whether as rivals, as enemies, or simply as unworthy of inclusion in the national community. Such an exclusion is in some sense a logical outcome of the Revolution's absolutizing of the boundary of the national community. Yet the French revolutionaries largely avoided the national chauvinism we have come to associate with the nation form. This was not because the French revolutionary conception of the nation was particularly "humanitarian," as Carleton Hayes argued—it was, after all, the French revolutionaries who perfected the modern notion of systematic political terror. Rather, the French model avoided national chauvinism because revolutionary discourse about the nation made other exclusions that were sharper and more prominent than any exclusion of foreigners. These went back to the very beginning of the revolution. *What Is the Third Estate?*, the revolutionary pamphlet published by the abbé Sieyès in January 1789, was the classic text of the revolutionary discourse of the nation. This great pamphlet, which ringingly declared the nation to be the source of all sovereign power, actually began by excluding French aristocrats from the nation—on the grounds that they did not participate in the nation's work and insisted on being governed by their own privileges rather than by "the common law." Aristocrats, Sieyès claimed, were "a separate people within the great nation"; they were "foreign to the nation" and "no less enemies than the English are of the French in times of war."[42]

From the very beginning of the Revolution, then, the French nation's enemy of choice was not a rival nation but an internal enemy of aristocrats who had, supposedly, by dint of their idleness and privileges, seceded de facto from the national community of mutual recognition. When Louis XVI was deposed and a republic was declared in 1792, the nation came also to be defined by a second exclusion—the nation was henceforth incompatible with kings. As the Revolution went forward, the term "aristocrat" was used to cover an ever larger category of persons, until, under the Terror, "moderates" or simply those with whom one disagreed, were regularly denounced as aristocrats, whatever their prerevolutionary social status. In short, during the French Revolution, the nation was defined far more by its antagonism with aristocrats and royalty than by an antagonism with foreigners.

Moreover, the nation form elaborated in the French Revolution was inseparable from an insistently universalistic ideology. The Revolution's principles were thought to be applicable to people living anywhere in the world, and the revolutionaries expected other peoples, sooner or later, to follow their example and rise up to claim their liberty. The American Revolution, risings in the Low Countries, and the burgeoning of English radical movements after 1789 made such a prospect seem likely at the beginning of the 1790s. In 1792, the Republic, already at war with the surrounding monarchical states, displayed its internationalism by inviting three non-French patriots to sit in its legislative body, the Convention. These were Anacharsis Cloots, an internationalist visionary from Holland; Joseph Priestly, an English radical; and the Anglo-American revolutionary Thomas Paine. Cloots and Paine actually took their seats and participated in the Convention's debates. In the heady early days of the war, the French expected patriots in surrounding countries to establish "sister republics" once the French armies struck the first blows against their tyrants. When they entered Belgium and the German Rhineland early in 1793, the French slogan was "war to the castles, peace to the cottages"; as they saw it, theirs was a war against aristocrats and monarchs, not against ordinary Germans or Belgians. These evangelical expectations seemed to be answered when local enthusiasts for liberty took advantage of the French occupation either to declare the establishment of sister republics or to ask for adhesion to the French republic itself.[43] Until the war began to turn against the French in the spring of 1793, the revolutionaries were largely able to ignore the implicit contradiction between the intrinsically bounded character of the national community and the universalism of the revolutionary ideology.

When the war turned desperate in the spring of 1793, the Revolution's attitude toward foreigners hardened significantly. The French were expelled from Belgium and the Rhineland, and, with the Vendée uprising in the west and the Federalist revolt in several provincial cities, the Republic was also engulfed in civil warfare. This was the situation that led to the institution of the "Terror"—that is, to an emergency government headed by the Committee of Public Safety and increasingly dominated by Maximillien Robespierre. As Sophie Wahnich has demonstrated in an exhaustive recent study of the discourse on foreigners during the Terror, this period was marked by increasing verbal hostility to foreigners and increasing controls on nonnationals living in the Republic.[44] To avoid being imprisoned, foreigners who were citizens of enemy powers were required to obtain and carry on their persons "certificates of hospitality" issued by the council of the commune or section in which they lived—bodies that could generally be counted on to apply stringent tests of loyalty to the Revolution.[45] The ascent of the Robespierrists also corresponded to a change in public representations of the enemy, especially the English. Initially, revolutionary orators carefully distinguished between the despotic English government, on which they declared war to the death, and the English people, whom they treated as potential friends and allies. But by the winter of 1794, the Robespierrists began to declare their hatred of the English people as well. Bertrand Barrère, always a master of extravagant rhetorical violence, chillingly declared that the English were "a tribe foreign to Europe, foreign to humanity. They must disappear."[46]

Yet I think that Wahnich's account tends to exaggerate the hostility toward foreigners. The "certificates of hospitality" that foreigners had to get from the sectional authorities were not very different from the "certificates of civic virtue" required of French citizens. Nor does Wahnich point out that the same orators who declaimed violently against the English far more frequently used the same language against nobles, non-juring clergy, and grain speculators, all of whom were repeatedly marked out rhetorically for extermination.[47] This was, to be sure, a period of escalating state violence, but it is important to recognize that rhetoric escalated far more uncontrollably than actual violence. Wahnich, in my opinion, takes the discourse about foreigners too much at face value, failing to take into account the reduced semantic weight of violent talk in this era of generalized rhetorical inflation.[48]

Indeed, what strikes me most about the denunciations of foreigners cited by Wahnich is how often their denunciations are nuanced by a recognition that even the most debased of peoples might yet free themselves and become allies and brothers of the French. Thus, on January 30, 1794, in the Jacobin club, Robespierre publicly proclaimed, "As a Frenchman, as a representative of the People, I declare that I hate the English people." But he quickly went on to explain himself:

> I avow that it is my hatred for their government that makes me hate this people; Let them destroy it, then, let them break it. Until then I vow to them an implacable hatred. Let them annihilate their government and perhaps we can love them again. . . . Let us see this people free themselves and we will render them all our esteem and friendship.[49]

Here Robespierre denounces the English people, but the hatred he declares is clearly conditional. The English are to be hated not because they are English but because they lack the courage to throw off their tyrants and have basely followed them into warfare against the Republic. If they should succeed in seizing their liberty, they would quickly become friends and allies of the French. Similarly, the popular society of the Franciade section of Paris declared on February 28, 1794, "We wish peace but we will only extend it to peoples who have broken their chains and thrown off the yoke of tyranny."[50] In the heady early days of the war, it was taboo to declare a hatred of the people against whom one was fighting because they were potential converts to the revolutionary cause. As the war ground on, it became acceptable to voice a conditional hatred of the enemy people, but only because of their stubborn refusal to overthrow their own tyrants and recognize that the French were in fact their liberators. Foreigners were denounced as the dupes and lackeys of kings and aristocrats, not as foreigners per se.

Thus, even under the stress of deadly warfare, the French continued to recognize their enemies as potential allies in a universal revolution against aristocracy and despotism. In this sense, the French concept of the nation remained, even under the Terror, more fundamentally defined by its opposition to aristocracy and monarchy than by its opposition to the people who lived beyond France's borders. And once the Terror had passed and the Republic's armies advanced again—into Belgium, the Rhineland, and eventually portions of Switzerland and Northern Italy—the Republic annexed these lands and their people to France, extending to them the entire revolutionary package of regenerated institutions. Their rulers were deposed, their aristocracies were stripped of privileges, and all citizens became equal before the law. The welter of Episcopal cities, kingdoms, margravates, dukedoms, counties, free cities, and so forth that made up these territories were divided up into departments, with their subordinate districts and municipalities, identical in form to those elsewhere in the Republic.[51] This policy of making conquered territories integral parts of the French Republic indicates that the nation continued to be defined as an antiaristocratic and antimonarchical community of egalitarian mutual recognition. As such, it was, in principle, indefinitely extendable in empty, homogeneous space—able to take in Flemish-speaking Belgians, Germans, or Italians as French citizens while denouncing French-born and French-speaking aristocrats and monarchists as foreign.

Thus, the French revolutionaries' declarations of hostility to foreigners may superficially resemble the kinds of national hatreds that developed in the nineteenth and twentieth centuries, but they actually reveal a very different concept of the nation and its relationship to foreigners. Similarly, the revolutionaries' views about the French language appear to presage nineteenth-century linguistic nationalism but in fact do not. During the period of the Terror, the revolutionary leadership made powerful claims about the value of the French language and argued for the suppression—"annihilation," as the abbé Grégoire put it—of the other languages and dialects that were spoken by citizens of the republic. Once again, the lead was taken by Barrère, who, on January 27, 1794, delivered to the Convention a "Report on dialects" on behalf of the Committee of Public Safety. He argued that those citizens who spoke languages other than French tended to be counterrevolutionary and therefore requested that the Convention establish elementary instruction in French in the nine departments where Breton, Basque, German, and Italian were spoken as mother tongues—that is, in the regions of Brittany, the Pays Basque, Alsace, Lorraine, and Corsica.[52]

The abbé Grégoire, speaking a few months later, in June 1794, went further than Barrère in attempting to impose a single national language. He argued that only three million citizens of the republic (of roughly twenty-four million) could speak French well and that six million could not speak it at all. Unlike Barrère, who was confident that the Revolution was bringing a working knowledge of French to the millions of peasants who spoke French-related dialects, Grégoire argued that it was necessary to "annihilate" such patois. He proposed not only universal instruction in French but also a reform of spelling and grammar and a multiplication of French-language writings and dramatic performances. He even suggested that no one should be able to get married until they had proven their ability to speak the national language.[53] In fact, it was not until the late nineteenth century, when the Third Republic established universal and compulsory state primary schooling, that the program of suppressing patois would be definitively put into effect.[54] The downfall of the Terror in the summer of 1794 and the paucity of means for carrying out ambitious programs of educational reform meant that Barrère's and Grégoire's proposals remained a dead letter for nearly a century. But on the face of it, the program itself seems quite in tune with nineteenth- and twentieth-century linguistic nationalisms.

This may be true at the level of programs, but Grégoire, Barrère, and the other revolutionaries thought about language very differently than did,

In the world envisioned by nineteenth-century nationalists, the national language was identified above all with the peasantry, whose folk tales, dances, and music expressed the pure, uncorrupted spirit of the people.[63] In Grégoire's world, the peasants were the antithesis of the nation. Their tales and lore were a product of ignorance and superstition, a barrier to the rational understanding that alone could make a people into a nation. As Grégoire understood it, the nation was literally inconceivable in the peasant dialects of Gascon or Provençal or Picard or Breton. Only when peasants became fluent in French, a language purified by the patient artifice of rational speculation and ennobled by the oratory and legislation of the Revolution, would they truly become citizens of the nation. The object of linguistic unity, for the revolutionaries, was not the expression of the national soul but the extension of rational patriotism to those Frenchmen—including, eventually, those in the annexed territories—who were thus far rendered ignorant by their use of patois.

A third difference between the nation as instituted in the French Revolution and the nation form that became standard later in the nineteenth century concerned the relationship posited between the nation and history. If the differences on questions of foreigners and language are in some respects subtle, those on the question of the historical temporality of the nation are absolutely stark. Etienne Balibar, the scholar from whom I have pirated the term "nation form," begins his article titled "The Nation Form" as follows: "The history of nations, beginning with our own, is always already presented to us in the form of a narrative which attributes to these entities the continuity of a subject." One of the illusions on which the nation is premised, Balibar claims, consists in seeing "ourselves as the culmination" of a historical process, as the products of a "destiny." Although I think Balibar is right about the temporal assumptions underlying the nation form from the mid-nineteenth century forward, it is ironic that France, Balibar's own nation, conceived of itself during the French Revolution in a way that is sharply at odds with this account. Far from positing a long and teleological historical continuity, the French revolutionaries conceived of the triumph of the nation as an act of supreme discontinuity.

That French revolutionary discourse posited the Revolution as an absolute break with the past is, in fact, one of the central arguments of contemporary revolutionary historiography: one thinks, for example, of the works of Mona Ozouf, François Furet, Lynn Hunt, and Keith Baker.[64] And the revolutionary concept of the nation, far from indicating an exception to this general theme, entirely confirms it. In the course of 1789, the claim that the French nation had an ancient constitution that had to be restored or updated was certainly made, but it was also decisively defeated. As against this thesis of historical continuity, the National Assembly followed the reasoning that Sieyès had articulated in *What Is the Third Estate?* The nation, Sieyès argued, is subject to no historical form: "A nation is independent of every form, and, no matter how it wills, it is enough that its will be made apparent for all positive law to cease before it, as before the source and supreme master of all positive law."[65] The nation, as Sieyès and the other revolutionaries used the term, was not the nineteenth-century nationalists' nation, with its deep roots and primordial sentiments. It was a permanently immanent collective being that, on the occasion of the French Revolution, broke through the historical forms that had been supposed to contain it and willed a new form of common life. For the French revolutionaries, in short, the nation was essentially an atemporal or perhaps omnitemporal category: their sense of temporality was actually more eschatological than historical. The nation, as it emerged in the French Revolution, was the site and the subject of a radical break in history, one perhaps best symbolized by the new calendar that started time over again with a new Year One that began with the declaration of the French Republic.

VII

I hope to have shown that the French Revolution significantly transformed the concept of the nation as this concept had existed in 1788. It did so in at least four ways. First, it heightened the significance of the term "nation," making it a sacred source of sovereignty and power. Second, it established a profound link between the nation and the equality of citizens. Third, it provided a model for creating a unified nation, for destroying or delegitimizing the intermediate bodies that stood between the individual citizen and the nation as a whole. Finally, it reconceptualized the territorial basis of the nation as an empty, homogeneous space in which every territorial unit was morally equivalent to every other. All these innovations in the concept of the nation have proved durable and portable. They are constituent elements of the modular nation form that has subsequently transformed the political landscape of the entire world.

But the French Revolution marks only one moment in the evolution of the nation form, and there were important aspects of the nation as the French revolutionaries conceived of it that stand in sharp contrast to the nation form that became standard during the nineteenth century. The revolutionaries regarded the nation as a potentially universal and open category, not as a category that necessarily drew exclusive boundaries around each community and cast those on the other side of the boundaries as potential enemies. They thought of the French language not as an emanation of the soul of the French people but as an artificial construction whose rationality alone gave Frenchmen access to full participation in the nation. And they thought of the nation not as the necessary culmination of a long and continuous history but as the product and the producer of a necessary break in historical time.

The French revolutionaries did not invent the nation form, nor did they succeed in giving it its definitive shape. They took up existing discourses and practices about the nation and reshaped them to their own use. Their appeal to the nation as the source of sovereignty was, for example, clearly prefigured in the rhetoric of the British "Glorious Revolution" and the American Revolution.[66] And the Americans, in the Northwest Ordinance of 1785, carried out a more radical exercise in geometrical respatialization of national territory than the abbé Sieyès dared to propose for France—albeit in land as yet largely unsettled by Euro-Americans. The reshaped concept of the nation that the French Revolution bequeathed to the world provided a very powerful model of how one might organize and regenerate a political community. But those who took it up—in Spanish America, Poland, Ireland, Italy, Germany, India, or Japan in the nineteenth century or in Indonesia, Zimbabwe, Kazakhstan, Palestine, or Bosnia in the twentieth—reshaped it themselves in the course of applying it. In the long and still-continuing world history of the nation form, the French Revolution was an episode both consequential and unique. It opened up hitherto unimagined political possibilities that were eventually taken up in the Americas, in Europe, and eventually around the world. But it also proved not to be replicable without being significantly transformed.

Suggested Readings

Anderson, Benedict
Imagined Communities: Reflections on the Origin and Spread of Nationalism.
Rev. ed. London: Verso, 1991.

Baecque, Antoine de
Le corps de l'histoire: Métaphores et politique (1770–1800). Paris: Calmann-
Lévy, 1993.

Baker, Keith Michael
*Inventing the French Revolution: Essays on French Political Culture in the
Eighteenth Century.* Cambridge: Cambridge University Press, 1990.

Balibar, Etienne
"The Nation Form: History and Ideology." In *Becoming National: A Reader*,
edited by Geoff Eley and Ronald Grigor Suny. New York: Oxford University
Press, 1996, 132–50.

Bell, David A.
The Cult of the Nation in France: Inventing Nationalism, 1680–1800. Cambridge, Mass.: Harvard University Press, 2001.

Certeau, Michel de, Dominique Julia, and Jacques Revel
*Une politique de la langue: La Révolution française et les patois: L'enquête de
Grégoire.* Paris: Gallimard, 1975.

Furet, François
Rethinking the French Revolution. Cambridge: Cambridge University Press,
1981.

Furet, François, and Ran Halévi
La monarchie républicaine: La Constitution de 1791. Paris: Fayard, 1996.

Godechot, Jacques
*La Grande Nation: L'expansion révolutionnaire de la France dans le monde de
1789 à 1799.* Paris: Aubier Montaigne, 1983.

Hunt, Lynn
Politics, Culture, and Class in the French Revolution. Berkeley: University of
California Press, 1984.

Margadant, Ted W.
Urban Rivalries in the French Revolution. Princeton, N.J.: Princeton University Press, 1992.

Ozouf, Mona
L'homme régénéré: Essais sur la Révolution française. Paris: Gallimard, 1989.

Palmer, R. R.
The Age of Democratic Revolution. 2 vols. Princeton, N.J.: Princeton University Press, 1959, 1964.

Wahnich, Sophie
L'impossible citoyen: L'étranger dans le discours de la Révolution française. Paris: Albin Michel, 1997.

Notes

1. Carleton J. H. Hayes, *Essays on Nationalism* (New York: Macmillan, 1926), and *The Historical Evolution of Modern Nationalism* (New York: Macmillan, 1931); Hans Kohn, *The Idea of Nationalism: A Study in Its Origins and Background* (New York: Macmillan, 1944); *Nationalism: Its Meaning and History* (Princeton, N.J.: Van Nostrand, 1955); and *Prelude to Nation States: The French and German Experience, 1789–1815* (Princeton, N.J.: Van Nostrand, 1967).

2. Benedict Anderson, *Imagined Communities: Reflections on the Origin and Spread of Nationalism*, rev. ed. (London: Verso, 1991). For a recent critique of Anderson, see Manu Goswami, "Rethinking the Modular Nation Form: Toward a Sociohistorical Conception of Nationalism," *Comparative Studies in Society and History* 44 (October 2002): 770–99.

3. Anderson, *Imagined Communities*, iii.

4. Etienne Balibar, "The Nation Form: History and Ideology," in *Becoming National: A Reader*, ed. Geoff Eley and Ronald Grigor Suny (New York: Oxford University Press, 1996), 132–50. Originally published as "La forme nation: Histoire et idéologie," in Etienne Balibar and Immanuel Wallerstein, *Race, nation, classe: Identités ambiguës* (Paris: Editions La Découverte, 1988), 117–43.

5. Anderson, *Imagined Communities*, 51.

6. The other two occurrences are in *Imagined Communities*, 80, where Anderson argues that the French Revolution, thanks to its discussion in "millions of printed words," became a model for a new class of political realities: revolutions.

7. Anderson, *Imagined Communities*, 81.

8. Anderson, *Imagined Communities*, 81.

9. Anderson, *Imagined Communities*, 80. Moreover, the fact that France was not a republic hardly seems crucial in this context. Republicanism was by no means an indispensable component of the nation form that was generalized after 1870. Indeed, between the Latin American revolutions of the 1810s and 1820s and the aftermath of World War I, the new nation-states that emerged in Europe

were nearly always monarchies. The national unifications of Italy and Germany in the 1860s and 1870s were carried out under monarchical auspices, and all the new national states (such as Greece, Serbia, and Romania) that were created out of the decaying Ottoman Empire were established as monarchies. Although the early national states, both in the Americas and in France, were republican in form, this aspect of their model was rarely pirated by Europeans in the nineteenth century.

10. For an excellent bibliographic survey of works relevant to the idea of the nation in prerevolutionary France, see David A. Bell, "Recent Works on Early Modern French National Identity," *Journal of Modern History* 68 (March 1996): 84–113. On Britain, see Linda Colley, *Britons: Forging the Nation, 1707–1837* (New Haven, Conn.: Yale University Press, 1992).

11. Pierre Rétat, "Roi, peuple(s), nation à la fin de l'ancien régime," in *Les mots de la nation*, ed. Sylvianne Rémi-Giraud and Pierre Rétat (Lyon: Presses Universitaires de Lyon, 1996), 189–98.

12. David A. Bell, *The Cult of the Nation in France: Inventing Nationalism, 1680–1800* (Cambridge, Mass.: Harvard University Press, 2001).

13. Although Bell makes it clear that the Revolution marked an important change in the discourse of the nation in France, I do not think he fully recognizes the importance of this change in the semantic register of the term.

14. The term appears in the decree of August 11, 1789. Keith Michael Baker, ed., *Readings in Western Civilization*, vol. 7, *The Old Regime and the French Revolution* (Chicago: University of Chicago Press, 1987), 230.

15. Philippe Dujardin, who has recently published an exceptionally acute study of the linguistic performances that transformed the delegates of the Third Estate into the National Assembly, puts it this way: the Assembly "is obliged to devote itself to inventing that which is already there, to generating that which is supposed to be its condition of existence, to creating the referent that is invoked." "Des États Généraux à l'Assemblée nationale: Figures et formules de l'universalité de mai à juin 1789," in Rémi-Giraud and Rétat, *Les mots de la nation*, 258.

16. The concept of recognition has been used above all by such post-Hegelian theorists as Axel Honneth and Charles Taylor, principally as a means of thinking about problems of citizenship in modern democracies. My use of the term to think about the system of profoundly undemocratic social relations in the old regime represents a particular appropriation of their concept. See Axel Honneth, *The Struggle for Recognition: The Moral Grammar of Social Conflicts*, trans. Joel Anderson (Cambridge, Mass.: MIT Press, 1996), and *The Fragmented World of the Social: Essays in Social and Political Philosophy* (Albany: State University of New York Press, 1995). See also Charles Taylor et al., *Multiculturalism: Examining the Politics of Recognition* (Princeton, N.J.: Princeton University Press, 1994).

17. One recent book that has emphasized the corporate character of old regime societies is Gail Bossenga, *The Politics of Privilege: Old Regime and Revolution in Lille* (Cambridge: Cambridge University Press, 1991). For a more formal analysis of old regime French social categories, see William H. Sewell Jr., "État, corps, and ordre: Notes on the Social Vocabulary of the Old Regime," in *Sozialgeschichte Heute: Festschrift für Hans Rosenburg zum 70 Geburtstag*, ed. H. U. Wehler (Gottingen: Vandenhoeck and Ruprecht, 1974), 49–68.

18. For a classic statement of the old regime concept of order, see Charles Loyseau, "Traité des ordres et simples dignitez," in *Les oeuvres de maistre Charles Loyseau* (Paris: A. Lyon, 1666). This work is available in English as Charles Loyseau, *A Treatise of Orders and Plain Dignities*, trans. and ed. Howell A. Lloyd (Cambridge: Cambridge University Press, 1994).

19. Anyone who reads the debates of the National Assembly in the summer of 1789 will be struck by how much the Assembly, which was engaged in the project of defining the rights and powers of the nation as a sovereign body of citizens, nonetheless obsessively enunciated the myth that everything the Assembly did was simultaneously the will of the king. The association between the king and the nation was still extremely powerful. See *Réimpression de l'ancien moniteur,* vol. 1 (Paris, 1840).

20. Peter Sahlins's *Boundaries: The Making of France and Spain in the Pyrenees* (Berkeley: University of California Press, 1989), demonstrates that the national boundary between Spain and France became an increasingly important social as well as political boundary during the seventeenth and eighteenth centuries.

21. Mona Ozouf, *La fête révolutionnaire, 1789–1799* (Paris: Gallimard, 1976), 44–75. An English-language version is *Festivals and the French Revolution*, trans. Alan Sheridan (Cambridge, Mass.: Harvard University Press, 1988), 33–60.

22. From John Hall Stewart, ed., *A Documentary Survey of the French Revolution* (New York: Macmillan, 1951), 231.

23. P.-J.-B. Buchez and P.-C. Roux, *Histoire parlementaire de la Révolution française*, 40 vols. (Paris: Paulin, 1834–1838), 10:193.

24. On the notion of regeneration, see Mona Ozouf, *L'homme régénéré: Essais sur la Révolution française* (Paris: Gallimard, 1989); and Antoine de Baecque, *Le corps de l'histoire: Métaphores et politique (1770–1800)* (Paris: Calmann-Lévy, 1993). An English version is *The Body Politic: Corporeal Metaphor in Revolutionary France, 1770–1800*, trans. Charlotte Mandell (Stanford, Calif.: Stanford University Press, 1997).

25. Keith Michael Baker, "Fixing the French Constitution," in *Inventing the French Revolution: Essays on French Political Culture in the Eighteenth Century* (Cambridge: Cambridge University Press, 1990); François Furet and Ran Halévi, *La monarchie républicaine: La Constitution de 1791* (Paris: Fayard, 1996).

26. Establishment of a right to judgment by citizen juries in all criminal cases was, according to Thouret, essential "for the maintenance of individual liberty." Speech to the National Assembly of April 6, 1790, in Furet and Halévi, *La monarchie républicaine*, 488.

27. Baker, "Fixing the French Constitution," 262, 269, 266.

28. On theories of space, see Edward Soja, *Postmodern Geographies: The Reassertion of Space in Critical Social Theory* (London: Verso, 1989), and Henri Lefebvre's difficult but essential *The Production of Space*, trans. Donald Nicholson-Smith (1974; reprint, Oxford: Blackwell, 1991). For a helpful commentary on the latter, see Neil Brenner, "Global, Fragmented, Hierarchical: Henri Lefebvre's Geographies of Globalization," *Public Culture* 10 (fall 1997): 137–69.

29. For extensive documentation of the revolutionaries' point of view, see Marie-Vic Ozouf-Marignier, *La Formation des départements: La représentation du territoire français à la fin du 18e siècle* (Paris: École des Hautes Études en Sciences Sociales, 1989). For a study of the local politics of the division of national territory, see Ted W. Margadant, *Urban Rivalries in the French Revolution* (Princeton, N.J.: Princeton University Press, 1992).

30. Anderson, *Imagined Communities*, 24–36.

31. Baker, *Readings*, 7: 230.

32. The quotation is from the anonymously published pamphlet *Observations sur le rapport du comité de constitution, concernant la nouvelle organisation de la France* (Versaille, 1789). This pamphlet is republished in Emmanuel-Joseph Sieyès, *Ecrits politiques*, ed. Raberto Zapperi (Paris: Editions des Archives Contemporaines, 1985), 245–71 (quotation at 247).

33. Sieyès, *Ecrits politiques*, 248.

34. Sieyès, *Ecrits politiques*, 249–51. In the version of this legislation passed by the Assembly, the term "commune" was used for the smallest divisions, and the next larger divisions were called "districts."

35. Frederick D. Williams, ed., *The Northwest Ordinance: Essays on Its Formulation, Provisions, and Legacy* (East Lansing: Michigan State University Press, 1989).

36. Sieyès, *Ecrits politiques*, 247.

37. Quotes from Ozouf-Marignier, *La Formation*, 63, 48, 65.

38. Margadant, *Urban Rivalries*, esp. part 2.

39. Ozouf-Marignier, *La Formation*, 292.

40. Ozouf-Marignier, *La Formation*, 295.

41. As Ted Margadant demonstrates, the jurisdictions of the new territorial divisions remained major issues in urban politics through the 1790s, into the Napoleonic era, and even into the Restoration. Margadant, *Urban Rivalries*.

42. Emmanuel-Joseph Sieyès, *Qu'est-ce que le Tiers Etat?*, critical ed. with intro. and notes by Roberto Zapperi (Geneva: Droz, 1970), 126, 140.

43. R. R. Palmer, *The Age of Democratic Revolution*, 2 vols. (Princeton, N.J.: Princeton University Press, 1959, 1964). For the situation in the early months of the war, see vol. 2, 50–65.

44. Sophie Wahnich, *L'impossible citoyen: L'étranger dans le discours de la Révolution française* (Paris: Albin Michel, 1997).

45. Wahnich, *L'impossible citoyen*, 34–44.

46. Discourse to the Convention on the Crimes of the English, May 26, 1793, quoted in Wahnich, *L'impossible citoyen*, 256.

47. On the rhetorical excesses of the Terror, see William H. Sewell Jr., "The Sans-Culotte Rhetoric of Subsistence," in *The French Revolution and the Creation of Modern Political Culture*, vol. 4, *The Terror in the French Revolution*, ed. Keith M. Baker and Colin Lucas (Oxford: Pergamon Press, 1994), 249–69.

48. The same could be said of David Bell in *Cult of the Nation*, 100–101.

49. Quoted in Wahnich, *L'impossible citoyen*, 307.

50. Quoted in Wahnich, *L'impossible citoyen*, 332.

51. Jacques Godechot, *La Grande Nation: L'expansion révolutionnaire de la France dans le monde de 1789 à 1799* (Paris: Aubier Montaigne, 1983); Robert Devleeshouwer, "Le cas de la Belgique," *Occupants-Occupés, 1792–1815*, Colloque de Bruxelles, 29 et 30 janvier 1968 (Brussels: Université Libre de Bruxelles, Institut de Sociologie, 1969), 43–65; Roger Dufraisse, "De la Révolution à la patrie: La rive gauche du Rhin à l'époque française (1792–1814)," *Patriotisme et nationalisme en Europe à l'époque de la Révolution française et de Napoléon*, Actes du Colloque, XIIe Congrès international des Sciences historiques (Paris: Société d'Études Robespierristes, 1973), 103–42; Roger Dufraisse, "L'installation de l'institution départementale sur la rive gauche du Rhin (4 novembre 1797–23 septembre 1802)," in *L'Allemagne à l'époque napoléonienne: Questions d'histoire politique, economique et sociale. Études de Roger Dufraisse réunies à l'occasion de son 70e anniversaire par l'Institut Historique Allemand de Paris*, n. 34 of *Pariser historische studien* (Bonn: Bouvier Verlag, 1992), 77–104.

52. Barrère's report is published in Michel de Certeau, Dominique Julia, and Jacques Revel, *Une politique de la langue. La Révolution française et les patois: L'enquête de Grégoire* (Paris: Gallimard, 1975), 291–99.

53. Grégoire's report has also been published in Certeau et al., *Une politique*, 300–317. See esp. 302, 310–11.

54. Eugen Weber, *Peasants into Frenchmen: The Modernization of Rural France, 1870–1914* (Stanford, Calif.: Stanford University Press, 1976).

55. Quoted in Kohn, *The Idea of Nationalism*, 432.

56. Certeau et al., *Une politique*, 291.

57. Certeau et al., *Une politique*, 297–98.

58. Certeau et al., *Une politique*, 302.

59. Certeau et al., *Une politique*, 306, 308.

60. Certeau et al., *Une politique*, 296.

61. Certeau et al., *Une politique*, 301, 304.

62. Certeau et al., *Une politique*, 304.

63. For a discussion of the role of music in nationalism, see Benjamin Curtis, "On Nationalism and Music" (Ph.D. diss., University of Chicago, 2002).

64. Ozouf, *La fête* and *L'homme régénéré*; François Furet, *Rethinking the French Revolution* (1979; reprint, Cambridge: Cambridge University Press, 1981); Lynn Hunt, *Politics, Culture, and Class in the French Revolution* (Berkeley: University of California Press, 1984); Baker, *Inventing.*

65. Sieyès, *Qu'est-ce que le Tiers Etat?* 183.

66. Gordon S. Wood, *The Creation of the American Republic, 1776–1787* (Chapel Hill: University of North Carolina Press, 1969), esp. 344–89; Steven Pincus, "To Protect English Liberties: The English Nationalist Revolution of 1688–89," *Protestantism and National Identity: Britain and Ireland, c.1650–c.1850,* ed. Tony Claydon annd Ian McBride (Cambridge: Cambridge University Press, 1998), 75–104.

CHAPTER FOUR

"TO THROW OFF A TYRANNICAL GOVERNMENT": ATLANTIC REVOLUTIONARY TRADITIONS AND POPULAR INSURGENCY IN MEXICO, 1800–1821

Eric Van Young

Top: seal used by insurgent chieftain José María Villagrán, who was executed with forty-one other insurgent leaders in 1813. Bottom: handwritten account of his arrest and execution. Courtesy Centro de Estudios de Historia de Mexico Condumex.

The Mexican struggle for independence from Spain (1810–1821) falls temporally near the midpoint of what historians of the modern world sometimes call "The Age of Revolution" (1750–1850) or, more sanguinely, "The Age of Democratic Revolutions."[1] The heavily Eurocentric worldview on which this periodization rests, however, has meant the substantial exclusion (with some exceptions) of Spain and its American dominions from larger interpretive treatments of the period as part of Western history as well as from social science model building about revolutionary processes.[2] Even when this periodization is adopted for thinking about Latin American history, it tends to beg the question of the distinctly undemocratic outcomes of much political change in the era by confusing liberalism, republicanism, federalism, regionalism, and even forms of populist dictatorship with democracy. When such comparisons are sometimes made—as between, say, the French or the American Revolution and the independence struggle in Mexico—they often rest on analogies or linkages to elite political ideologies in the Atlantic revolutionary traditions, institution building, or styles of political leadership rather than on any detailed view of what common people were thinking or doing.[3]

To interpret any process of large-scale, protracted political violence as monolithic, whether a revolution or not, is surely incautious. Only at the peril of misunderstanding the deep historical dynamics of such social upheavals do we take elite political thinking as a proxy for popular political thinking or as necessarily its prime mover. Even more is this the case with a society like Mexico at the close of the eighteenth century, in many ways ill-integrated spatially, economically, culturally, and politically. When one looks closely at the social forces in play in the country during this decade of internal war and national liberation struggle, one gets the impression that popular and elite insurgency aspired to quite different goals, while the ideological elements of popular collective action had, on their face, a markedly atavistic look. If the "Age of Revolution" is thought to be the avatar of modernity, therefore, from the point of view of popular groups in Mexico the independence struggle there does not look very modern.[4]

The main focus of this chapter is on the ideological dimension of popular participation in the Mexican wars of independence at the beginning of the nineteenth century and in particular on how and why the thinking underlying popular insurgency should appear quite "traditional" and only tenuously linked, if at all, with an Atlantic revolutionary tradition in the dimension of ideology or political practice.[5] I will trace primarily the ways in which popular and elite ideas about politics related to each other, and I will try in passing to situate both in relation to the larger Atlantic world from the mid-eighteenth century onward. To begin with, let me put aside for the moment my own caveat about essentializing these positions in a culturally complex colonial society in order to establish a sort of heuristic baseline for the discussion that follows. The nominal leaders of the Mexican independence movement, many of them creoles (New World–born whites) or *mestizos* (men of mixed blood), espoused a proto-nationalist vision of Mexico's future (and arguably of its past) embodying what has been called creole patriotism. This loose affective and discursive posture tended to evolve ever more overtly toward political independence and a nation-building project as the early autonomist leanings of their movement receded during the course of the decade 1810–1821.[6] The relationship between this creole protonationalism and the political thinking of Mexico's country people, especially the indigenous villagers who mostly filled out the insurgent ranks, was primarily one of opposition because their ideas were built on very different cultural assumptions and views of the colonial state. I will have more to say later as to why this ideological parallax should make the case of the Mexican independence struggles comport so ill with much recent thinking about the nature of revolutions in general and large-scale peasant movements in particular.

In exploring these issues, I shall interpret this volume's central theme, the relationship between revolution and nation building in the Atlantic world, in a plastic and inclusive fashion. As originally posed at the scholarly encounter where the chapters in this volume were presented and discussed, that theme was embraced by the title "revolutionary traditions," and I have retained that phrase. The term "revolutionary traditions" is used here in three ways, the first two fairly conventional, the third perhaps idiosyncratic. The first is to understand "revolutionary traditions" in the sense of actual history, specifically as designating a historical class of large-scale social upheavals genealogically and morphologically related to each other. Related to this use of the term would be a second, embracing the accompanying and derived discursive and intellectual elements—"traditions," if you will, in a more folkloric sense—that have articulated, shaped, and represented those upheavals as historical actors and legatees have thought about them; the term "revolutionary ideology" is a more conventional way to express this. Among these elements would be ideas of how the relationships among state, society, and individual are to be mediated. Such notions would include social contractualism, the consent of the governed, popular sovereignty, republicanism, natural law and the law of nations, individual liberty, equality before the law (if not before market forces), and so forth as these worked themselves out in different historical contexts. The third interpretation would look to traditional wisdoms *about* Atlantic revolutions, especially as reflected in contemporary works of scholars in the human sciences describing and explaining these great political upheavals.

I

I have already alluded to the fact that the Latin American independence struggles, in this case specifically Mexico's, are most often passed over not only in large-scale interpretive histories of the Western experience during the "Age of Revolution" but also in social science model building of revolution and other forms of violent political change. One notable exception here would be Benedict Anderson's thoughtful and highly influential essay on the modern nation-building process, *Imagined Communities*.[7] He proposes in a widely cited chapter of the book that modern nationalist sensibility was in fact imported into the center of the Atlantic world from its periphery, Spanish America, as a result of the independence movements there at the beginning of the nineteenth century. This may very well be, but Anderson's effort to integrate this region of the world into a larger scheme falls somewhat short of an informed interpretation of political and social processes in Spanish America generally and Mexico in particular. In part this is due to his having based his argument on a very limited and rather monochromatic range of published works. Much more important than this, however, is the fact that Anderson locates the dramatic center of his story in the creole elite and imperial officialdom of Mexico and the other soon-to-be-nations of the Iberian Atlantic empire rather than taking into account the sort of broader social and cultural dynamic being advocated here, in the absence of which it is impossible to understand completely the nature of the new polities that emerged from the Spanish Empire or their subsequent histories. When Anderson claims, for example, that "language was never even an issue in these early struggles for national liberation," he throws a veil of obscurity over the very real historical experience of cultural difference *within* several of the colonies, most especially Mexico, whose population was primarily indigenous in 1810 and where linguistic and other sorts of differences between creole directorate and popular masses all but choked off the communication of a common political program. Nor is it an accident that in the one paragraph Anderson does devote to the issue of potentially wide social mobilizations in Spanish America (aside from a passing reference to the great pan-Andean revolts of the early 1780s) he concentrates on creole elite fears of *slave* rather than Indian uprisings, at a stroke erasing much of what occurred in Mexico and the Andean region between about 1810 and 1825. When he comes to note "a certain 'social thinness' to these Latin American independence movements," therefore, he is simultaneously correct and completely mistaken: correct in the sense that independence as such was (substantially but certainly not exclusively) a creole project, mistaken in the sense that a broader social mobilization was occurring whose goal was neither independence nor nation building but that touched at a great many points the creole-led movement.[8] Anderson has thus displaced the conventional narrative of nation building outward but not downward.

Yet Benedict Anderson is correct in insisting that the war for independence waged by New Spain (as Mexico was known during the colonial period) against old Spain must be reckoned in that company of world-historical, seismic upheavals that have created, destroyed, or reconfigured entire polities, among them the major nation-states of the modern era. Certainly the conflict encapsulated many of the social contradictions and resultant strains within the Spanish American colonial regime as a whole—of race and class, wealth and poverty, center and periphery, authoritarianism and political opening, tradition and modernity—while at the same time epitomizing the collapse of Spain's transatlantic empire, one of the great colonial projects of world history. Furthermore, Mexico's independence struggle was arguably the first great war of national liberation of the post-Columbian age in which the ethnic difference between colonizers and colonized was a major political issue.[9] Certainly in some ways its position among such movements is equivocal since it was neither the first nor the last anticolonial war. It was preceded by the American Revolution, whose influence on the independence movements in the Spanish colonies is hard to deny, although in Latin America as a whole it did not find the deep resonance of the French Revolution.[10] And it was contemporaneous with the late consolidation of British colonial domination in South Asia, at the start of a long century that was to see European colonial powers come into direct or indirect control of most of the non-European world. This is not to assert that the struggle of the British North American colonies against the colonial regime lacked a racial element or even more strongly marked signs of class antagonism within the movement itself but only that these did not primarily fuel popular participation or infuse it ideologically to the same degree as they did Mexico's struggle against Spain, which actually embraced two wars—one anticolonial, the other internecine. Nor was the Mexican independence movement the first racially tinged social upheaval in the Spanish colonial world since the uprisings of Andean indigenous peoples during the eighteenth century, most notably those of Túpac Amaru and Túpac Catari in the early 1780s, were rife with fearful interethnic violence and had been in their turn preceded by smaller outbursts over the centuries of colonial rule.[11]

The Mexican independence struggle was the first mass rebellion of the nineteenth century, however, to combine within an incipient (and socially highly localized) nationalist context elements of ethnic confrontation between colonially dominated indigenous peoples and descendants of settler colonists, with a frontal assault against the colonial regime and its representatives (including recent immigrants from Spain). Moreover, the issues were more starkly delineated here than in most of the other Ibero-American independence movements.[12] The insurgency in New Spain, then, foreshadowed the death of a European colonial project, in some ways growing necrotic even as it expanded into new areas of the world.[13] Autopsies of the colonial order are therefore much illuminated by attending in a comparative context to the Mexican insurgency, which anchors in certain interesting ways one end of the protracted process of decolonization so central to the history of the modern world, even while colonial expansion itself was to enjoy more than another century of robust life.

Why, then, is the Mexican independence struggle so often ignored by historians and social scientists (with the previously noted exception) whose attention is focused on larger questions of revolution and social change or, more specifically, on exploring an Atlantic revolutionary tradition? There are several reasons, of which three especially bear mention here. First, central as they have been to the developmental experience of the Euro-Atlantic world in terms of the human and natural resources they have contributed, the former Ibero-American colonies have remained peripheral in most Western thinking about political and social processes except possibly as negative examples, as, for instance, in dependency theory or in thinking about authoritarian political rule and the failure of democracy. On this view their history is more effect than cause since the historical narrative of modernity is generally thought to have told itself outward from the Euro-Atlantic center, for the most part, rather than inward from the periphery.[14]

Second, the outcomes of these movements for the most part fit badly with the basic model of revolution, especially social revolution, as a deep restructuring of a society by means of widespread and prolonged political violence, even where such an end might require some time to be achieved and fall some distance short of a total social change. Certainly from the perspective of the great majority of Mexico's population—mostly rural, peasant, and nonwhite—little would be gained after 1821 in the separation of colony from metropolis. Fundamental property rights or the distribution of landed wealth, for example, were not really on the agenda of the creole rebel leadership, who were quite socially conservative for the most part; it would take the Revolution of 1910 and the regimes after 1920 to dismantle the traditional Mexican latifundium. The position of subaltern groups may even have deteriorated in the decades following 1821. This was owing to economic stagnation and the incremental breakdown of certain customary and legal protections for forms of communal property (a change not completely consummated until well past midcentury) still very important in the rural economy at the close of the colonial era and traditionally associated with the Spanish monarchy but increasingly at odds with the doctrines of nineteenth-century liberalism. Although the "political nation" may have expanded somewhat in numbers in the aftermath of independence, furthermore, the huge majority of Mexicans long remained in a political shadow, at least as far as national-level public life was concerned. If not disenfranchised in the narrowest sense of the term, they were at least dominated by clientelistic relationships centering on local or regional political bosses. Taken as a single epoch, the eighty or one hundred years embracing the crisis of the colonial regime, the protracted insurgency itself, and the subsequent decades during which periods of tentative state building repeatedly gave way to episodes of political meltdown wrought no deep change in Mexican political or popular culture, even in the long drawn-out manner, for example, alleged of the process of English state building.[15] Finally, the country's system of class or ethnic stratification was not altered significantly except at the upper and upper-middle levels. Although some Mexicans of mixed socioethnic background did manage to force their way into positions of political power and material prosperity during the independence struggle and over the ensuing decades, the vast majority did not.[16]

The third and most important reason for the neglect of the independence movement in Mexico by the larger social science/historical literature, finally, is that it presents an analytical difficulty for the comparative treatment of political upheavals since 1500 or so. The deep ethnic and cultural division cutting across Mexican society until fairly recent times and manifestly persisting in more attenuated forms even today corresponds to a historical experience among Mesoamerican indigenous peoples and the descendants of their conquerors different from that of the relatively more homogeneous culture areas of much of the Old World.[17] This naturally makes classical theories of social upheaval difficult to apply to Mexico or other regions of Indo-America, such as the Andes. In both Mesoamerica and the Andes, native state-level societies were highly developed at the advent of the Europeans, New World peoples were very dense in numbers, and the postconquest survival of indigenous cultures was longer than elsewhere in the Americas, if in somewhat reduced forms.[18] Even when not avowedly Marxist in their underpinnings, many models of massive political violence and social revolution at bottom invoke forms of class conflict as their explanatory bedrock. But in the societies of Indo-America the scars of Spanish military conquest in many ways remained long unhealed, so that by the late colonial period (and beyond), in addition to contention over economic and political power, deep running ethnic and cultural differences and antagonisms still separated elites and dominant regimes from disaffected middle sectors and masses.[19] To put this in more traditional fashion, we are faced in these multiethnic colonial societies with the difficult question of the degree of congruence between "race" and "class," to which must be added the problematics of a war for decolonization within a putatively universal Catholic monarchy. Under such conditions, theories of class conflict as an etiology of social upheaval or of antiregime cross-class alliance as one of that conflict's articulators are less than fully convincing. They may explain neither why large groups in the population mobilized or failed to mobilize under a particular conjunction of circumstances nor the nature of their movements once under way. Given this problem, scholars of popular ideology and political violence are well advised to focus their attention on issues such as ethnic identity, community solidarity, and religious belief, seen not just as proxies for economic or class interests but also as major cultural factors in themselves.[20]

II

With these considerations in mind, let us now undertake a reconnaissance of the ranks of the Mexican rebels of the independence period for evidence as to the forms and sources of insurgent ideology and for how these might or might not be related to a broadly Euro-Atlantic tradition of political thinking as exemplified in eighteenth- and nineteenth-century revolutionary upheavals in the New World and the Old. Our route of march will lead us first quickly across the already much-reconnoitered territory of the creole protonationalism characteristic of the Mexican independence movement's nominal directorate. Next we will explore the ideas of middle- and lower-level insurgent chieftains, a pivotal group sandwiched between creole directorate and mass rural following, as exemplified in a fascinating letter of 1812 sent out over the signature of Field Marshal José María ("Chito") Villagrán, a small-town delinquent, cast during his brief military career as a major regional insurgent leader. We will end with a sprint through forms of popular insurgency and political ideology, observing how tenuously connected these were with the creole nationalism held by the conventional wisdom to have encapsulated the thinking of all Mexicans. These three insurgent moments reflect with considerable clarity the internal schisms within the insurgent ranks and the quite distinct political goals of different sectors of the Mexican population, suggesting why it is appropriate to describe the independence struggle as just as much an internal conflict as a war of national liberation. Furthermore, we will note that the further down colonial Mexico's socioethnic hierarchy we travel, the more remote the relationship of an Atlantic revolutionary tradition to the wellsprings of the popular insurgency appears to become.

First Moment: Creole Nationalism

The burgeoning nationalism that undergirded creole projects for independence from Spain was not necessarily linked to republicanism, and indeed an important subset of Mexican thinkers and statesmen, right through the mid-nineteenth century, advocated monarchism constrained within constitutional forms and at least limited popular political representation.[21] A preference for monarchy was the rule within the ranks of the early autonomist thinkers before the actual outbreak of the rebellion of 1810, a violent eruption spearheaded by Father Miguel Hidalgo y Costilla—a country curate with urban tastes, a sometime heterodox with advanced ideas, a former seminary president and sympathizer with the rural poor. Hidalgo initially espoused the candidacy of King Ferdinand VII of Spain to be monarch of New Spain, provided his legitimacy could be proved uncompromised, while monarchical projects were frequently proposed by other creole thinkers as well. Because of the unsettled situation in Spain the issue remained murky until the restoration of Ferdinand in 1814.[22]

Royalist thinkers and propagandists on both sides of the Atlantic also stressed the religious underpinning of the Spanish Bourbon monarchy and the king's authority, attempting constantly to hammer this home to the "humble portion of the people." Pamphlet literature published by elite writers for literate audiences in both Spain and Mexico in the years 1808–1810, during the accelerating political crisis in the peninsula and the colony, shared this preoccupation with the person and quasi-mystical powers of the Spanish monarch.[23] The Iberian tradition of mystical kingship embraced myths about Sebastianism, "el encubierto," and other mythified monarchs. Even so, royalist propaganda appeals to these principles of social authority had about them a corporatist, secular, and peculiarly bloodless quality that may well have represented the authors' thinking but that were based on a fundamental misapprehension of what the popular classes believed and how they believed it.[24]

In this light the continuing discussion of the possibility of inviting King Ferdinand to rule the colony (as the Brazilians had done with the Portuguese King João VI) appears more natural and his wide popular acclamation as a messianic figure less bizarre. Furthermore, a constitutional monarchy of some sort linked indissolubly to religious sanction seemed to many Mexican autonomists the logical solution to the problem of state building. Thus, the short-lived Mexican Empire (1821–1822) of Agustín de Iturbide seems less cynical and idiosyncratic when it comes along at the end of the independence struggle.[25] On the whole it seems fair to say, however, that more than monarchy or republicanism or the instrumentalities of state making, what engaged the attention of creole thinkers most centrally was the concrete issue of political autonomy and behind it the larger question of Mexican nationhood.

Nor was radicalism, whether within a monarchical or a republican framework, a notable characteristic of early Mexican political thought. Although there was a great deal of Sturm und Drang about constitutional forms, the rebel Act of Independence of 1813, the constitution that took shape in the following year, and the loose program associated with them were anything but Jacobin.[26] There is controversy among modern scholars as to the liberal content of these documents, some claiming that they were essentially quite conservative, others that they followed closely the lines of the French revolutionary constitution of 1793.[27] One reason for the difficulty of characterizing creole political thought is that after the initial crisis of 1808, the intellectual community of New Spain was splintered along political lines, many creole intellectuals and public figures switching sides back and forth or trying to hedge their bets by adhering to both parties.[28] What one sees in the 1814 Constitution of Apatzingán is an insistence on political autonomy from Spain, popular sovereignty, representative forms, separation of powers, an established and exclusive Catholic Church, and so forth.[29] Although the issue of state building was of considerable importance to the directorate of the independence movement, however, there is little if any evidence to indicate that it mattered at all to their popular following.

More interesting from the perspective of comparing elite creoles with popular worldviews and, in turn, both with an Atlantic revolutionary tradition is the question of emerging Mexican nationhood and its place in the respective thinking of the two Mexican groups. In the thinking of elite creole ideologues, the concept of nationhood occupied the central place that loyalty to the natal community and messianically tinged mystical kingship were to occupy in the thinking of the popular rural masses of the country, as we shall see. The belief in the historical role of the nation-state surely constituted one important point of convergence between Mexican creole insurgents and the greater Atlantic revolutionary tradition within which their thinking was in part formed, although it was almost entirely absent from popular political thinking and forms of group identification, as was state making.[30] In creole thinking the idea of the nation emerged most clearly in propositions about popular sovereignty and state legitimacy, initially during the period of the 1808–1810 political crisis in the Spanish Empire triggered by the interference of Napoleon Bonaparte in Iberian politics. In 1808 the creole-dominated city council (*ayuntamiento*) of Mexico City argued in the face of the crisis of the imperial monarchy that the coerced abdications of Spanish monarchs Charles IV and his son Ferdinand VII were null because they were acts of usurpation. Furthermore, the imposition of Joseph Bonaparte as king of Spain was in the *ayuntamiento*'s words "contrary to the rights of the nation to which no one can give a king if it is not itself by the universal consent of its people."[31]

A contractualist view of monarchical authority and the idea of immanent popular sovereignty associated with it can be traced back in Spanish
political thinking to the sixteenth-century political thinkers Francisco de
Vitoria and Francisco Suárez. These ideas were reinforced and elaborated
in the eighteenth century in the writing of natural-law theorist Samuel
Puffendorf and others and were espoused strongly in Mexico by the creole patriots Francisco Primo de Verdad, Juan Francisco Azcarate, Melchor
de Talamantes, and Servando Teresa de Mier, becoming in their hands an
explicit doctrine of national self-determination, later echoed by various
pronouncements of Father José María Morelos and in the official discourse of the nation. This rather abstract idea was buttressed in the Mexican case by the notion that Mexico was not a *new* nation but an ancient
one whose rightful monarchs and people had been usurped and subjugated illegitimately. Thus, the 1813 Mexican declaration of independence
specified that the country was to "recover the exercise of its usurped sovereignty."[32] As with constitutional forms, however, there is little if any evidence to indicate that creole ideas about nationhood, popular sovereignty,
emerging Mexicanness, or citizenship resonated in any but the dullest register with popular concepts of personal or community identity.

Popular and elite rebels were sometimes able to unite under the banner of the Virgin of Guadalupe and a fairly virulent anti-*gachupin* (peninsular Spaniard) sentiment, though Guadalupanismo was a far less potent
unifying political formula than is generally supposed. Father Morelos and
others of the insurgent leaders attempted to foster explicitly such a unity
among the various sectors embraced by their cause, but they met with only
modest results.[33] In March 1813, for example, Morelos decreed that the
men in his army should wear in their hats a device proclaiming their loyalty to La Guadalupana, and in his *Sentimientos de la Nación* of 1813, he
proposed establishing through constitutional law the celebration of December 12 as the day of the Virgin of Guadalupe.[34] But there is precious
little evidence of a positive response by Mexican country people, Indians
in particular, to the brandishing of the Virgin of Guadalupe as at once a
banner of popular rebellion and an umbrella for a cross-class, cross-ethnic
alliance between creoles and indigenous insurgents.[35] Such symbols and
their associated behaviors represented different things to different groups.
In the case of the Virgin of Guadalupe, creole patriots tended to see in her
advent and cult evidence of the providentialism associated with the his-

torical formation of the Mexican nation. To the contrary, popular groups, when they did not instead exalt local patron saints or other divine interventors, saw in her in particular a protectress and in Marianism in general an echo of ancient mother-gods.[36] The victimization of European-born Spaniards, occasionally in the Virgin's name, represented for the creoles the working out of a fraternal struggle over concrete political prizes, while for the rural masses of the colony, and indigenous peasants in particular, it functioned in some cases as a displaced frontal attack on dominant white society in general.

The creole patriotism whose origins David Brading has traced so interestingly and that began developing into a genuine nationalism in the decades after independence was a very different ideology from the localist rural and indigenous worldview often linked to messianic expectation and mystical kingship. In fact, creole patriotism was undergirded by certain racist ideas regarding the indigenous peoples of New Spain and their "degraded" condition at the close of the colonial period, even while many creole thinkers attempted to appropriate a noble indigenous past for purposes of state making and nation building. Creole ambivalence about indigenous Mexicans originated in the attempt of creole ideologues to distance themselves from the stain of *mestizaje* (race mixture) and the prevailing negative pseudoscientific ideas about the nature of man in the New World, concepts popularized by such European writers of the time as Buffon, Raynal, de Pauw, and Robertson.[37] Creole thinking of the independence era was shot through with an attempt to create a Mexican nation, even if not yet with coherent nationalist imagery. The locus of community for most creole autonomist thinkers was in the nation, and their struggle throughout the next 150 years was to invent a coherent ideology and a state structure congruent with their community of sentiment.

Second Moment: Chito Villagrán Writes to the Curate

Our second insurgent moment takes us into the middle reaches of the rebellion, to the thinking of its local and regional leadership cadres and therefore closer to the heart of popular ideology and in keeping with my central thesis, further away from any recognizable Atlantic revolutionary tradition. It is risky to make too great a claim for the representativeness of the document being analyzed here since it is nearly unique of its kind. But I would suggest that it bears a close relationship to what one might call

educated popular opinion on political questions of the time, most particularly on the illegitimacy of the Spanish colonial order and the justification for rebellion to bring that order down.[38]

The document's nominal author was José María ("El Chito") Villagrán (ca. 1780–1813) and his famous father, Julián Villagrán, a prominent
insurgent chieftain (*cabecilla*) of the early independence struggle.[39] Because of their brutality toward their opponents and civil populations, the
nakedness of their personal opportunism, and their apparent lack of any
principled political stance, neither Chito nor Julián Villagrán have fared
well at the hands of historians of the independence struggle. Their base of
operations was their natal town of Huichápan, to the northwest of Mexico City. Their zone of military influence at times extended as far as the
Huasteca region to the east and even to San Luis Potosí. Countrymen of
rough habits and limited education, they managed to mobilize insurgent
bands of three thousand men or more at a time. These forces were composed largely of indigenous villagers and other humble rural people gathered from pueblos and rural estates in the Huasteca uplands, the silver
mining areas of Zimapán and Pachuca, and centers of Indian population
such as Ixmiquilpan. Unruly, bold, touchy, jealous of their military autonomy, but also talented, Chito and his father bridled under the dictates of
the peripatetic insurgent governments of the time and seldom cooperated
for long with other rebel chieftains, seeking instead to carve out for themselves their own spheres of dominance in the countryside.

More colorful and in some ways more interesting than his father,
Chito Villagrán was about thirty years old when he joined the insurgency.
He was famously precipitated into rebellion by his attempt to evade prosecution for the murder on September 20, 1810 (just four days after the
outbreak of Father Hidalgo's rebellion), of a local hacendado and minor
civil official who had been amorously involved with Chito's wife. There is
little indication that Chito Villagrán was any more ideologically sophisticated than his father or any less driven by personal ambition. As a youth
in Huichápan, he was basically a local delinquent, continually getting into
minor scrapes with the law and protected by his father and uncle Rafael
(also a militia officer and insurgent but pardoned by the crown in 1816).
He later worked as a foreman on rural estates in the area. More than one
citizen of Huichápan thought him "a man of barbarous and bold habits
. . . feared in this town and its district."[40]

Aggressive, ungovernable, and impulsive, even before the rebellion Chito Villagrán had acquired a reputation for brutality and daring. He and his father instituted a sort of reign of terror in Huichápan when they held the town, executing a number of European Spaniards there and appropriating their wealth. A natural and skilled guerrilla fighter, Chito sometimes acted in concert with his father and other kinsmen, sometimes independently, disrupting communications between the capital and the center of the country and briefly capturing and holding important towns such as San Juan del Rio. He was promoted field marshal by the rebel Junta de Zitácuaro, but in 1812 Chito had a falling-out with Ignacio López Rayón, the nominal leader of the insurgent rump government. Chito reoccupied and heavily fortified Huichápan, which he held until the spring of 1813, but a concerted military effort by the royalists to break his influence brought him into their hands. Since his father Julián refused to save him by surrendering and accepting a royal pardon, Chito was executed on May 14, 1813.

Chito Villagrán's personal trajectory seems clear enough: from local delinquent and town bully, to criminal of passion, to rebel, to a figure of at least partial apotheosis among insurrectionary heroes after his death. His career would lack any explicit ideological content at all were it not for the survival of a document that gives Chito's story an odd twist. This interesting letter was written to the curate of the village of Atotonilco el Grande, Dr. Diego Antonio Rodríguez, ostensibly by Mariscal de Campo José María "Chito" Villagrán himself, and dated at Zimapán, April 14, 1812.[41] The occasion for the letter was the capture of Atotonilco by rebel forces under Villagrán's command on April 6, 1812. Resistance to the rebel attack had been strong, and in the process more than a hundred local Indian defenders had been killed in battle, many houses burned, and the town completely sacked.[42] After taking Atotonilco el Grande, Chito Villagrán threatened to raze the town if all absent white householders did not immediately present themselves at his camp with their weapons. Father Rodríguez refused to cooperate with this order and engaged in an epistolary exchange with Villagrán in which the rebel chieftain repeated his order a number of times and the priest stalled with long-winded replies expounding on doctrinal and political matters. In late May, Rodríguez escaped to the royalist stronghold of Pachuca, eventually transmitting Villagrán's letters to the ecclesiastical authorities in Mexico City under his own cover letter of June 8, 1812.[43] Here is the text of Chito Villagrán's letter to Father Rodríguez:

> Supposing [it were true] that our insurrection were against our legiti-
> mate King and beloved monarch the Lord Don Ferdinand VII, and that
> we intended to throw off the yoke of his domination; and supposing that
> the Lord Pope Alexander VII [*sic*] and his successors had authority over
> the distribution of the Kingdoms of the earth as is argued, since his
> Kingdom is purely spiritual according to the teachings of Jesus Christ in
> the Gospels, and that the Bull were not fraudulent in which His Holi-
> ness orders that two mental lines be formed so that what is conquered
> on one side belongs to the King of Spain, and that conquered on the
> other side belongs to the King of Portugal, as is treated at length by Fray
> Josef Torrubia in his work on general history, where he includes the
> complete Bull of Alexander VII [*sic*] that you cite in your letter; and sup-
> posing that Cortes had not been sent by the ambition of [Diego]
> Velásquez, as Solís says, to the conquest of this Kingdom, but by Charles
> V, and that the embassy to Moctezuma had been genuine, and not in-
> vented in his [Cortes's] head; and supposing that it were legitimate for a
> Christian King to despoil of his dominions a gentile King so that his
> vassals embrace the catholic religion, since Moctezuma was as much nat-
> ural lord of these kingdoms as Charles V was of his (Solórzano treats of
> this at length—James the Apostle brought religion to Spain, but did not
> because of that despoil its Kings of their Crown); and supposing that
> this were not the time determined by God for the Europeans to pay for
> the iniquities, robberies, cruelties, and deaths that with such impiety
> they committed in the Conquest of these Kingdoms, as noted in the rep-
> resentations of Bishop Las Casas, of Garcilaso de la Vega, of the cited
> Solís, and of many other authors; and supposing, finally, that all this were
> true, and that the entire American Nation had risen in mass as they
> have, asking a new government that will not overturn or suppress the
> edicts and laws of the Sovereign, or asking a King of the nation itself,
> and not a foreigner [or de fee], according to the expression of Padre
> Vieira in favor of the Americans of Brazil; I ask you, according to what
> has been said, upon what basis rest the censures fulminated against
> Señor Hidalgo and those who follow his party by the Holy Tribunal and
> the so-called Bishop of Valladolid? If the Church does not hurl anathe-
> mas against the infamous Napoleon because, being a Corsican, he takes
> control of the Kingdom of France, nor against his brother Joseph who
> was crowned in Spain, nor against the Dutch who, renouncing their Na-

tional Government, acknowledge [as monarch] the intruder Louis Bonaparte, why does it hurl anathemas against a nation that, to maintain pristine the catholic Religion it professes, takes up arms to demand and acquire the rights usurped from it so long ago, to throw off a tyrannical government, and to take unto itself the sovereignty of its King, don Ferdinand, whom Napoleon and his emissaries (most of the Europeans [in New Spain]), after persecuting and almost decapitating, are trying to despoil of his rights? I cannot persuade myself, Señor Priest, that the anathemas fulminated by the Church fall on the defense we are making of Religion, and Liberty, and thus I believe firmly that we are not comprehended in their penalties.

I assume you are informed that the Edict of the Holy Tribunal of the Faith, and the proclamation of the late Archbishop, tell us that Napoleon has despoiled our Ferdinand of his Kingdom; that his brother Joseph is King of Spain and proclaims himself also King of the Indies; that there are five hundred Spanish emissaries in our Kingdom, sent to seduce us; and finally that we should prepare to defend ourselves because all this threatened total ruin to our Religion. According to what I have said, which you cannot deny, tell me, Señor Priest, should we permit our Religion and our liberty to perish, or should we not take up arms to defend both? If from fear of censure we had not followed our generals, what would our fate have been by now? You, with your fervor, can infer the result. God's Law commands us not to take the life of our neighbors, and that we are forbidden to take what is not ours, and that he who denies this is a heretic because he denies the precepts of the Decalogue. Furthermore, it is the case that the Europeans are our neighbors, as are all the sons of Adam be they of any nation or religion—this is true. But tell me, Señor Priest: a Jew, an Aterite, a Calomite, or a Lutheran—are they our neighbors? There is no doubt that they are. And would you fail to hand over one of these people, if you saw him, to the Holy Tribunal of the Faith, or inform it of his presence, so that he be killed, burned, punished, and all his possessions confiscated? There is no doubt. But is not this man your neighbor? Does not the Divine Law command that you see him as yourself? This means that for them there is no law, nor are they protected by the laws of charity. And why? So that their false doctrines not contaminate others. And should not these principles operate against the European [Spaniards], and should they not be destroyed, whose unjust possession of the government not only deprives our King of his rights, and tyrannizes us, but also threatens the loss of our Religion, and that we remain slaves forever—should they only be seen as our neighbors? Ah, Father Priest, how little you know of this matter of the Catholic, Christian American Nation of today!

I assure you that if you scruple to discuss and communicate with the Americans for fear of anathemas, how much more scruple should we have in discussing with the Europeans, and with those of their party. Because it is doubtful if we are included in the anathemas, which are inspired by the passion of partisanship and the defense of material interests which the Europeans did not bring with them from their own land; but the Europeans and their allies are included in the anathemas of the sacred canons and councils of the Church, hurled against those who burn homes, lay waste fields, profane churches, etc. Assume that not Saint Thomas the Apostle but the Europeans brought the Faith to these regions, but seeing that they intend to destroy that which they have built, it is necessary to persecute them and drive them out. The Jews were the people beloved of God, those entrusted with the Religion, and from whom the Messiah came, but not because of that do we forbear to burn them when we see them. I could say much to you in answer to your letters.

Within the context of Chito Villagrán's career, this letter presents certain difficulties. There is no question that the letter to Rodríguez went out over Chito's signature. The letter was probably written by a well-educated priest in Villagrán's entourage, however, since the insurgent chieftain's personal history, rustic background, and limited education make it virtually impossible to believe that he composed the text himself. Exchanges of this sort between rebel chieftains and loyalist priests, officers, or civil officials were not so exceptional judging by some remaining evidence, but they had more often to do with negotiations for royal pardons or the surrender of besieged towns than with ideological colloquies.[44] Given the unlikelihood of Villagrán's personal authorship of the letter, I am not suggesting that he underwent some kind of backwoods epiphany but simply (whatever the autonomy of the author in writing the letter in the chieftain's names) that these doctrines must have been "in the air" around him and others of his social background and that he must have absorbed them at least to a minimal extent. Perhaps a priest in the leader's entourage preached homiletic sermons to Villagrán's insurgent band after Sunday Mass or tried to educate Chito politically at his table. Whether Chito Villagrán understood these somewhat arcane musings about sovereignty, the public good, the sanctity of religion, and so forth as civilized pretexts for the commission of atrocities and the satisfaction of his personal appetites and ambitions, as his detractors invariably claimed, or whether they really formed an ideological superstructure for a politicomilitary policy is impossible to say.

The content of the letter evinces little unusual either in format or in argument, even down to its highly rhetorical style, and is much of a piece with the abundant pamphlet literature of the time. The positions taken by the writer are certainly familiar enough: the questioning of the juridical status of the Spanish conquest of Mexico itself and of the putative universality of papal authority that underlay it; the cultural relativism (if one may call it that) linked to Christian humanism and the criticism of the doctrines of "just war" undergirding the Spanish conquest, along with the paradoxically unselfconscious ethnocentrism and xenophobia (against the Jews, the French, and so forth) that accompany them; the doctrine that sovereignty is rooted in the governed; the monarchical legitimism focused on King Ferdinand VII; the notion of the personal union of the empire in the monarch; and so forth. Also familiar are the rhetorical flourishes, the invocation of scholarly authority (quite wide ranging, at that) to buttress the argument, and the elaborate counterfactual constructions. These themes need not detain us long here since they have been written on at length and with great ingenuity by a number of scholars. It is worth noting briefly, however, a few aspects of the writer's thinking and of the rhetoric, which occasionally betrays a subtext somewhat out of keeping with the letter's manifest content.

First, the ideas called on to justify the insurgency are standard. This is hardly surprising, but it is certainly in keeping with the deep conservatism of popular rebellion and indeed of the insurrection as a whole. The writer does not anticipate any "modern" doctrines—liberalism or republicanism, for example; nor does he even really look sideways to eighteenth-century notions of natural law or jus gentium. He looks backward to illegitimate conquest, the impious motives of Hernán Cortés and his sponsors, and the evangelization of Mexico by St. Thomas the Apostle. Second, there is a move to separate loyalty to the monarch from the religious legitimating generally claimed for it. This is achieved, first, through impugning the authority of Pope Alexander VI to divide the earth into Spanish and Portuguese spheres (or hemispheres, really) of domination since papal authority is/was not of this world but purely spiritual.[45] It is achieved,

145

second, by suggesting that St. Thomas the Apostle and not the Spaniards initially brought Christianity to the Aztecs and therefore that Spanish political stewardship of the Indies based on the Christianizing mission was an illegitimate arrogation of authority predicated on a false historical premise.[46] Third, there is an implicit question (denial would be too strong a word) asked of the Spanish right, even the deposed legitimate monarch's right, to govern Mexico at all, religious justification or no. There is some hint in the initial counterfactual statement—"Supposing [it were true] that our insurrection were against our legitimate King and beloved monarch Lord Don Ferdinand VII, and that we intended to throw off the yoke of his domination ('el yugo de su dominación')"—that that is precisely the goal of the insurrection.

Particularly revealing in Villagrán's letter to Dr. Rodríguez, however, is the presence of two ideological elements that resonate strikingly with his own career in rebellion and more broadly with the insurrectionary movement in general. First, the letter expresses a kind of quasi-utilitarian, communalist view of political legitimacy and the efficacy of political action. This emerges clearly in the discussion as to whether God's injunction regarding the sanctity of individual human life, as expressed in the Decalogue, can be overridden by a clear and present danger to the integrity of the state and religion. The writer's answer is an unequivocal yes. Though this is hardly surprising with regard to Jews, Lutherans, and others who are ipso facto defined as threats to the community, the author goes on to extend the doctrine to the European Spaniards in New Spain through an ingenious implicit parallelism with the Jews. The privileged position of both peoples in the eyes of God and their earthly inviolability, he writes, were contradicted by their immoral actions. Although the crime of the Jews is not explicitly stated, we may presume it to have been their rejection and betrayal of Christ despite the fact that they were "the people beloved of God, those entrusted with the Religion, and from whom the Messiah came." The crimes of the European Spaniards are spelled out in the letter at some length, however. The list begins with "the iniquities, robberies, cruelties, and deaths that with such impiety they committed in the Conquest of these kingdoms"; continues through the persecution by Napoleon (implicitly with the support of many Spaniards in Spain itself and in Mexico of King Ferdinand), the despoliation of the legitimate monarch's rights, and the sending of five hundred "Spanish emissaries . . .

to seduce us"; and culminates with the *gachupines'* "unjust possession of the government [that] not only deprives our King of his rights, and tyrannizes us, but also threatens the loss of our Religion, and [threatens] that we remain slaves forever." This formulation draws attention to the painful and fratricidal nature of the independence struggle, emphasizing the moral imperative behind it and stressing that it was not undertaken lightly. The writer does not dwell at all on how or by whom the good of the community (of New Spain) is to be construed but implicitly invokes the spontaneous expression of some sort of popular will.

As a personal pronouncement of Chito Villagrán, there is some irony in this doctrine since his own career demonstrates an extreme unwillingness to subordinate himself or his actions to any conception of community well-being larger than his own. As a general political doctrine, however, this communalist view evokes on an ideological plane the manner in which the movement worked in actuality, particularly in manifestations of popular rebellion: it was fragmented, feudalized, localized—often more clan feud and riot than mass mobilization. This is not to say, on the one hand, that formal ideology or programmatic elements, even in the sort of backwoods theology and politics vented in Villagrán's letter, were drawn from or necessarily heavily influenced by an inchoate popular Weltanschauung regarding political institutions. Nor is it to suggest, on the other hand, that popular practice was based primarily on an idiosyncratic, parochial reading of the formal doctrines of high politics and theology. The letter's approach does indicate, however, that the great and little traditions resonated with each other at least a bit and that they may even have had common roots in the sociopolitical structure of colonial Mexico.

Second, it is clear from the letter that the writer sees religion and sovereignty as very closely related though not bound up logically or inextricably. The relationship seems almost to be one of analogy (of two entities having the same or similar properties) rather than of identity or conflation. It is true that sovereignty (whether in the form of the king's right to rule or that of a diffuse popular "liberty") and religion are repeatedly invoked by the writer in the same breath and that two items on his agenda are the enjoyment of an uncompromised, legitimate political sovereignty and the free practice of true religion. These are not seen to be linked logically in any coherent fashion, however. It is the burden of the letter, in fact, substantially to *disconnect* religion and sovereignty in ways harking

147

back to their *connection* in the sixteenth-century debate over the justification of the conquest. This is rather odd especially in view of the intensely
religious character of much of the symbolism associated with mass rebellion in the years between 1810 and 1821, a movement permeated (at least
in the hopes of its creole directorate) with the Guadalupe cult, replete with
references to the Godless French and their *gachupin* minions and so forth.
This ideological rupture in the old linkage between religion and sovereignty—between God and the Spanish state—suggests a duality in forms
of rebellion as well in which much of popular rebellion was religious or
quasi-religious in essence but political in appearance and in which much
of elite rebellion and formal ideology were religious in appearance but political in essence. This further suggests divergent understandings between
the elite leadership stratum and mass following as to how the world itself
was constituted and what was at issue in the wars of independence in New
Spain, putting popular rebellion and political thinking even further outside a secularized Atlantic revolutionary tradition.

Third Moment: Popular Violence and Ideology

Further yet removed from any clear relationship to an Atlantic revolutionary tradition, the popular insurgency of 1810–1821 was overwhelmingly peasant, substantially indigenous in composition, local and
contingent in occasion and form, and largely cultural in content although
nonetheless political in the broadest sense of the term. Popular ideology
was focused on the defense of community rather than on emerging notions of the distinction between colony and nation, state and civil society,
or nation and "other." Communalist thinking and politics depended in
large measure on sources of religious legitimation and were linked to the
monarchy-as-protector by a sort of primitive fusion that transcended
spheres of state activity at local and colony-wide levels—the very political
and ideological space, between the village community below and the imperial structure above, in which the Mexican nation-state was shortly to
be cobbled together.[47] Evidence strongly suggests that the goals of popular politics and violent protest diverged considerably from those of the creole directorate of the independence movement. I would like to lay out two
of the most important of these—forms of village collective action and
messianic belief—and then finally pass on to a social profile of popular in-

surgents in order to locate ideological elements in social circumstance. Here the evidentiary ground has obviously shifted from the exegesis of texts to the description of collective behavior, with all the interpretive slipperiness such a move entails.

Localocentrism and the integrity of community were features of village riot and protest right through the late eighteenth century and into the internal war period of 1810–1821 and beyond. It has often been noted of the colonial countryside that rural disturbances tended to remain localized for the most part, only infrequently coalescing into broader insurrection, and conventional wisdom to the contrary notwithstanding, this was also true of the independence period.[48] As to forms of collective violence, the organization of many village uprisings both before and after 1810 resembled nothing less than rural soviets or perhaps free communes along Fourierist lines. These cases consisted of short-lived attempts by rural communities apparently to cut their political and other bonds with the outside world and govern themselves in utopian independence. Occasionally one sees in such episodes hints of attacks on local systems of privilege and property, such as occurred in the village rising at Chicontepec, in the Huasteca zone of the modern State of Hidalgo, in May 1811, where the evidence of an insurgent program focused on the local landholding structure as the most specific immediate issue of grievance.[49] This sort of local mobilization was occasionally accompanied by actual or threatened violence directed against non-Indian racial groups and a highly amplified, almost obsessive concern with local political legitimacy and forms of authority.

One fairly vivid example of the pueblo-as-soviet during the insurgency is that of the village of San Lorenzo Ixtacoyotla, in the district of Zacualtipan, near Metztitlán and not far from Chicontepec, to the northeast of Mexico City, taken by force of royalist arms on November 15, 1811. Although the defenders of the town had virtually no firearms, they had held it as an avowedly insurgent commune for some two months. Leadership seems to have come not from outsiders but from the Indian governor of the pueblo and the local *cabecillas* Luis Vite and Vicente Acosta, both Indians. Local men were recruited to steal maize from nearby haciendas. Other villages in the area were known to the rebels as "cantons," though there was no action in concert with them. Local roads connecting the insurgent villages with other areas were cut, the rebels "thinking with this that the pueblo would remain safe," in the words of one local observer—not only, one suspects, for tactical reasons but also to underline the indigenous nature of the uprising. Acosta urged the village rebels not to believe in or acknowledge the authority of King Ferdinand VII (an unusually radical stance), while Vite convinced them that the royalist troops operating in the region "came killing everyone because since they were *gachupines* they did not like the local men ('*los hijos [del pueblo]*') because they are Indians." It was also widely believed by village insurgents in the area that the *gachupines* and other non-Indian locals were allied against the Indian villagers, "and if the non-Indians help the *gachupines*, we have no other support than our Lady of Guadalupe."[50] So we have here and in other cases what looks to be the embryonic stage of an insular village utopia, substantially cut off from other such communes, acting to expropriate property from non-Indians and following at least to some degree an ideology of American religious legitimation, ethnic exclusion, and rejection of a top-down colonial state.[51] What we might call the internal choreography of these village uprisings—their interior logic, the patterns of movement of their participants, and the sites of public action—also reflects this same localocentrism. They demonstrated a marked tendency to turn inward to protect community integrity instead of a turning outward to form tactical alliances or change the external political world. In this manner, they resembled social implosions more than the explosions and insurrectionary contagions colonial authorities so feared.

Another line of evidence—the dramatic strain of messianic expectation to be found in the plebeian ideology of rebellion—can be linked to what I have been calling the localocentrism of rural Mexican popular culture. A widespread belief in the messianic attributes of the Spanish monarch prevailed among many popular rebels and rioters in New Spain even before the outbreak of the independence rebellion in 1810 and was specifically attached in the following years to the reactionary figure of King Ferdinand VII.[52] Many Indian insurgents, in particular, believed that the king himself was in Mexico and that he not only condoned but actively led the rebel armies. His person and powers were not bound by time and space, furthermore: he performed prodigies of travel, appeared in widely separate locations simultaneously, deflected royalist cannonballs from their targets, and intervened to change the course of battles. Rural people flocked to the insurgent standard when canny rebel leaders invoked the king's name. Those same leaders were known to have suppressed the news of Ferdinand's restoration to the Spanish throne in 1814 for fear that the loyalty of their Indian followers would ebb if it were known.

Although it is true that this kind of naive legitimism may be seen as a cross-cultural characteristic of peasant rebellion and also true that it mimicked elements of Iberian and European political culture going back to the medieval period, there are several aspects of popular messianism in the Mexican case that link it not to an imported or superimposed ideology but to an enduring popular culture. It is pretty clear that a messianic expectation focused on the Spanish king resonated with a precolonial, indigenous cyclical cosmogony widely typical of Mesoamerican cultures. It is equally clear that the less acculturated Indian villagers of the more northerly, mountainous, and isolated coastal zones of the colony were inclined to cast Indian prophet–kings in the role of messiah, while the settled peasant villagers of central Mexico were more likely to select King Ferdinand VII for the role or on occasion the creole leader Ignacio Allende or other surrogate figures. My interpretation of this difference is that although a native, popular tradition of messianic expectation survived in many areas of the country, it was more truncated in the Mexican *oikumene* by long exposure to Spanish evangelization, urban culture, and economic subordination. Veneration of the Spanish king and the conversion of Ferdinand VII specifically into a messianic figure, however, were also rooted in the practical policies of the colonial period. From the sixteenth century on, the political and juridical stance of the monarchy had been at least nominally dedicated to protection of indigenous communities against the rapacity of the colonists, thus cementing an ideological alliance between Spanish monarch and Indian vassals. Moreover, although there emerged in creole insurgent pamphletry and other forms of propaganda a strain of messianic thought, it was bloodless and formalized in comparison to the vividness and immediacy of popular messianism. The elements of a village millennium were readily at hand, therefore, especially for Indian peasants: a messianic object (the Spanish king or his surrogates) and a millennial space (the embattled village itself).

The third line of evidence I offer, touching on the nature of popular participation in the insurgency, consists of a very abbreviated statistical profile of the insurgents. The supposition here, obviously, is that there exists some correlation between certain social and cultural markers and the propensity to think and act in a certain manner. What follows is a statistical profile of the popular insurgents, based on a collection of data concerning about 1,300 individuals captured for insurgent activity, the majority between 1810 and 1812, although the sample extends to 1821. The sample would represent perhaps 1 percent of the total male combatant population in New Spain during the period 1810–1821 and is based on heterogeneous but reasonably reliable data. The variables include gender, age, ethnicity, occupation, civil status, place of habitual residence and/or birth, distance between place of capture and place of residence/birth, and some other variables of little immediate interest here. The sample is made up almost exclusively of men.

To begin with the age variable, it turns out that young adults, between fifteen and twenty-four years of age, make up almost 35 percent of the sample, with mature adults of between twenty-five and fifty years of age making up something in excess of 60 percent. This distribution yields an average age of almost thirty years. The most striking thing about this finding is the relatively advanced age of the majority of individuals in the sample compared with the life expectancy of the Mexican population as a whole during the period. That population demonstrated the characteristics (high birth and death rates, relatively high infant mortality and low average age at death, and slow growth) of a typically "ancien régime" demography.[53] As a result, by Mexican standards of the time, the thirty-year age of the average rebel was hardly that of a young man and might be considered quite mature. This means that the average insurgent should probably have been settled as an adult: he was very probably married, if he was going to marry at all; he was likely a father; and he had already inherited all the property he would inherit given the practices of equal partible inheritance prevailing at the time. In other words, our average rebel was likely no callow youth buffeted by the violent emotional and hormonal storms of adolescence and early adulthood typical of many Western cultures—marginal, liminal, or struggling to assert his personal and social identity against parents, community, or rigid social norms—but a mature individual with established social ties.

Let us now turn to the second important variable, that of ethnicity. The opinion held by many since the nineteenth century, that the Mexican movement for independence from Spain was in some meaningful sense

predominantly mestizo in social composition, especially after the disper-
sion of Father Miguel Hidalgo's army by royalist forces at the beginning
of 1811, cannot be connected with the actual social profile of the insurgents. The percentages of major ethnic groups present in the Mexican
population as a whole are reflected quite closely in the proportions of
those same ethnic groups within the sample of insurgents: 18 percent
whites (both European and creole), 22 percent "castas" (people of mixed
blood), and 60 percent indigenous.

In the sample are included several other interesting variables, such as
occupation and civil status, but these are best left aside in this chapter.
What is of considerable interest in the sample is the spatial relationship
between place of birth or habitual residence and place of capture of rebels,
that is, the distance between these two points. The analysis of the sample
for this variable indicates that about 20 percent of the accused insurgents
were captured near their homes, within a distance of 1 to 14 kilometers;
another 20 percent fell into the hands of the royalists within an easy distance of their villages, within a range of 15 to 40 kilometers; 40 percent
within a medium distance, 41 to 160 kilometers; and the last 20 percent
within a long distance, at more than 161 kilometers.[54]

Cross tabulations of these variables produce interesting results, some
of them hardly surprising. When we cross occupation and distance variables, for example, we find that farmers were captured close to their natal
villages, professionals (mostly whites) and transport specialists (above all
mule skinners) farthest away. Married men were captured nearer their
homes and bachelors farther away. On the other hand, some of the inter-
relationships are less predictable. Those among age, occupation, and civil
status suggest a possible blockage in the life course for men accused of insurgency, which I have suggested in other work of my own. This makes
the relatively mature age of the insurgents at capture (about thirty years,
it will be recalled) a potentially revealing factor in a society in which individuals could generally expect to have established families and adult social
and political responsibilities by the time they reached their early twenties
or so. Given their chronological maturity, for example, it is interesting to
note the unusually high rate of bachelorhood among the sample of insurgents as compared to the general population.

For present purposes, however, the most suggestive relationship is that
between ethnicity and distance between place of birth or habitual residence

153

and place of capture. The statistics show substantially significant differences between ethnic groups in terms of the distance from place of birth or
habitual residence to place of capture. The clearest of these differences is
between Indians and whites. Indigenous people were four times as likely as
whites to be captured within a short distance of their homes (say, three
hours or so by foot travel). In this first and shortest range of distance, blacks,
mestizos, and other mixed-blood groups were to be found statistically in the
middle, between the Indians and the whites. A bit farther out from home
but still within a day or so journey by foot, all the major ethnic groupings
show similar percentages. Captures in the middle distance (a two- or three-
day trip by foot from home) demonstrate a slight echo of the "near home"
distribution, but the spread in percentages is too small to make much of. At
more than a four days' walk from home, however, a rough ethnic differen-
tial reasserts itself, with indigenous people and mestizos about half as likely
as whites to be captured and blacks nearly in between.

On the whole, these findings, especially those relating ethnicity to distance between place of birth/residence and place of capture, suggest a sort
of a ringlike arrangement of various overlapping groups in the insurgent
population to act in a spatial field centered on their home towns, villages,
and hamlets.[55] The most likely explanation hinges on differences in worldview and mentality among the groups in question. Indian peasants, who
made up the largest group among the insurgents, were profoundly localist
in their worldview, and their actions tended to be constrained by the political and affective *campanilismo* characteristic of their mind-set.[56] On the
other hand, Spaniards (that is, whites) were much more likely to enjoy a
higher degree of physical and social mobility, to have experienced something of a wider world, and to be able to conceive of an abstract entity such
as a nation in whose nominal interest they might take up arms. Mestizos
and other mixed bloods in the population fell somewhere between these
two poles. There would appear to be a spatial continuum, therefore, corresponding closely to an ethnic one that reflected not the importance of race
per se in stimulating or constraining the forms and breadth of collective action but rather the often unarticulated views of different groups as to what
constituted the appropriate community of reference for action. Insofar as
the popular insurgency among village-dwelling Indians is concerned, this
line of evidence fits rather well the model of the imploding communal village fighting to maintain its autonomy and integrity because that village

was at the same time the locus of villagers' social identity and cultural identity as well as the main theater of their economic subsistence. In keeping with this, the appeal to the Spanish monarch, whether in public ritual and celebration, litigation in the colonial courts, or collective action with a messianic cast, was intended to provide not only political legitimacy but also leverage against communal enemies. The polity being defended, however, was not a real or imagined nation but a village.

One of the most strongly entrenched conventional interpretations of the movement for Mexican independence is that the primary object of both popular and elite rebels was national autonomy and the capture of state power. But whatever else they may be, states are also mental constructs, and one's perception of them is likely to change as one's structural perspective changes. Our modern preoccupation with the state as the most important locus of public life and as the instrument of profound social change—and our reification of it—have led us to the practice of what one historian of the Mexican Revolution of 1910 has aptly termed "statolatry."[57] I would add here that historians may so often focus on the state because we *can* focus on it. That is, we can follow the state's changes, as opposed to other, less visible but no less pervasive processes that may unfold in a local theater and that find, properly speaking, other than obviously "political" or instrumentalist forms of expression or that may not be traceable at all in subaltern groups. But for people even to conceive of a state, they are required to share a cognitive map that includes a view of a wider world beyond locality and of the integuments that hold it together. For much of the population of late colonial Mexico, such a vision did not exist, and to assume its presence is anachronistic. Furthermore, the objects of popular violence in 1810 and thereafter were not particularly representatives of the Spanish colonial state—local officials or priests, for example. Even where they occasionally were, there is a difference between figures of authority and the body of the state itself. What seems to have mattered to most people was not state, and still less nation, but community. In the case of early nineteenth-century Mexico, therefore, I am in favor, to paraphrase a sociological motto that gained some currency a few years ago, of taking the state back out or at least of reinserting it into our analysis only carefully and perhaps at an oblique angle.

When large-scale fissures appeared in Mexican society at the beginning of the nineteenth century, the cultural fault lines between the village-dwelling Indian population and the other sectors of the society opened a space for the emergence of a popular ideology saturated with an apparently atavistic religious imagery. This imagery was accompanied by popular mobilization and violence whose effective range and destructive energy were severely constrained by the very communalistic identifications that had engendered them. The contrast of these with the protonationalist and even protoliberal state- and nation-building program of the independence movement's creole directorate could not have been clearer. Within this framework it would be my contention that the critique of the late Bourbon state fashioned by the creole directorate of the independence struggles and the project for a national state experimented with in the decades following independence from Spain were artifacts of elite, essentially urban culture linked to a European great tradition. These could be contained, if with strain at some points, within an Atlantic revolutionary tradition. The assumptions and preoccupations of that culture and the political projects arising from it resonated only dully, if at all, with the popular culture of rural and predominantly Indian Mexico.[58]

Where does the decade of insurrectionary violence in Mexico (and its political legacy) stand, then, in relation to the revolutionary traditions (or currents) of the Atlantic world between the end of the seventeenth century and the beginning of the nineteenth? To relate my account to the themes of this volume as a whole, let me return to my initial discussion of the three somewhat distinct possible definitions of revolutionary "traditions," the trope around which the original academic event was formulated and to which the papers were addressed. In terms of the first definition I sketched—that of a revolutionary tradition as actual history, specifically designating a class of large-scale social upheavals genealogically and morphologically related to each other—the Mexican independence movement certainly swims in the same current with the other great revolutions of the "Age of Revolution," the American and French, and even bears some remote relationship with political change in seventeenth-century England. Genealogical connection is readily apparent since the Mexican independence struggle would surely not have occurred when it did absent the antecedent events in the Anglo-American colonies and France. Here demonstration effects were important (the corrosive tides of nationalism, republicanism, and even liberalism, after all, lapped at the Atlantic shores of New Spain after 1775), as were specific historical contingencies (the geopolitical expansion of revolutionary France creating a crisis of authority and legitimacy in the Spanish Empire, for example). This is not to discount a more internalist view of Mexican or Spanish American independence, the logic of Spanish imperial decay and defensive reform and repositioning in a changing international environment, or elements of political culture native to the Iberian world that might be mobilized to justify colonial self-determination, popular sovereignty, and so forth but only to concede influence and contingency their due. Key elements of morphology also unite the Mexican case with the other two in some measure, although here the convergence becomes a bit thinner: protracted military conflict, an attempt to reconfigure state structures, constitutionalism, and some common elements of Enlightenment-derived ideology, at least as the level of elites. The Mexican case shared with the American, moreover, the problem of reestablishing stability while decolonizing and with the French the difficulty of either suppressing or metabolizing elements of internal resistance and dissensus (for example, the Vendée, the Chouannerie) swirling about the sometimes incoherent program of regime change.

It is in connection with the second and third definitions of "revolutionary traditions"—the second, that of discursive, intellectual, and ideological elements attendant on such episodes, and the third, the traditional wisdom *about* such upheavals, which basically takes us into the interpretive register—that serious difficulties of "fit" between the Mexican experience and Atlantic-world revolutionary trends emerge. This is true especially with regard to the divergence within Mexico between the theaters, forms, and ideologies of popular collective action and elite political leadership; let me cite but three examples.[59] First, though there was significant rural participation in the American and French revolutions, these movements were primarily bred and carried forward in the cities; in Mexico the decade-long insurgency was overwhelmingly rural in character and concomitantly Indian in complexion in many areas of the country.[60] Second, in the Anglo-American colonies there was a good deal of public talk about God and the providential nature of the movement for independence, and in France the radical revolutionaries attempted to expunge or recathect religious affect (in the Cult of Reason and the *fête révolutionnaire*, for example) even as the forces of counterrevolution made much of its defense (in resisting the application of the 1791 Civil Constitution of the Clergy, for instance).[61] But in neither case did religious sensibility, symbolism, and discourse on the *revolutionary* side strike so loud a chord in popular ideology as it did among humble Mexicans, most of them Indians, whether they marched under the banner of the Virgin of Guadalupe or some local religious icon.[62] Finally, the notable strain of naive monarchism running through the ideology of popular insurgents in Mexico in the form of messianic beliefs focused on King Ferdinand VII or his surrogates found no parallel in the American or French movements.

These three contrasting ideological elements among the eighteenth- and early nineteenth-century Atlantic movements (and the first, rurality, should really be understood as more ideational than geographic since it reflected a communitarian sensibility—an ideology of local utopianism, in other words) point strongly to the existence of a much larger social and cultural space between popular and elite political groups *within* the insurrection in the Mexican case and to the importance of ethnocultural difference there—to the Indianness of much of popular rebellion, in other words. This brings us to consider the third definition of "revolutionary traditions" offered at the beginning of this chapter, that of conventional wisdoms *about* revolutions, the interpretive register. To recapitulate my introductory remarks: The case of Mexican independence offers a poor fit with the prevailing class-based, estate-based, or even interest-group models frequently invoked to explain revolutions or at the very least suggests that historical models that ignore ethnocultural difference or reduce it to a minor dependent variable have little explanatory power with regard to Mexico or other areas of Latin America that were colonized, governed, evangelized, and enculturated in a manner totally distinct from that of British North America.

Suggested Readings

Anderson, Benedict
    Imagined Communities: Reflections on the Origin and Spread of Nationalism, rev. ed. London: Verso, 1991.

Anna, Timothy E.
    The Fall of the Royal Government in Mexico City. Lincoln: University of Nebraska Press, 1978.

Archer, Christon I., ed.
The Wars of Independence in Spanish America. Wilmington, Del.: Scholarly Resources, 2002.

Guerra, François-Xavier
Modernidad e independencias: Ensayos sobre las revoluciones hispánicas. Madrid: Mapfre, 1992.

Hamill, Hugh M., Jr.
The Hidalgo Revolt: Prelude to Mexican Independence. Gainesville: University Press of Florida, 1966.

Katz, Friedrich, ed.
Riot, Rebellion, and Revolution: Rural Social Conflict in Mexico. Princeton, N.J.: Princeton University Press, 1988.

Lomnitz, Claudio
Deep Mexico, Silent Mexico: An Anthropology of Nationalism. Minneapolis: University of Minnesota Press, 2001.

Rodríguez O., Jaime E.
The Independence of Spanish America. Cambridge: Cambridge University Press, 1998.

——, ed.
Mexico in the Age of Democratic Revolutions, 1750–1850. Boulder, Colo.: Lynne Rienner, 1994.

Tutino, John
From Insurrection to Revolution in Mexico: Social Bases of Agrarian Violence, 1750–1940. Princeton, N.J.: Princeton University Press, 1986.

Uribe-Uran, Victor M., ed.
State and Society in Spanish America during the Age of Revolution. Wilmington, Del.: Scholarly Resources, 2001.

Van Young, Eric
The Other Rebellion: Popular Violence, Ideology, and the Mexican Struggle for Independence, 1810–1821. Stanford, Calif.: Stanford University Press, 2001.

Wolloch, Isser, ed.
Revolution and the Meanings of Freedom in the Nineteenth Century. Stanford, Calif.: Stanford University Press, 1996.

Notes

1. See, for example, R. R. Palmer, *The Age of Democractic Revolution: Political History of Europe and America, 1760–1800*, 2 vols. (Princeton, N.J.: Princeton University Press, 1959–1964); Eric Hobsbawm, *The Age of Revolution: Europe, 1789–1848* (London: Weidenfeld and Nicholson, 1962). The present chapter owes much to previously published work of my own, including my book *The Other Rebellion: Popular Violence, Ideology, and the Mexican Struggle for Independence, 1810–1821* (Stanford, Calif.: Stanford University Press, 2001).

2. See the generally thoughtful remarks on this issue in the editor's introduction to *Mexico in the Age of Democratic Revolutions, 1750–1850*, ed. Jaime E. Rodríguez O. (Boulder, Colo.: Lynne Rienner, 1994), 1ff.; for a similar periodization of economic history in Latin America, linking it to political developments in the wider Atlantic world, see Kenneth J. Andrien and Lyman L. Johnson, eds., *The Political Economy of Spanish America in the Age of Revolution, 1750–1850* (Albuquerque: University of New Mexico Press, 1994). There is some irony in the deployment of this periodization, however useful it may be for heuristic purposes. In attempting to break the bonds of traditional political periodizations (independence as end/beginning) we have adopted the "age of revolution" scenario, which reinforces political criteria for periodization while tying the history of Latin America ever more closely to events in the North Atlantic world (enlightened despotism/French Revolution–American Revolution/revolutions of 1848), quasi-universal nation-building processes, and the Whiggish teleology of liberalism. For a discussion of the "Age of Revolution" periodization for Spanish America from the point of view of cultural history, see Eric Van Young, "Was There an Age of Revolution in Spanish America?" in *State and Society in Spanish American during the "Age of Revolution": New Research on Historical Continuities and Changes, ca. 1750s–1850s*, ed. Victor Uribe Uran (Wilmington, Del.: Scholarly Resources, 2001), 219–46.

3. See, for example, Josefina Zoraida Vázquez et al., *Dos revoluciones: México y los Estados Unidos* (Mexico City: Editorial Jus, 1976); Peggy K. Liss, *Atlantic Empires: The Network of Trade and Revolution, 1713–1826* (Baltimore: The Johns Hopkins University Press, 1983); Isser Wolloch, ed., *Revolution and the Meanings of Freedom in the Nineteenth Century* (Stanford, Calif.: Stanford University Press, 1996); Robert M. Maniquis, Oscar R. Martí, and José Pérez, eds., *La revolución francesa en el mundo ibérico* (Madrid: Sociedad Estatal Aquinto Centenario, 1989); and Jaime E. Rodríguez O., *The Independence of Spanish America* (Cambridge: Cambridge University Press, 1998).

4. For an excellent study touching on these matters, see Francois-Xavier Guerra, *Modernidad e independencias: Ensayos sobre las revoluciones hispánicas* (Mexico City: Editorial MAPFE, 1993).

5. The effective conservatism of the colonial revolutions is quite notable, in fact, in the sense that colonial elites both in Spanish and Anglo-America used as ideological leverage the idea that they were vindicating traditional rights against oppressive regimes. In chapter 1, Lois G. Schwoerer traces the genealogy and seventeenth-century apotheosis of what she calls "jury ideology," with its linkage to the second "pillar" of political right, namely, parliamentary representation. These had no direct parallels in the Spanish Atlantic world, strictly speaking, but the implicit "colonial compact" between Spanish monarchy and colonies and the traditionalist, centuries-old critique of corrupt or inefficacious government in the Spanish realms embodied in the call of rioters and insurgents of "Long live the king! Death to bad government!" provided rebels with moral and political high ground from which to launch an assault against a colonial state thought to have forfeited its legitimacy.

6. One of the clearest and most thoughtful treatments of creole patriotism in Spanish America, but most particularly in Mexico, is that embodied in the many works of David A. Brading, of which see especially *The First America: The Spanish Monarchy, Creole Patriots, and the Liberal State, 1492–1867* (Cambridge: Cambridge University Press, 1991); on Mexico, see Luis Villoro, *El proceso ideológico de la revolución de Independencia* (1953; 2nd ed., Mexico City: Universidad Nacional Autónoma de Mexico, 1986); and for another area in the colonial New World, see Hans-Joachim König, *En el camino hacia la nación: Nacionalismo en el proceso de formación del estado y de la nación de la Nueva Granada, 1750–1856* (Bogota: Banco de la República, 1994).

7. Benedict Anderson, *Imagined Communities: Reflections on the Origin and Spread of Nationalism* (1983; rev. ed., London: Verso, 1991), esp. 47–66. For some examples of the "passover" phenomenon from among several generations of historians' and historical sociologists' model building about revolutionary phenomena, see Barrington Moore Jr., *Social Origins of Dictatorship and Democracy: Lord and Peasant in the Making of the Modern World* (Boston: Beacon Press, 1966); Theda Skocpol, *States and Social Revolutions: A Comparative Analysis of France, Russia, and China* (Cambridge: Cambridge University Press, 1979); Jack A. Goldstone, *Revolution and Rebellion in the Early Modern World* (Berkeley: University of California Press, 1991); Victor Magagna, *Communities of Grain: Rural Rebellion in Comparative Perspective* (Ithaca, N.Y.: Cornell University Press, 1991); and Sidney Tarrow, *Power in Movement: Social Movements, Collective Action and Politics* (Cambridge: Cambridge University Press, 1994).

8. For a considered but respectful critique of Anderson embracing these and other points, see Claudio Lomnitz-Adler, *Deep Mexico, Silent Mexico: An Anthropology of Nationalism* (Minneapolis: University of Minnesota Press, 2001), 3–34.

9. The implicit comparison group in this rather sweeping statement embraces the extra-European areas of the world. Within Europe or on the European periphery, one may cite anticolonial or anti-imperial insurgencies (some successful, others not), among them by the Irish against their English overlords and the Dutch and Portuguese against the Spanish. My characterization of the Mexican insurgency as an anticolonial war of national liberation is at odds with a number of recent scholarly works, among them Jaime E. Rodríguez O.'s major recent interpretive synthesis on the Spanish American independence struggles, *The Independence of Spanish America*; instead, Rodríguez links the various movements politically and ideologically to the "Age of Democratic Revolutions" and the protracted breakdown of the Spanish Empire.

10. See especially Guerra, *Modernidad e independencias*, 19–54, and Maniquis et al., *La revolución francesa*.

11. The literature on the "age of Andean insurrection" is large and growing. Some of the best modern treatments are Steve J. Stern, ed., *Resistance, Rebellion, and Consciousness in the Andean Peasant World, 18th to 20th Centuries* (Madison: University of Wisconsin Press, 1987); more recently Scarlett O'Phelan Godoy, *La gran rebelión en los Andes. De Túpac Amaru á Túpac Catari* (Cuzco, Peru: Centro Estudieos Regionales Andinos, 1995); and Charles F. Walker, *Smoldering Ashes: Cuzco and the Creation of Republican Peru, 1780–1840* (Durham, N.C.: Duke University Press, 1999).

12. I except the case of Haiti (1791) because although racial antagonisms were fierce in the Haitian independence struggle, the role of long-colonized indigenous peoples was nonexistent.

13. As John M. Murrin points out in chapter 2, one of the paradoxes of the American Revolution is that it occurred precisely at the time that the British Empire was growing ever more integrated.

14. Again, Benedict Anderson's interpretation is noted as an exception in this regard. My conceptualization of ultra-European historiography has been influenced by the intersection of subaltern studies and postcolonial criticism; see, for example, Dipesh Chakrabarty, "Postcoloniality and the Artifice of History: Who Speaks for 'Indian' Pasts?" *Representations* 37 (winter 1992): 1–26; Gyan Prakash, "Subaltern Studies as Postcolonial Criticism," *American Historical Review* 99 (December 1994): 1475–90; and many of the pieces in Bill Ashcroft, Gareth Williams, and Helen Tiffin, eds., *The Post-Colonial Reader* (London: Routledge, 1995). It does seem the case that even a major upheaval like the Mexican independence movement has not yet spawned the dense modern historiography or the well-developed interpretive debates devoted to the French, English, or Russian revolutions, for example, although there is a large traditional historical literature, some of which forms part of the canon of great Mexican works of narrative his-

tory. Chief among such works is the massive and still controversial work of the mid-nineteenth-century conservative statesman Lucas Alamán, *Historia de Méjico*, 5 vols. (1846–1852; 2nd ed., Mexico City: Editorial Jus, 1968). The Mexican Revolution is quite another matter, though it, too, is rather underdeveloped historiographically relative to Old World cases and continues to be mired in certain well-worn political ruts whose scholarship has not yet produced some of the basic social and economic analyses essential to pushing these debates onto more fertile ground. For an interesting comparative treatment embracing the historiography of the English, French, and Mexican revolutions, see Alan Knight, "Revisionism and Revolution: Mexico Compared to England and France," *Past and Present*, no. 134 (February 1992): 159–99.

15. Philip Corrigan and Derek Sayer, *The Great Arch: English State Formation as Cultural Revolution* (Oxford: Blackwell Publisher, 1985); and see also the suggestive way in which the formulations of Corrigan and Sayer (and those of James C. Scott on "everyday" forms of resistance) have been woven into the chapters in Gilbert M. Joseph and Daniel Nugent, eds., *Everyday Forms of State Formation: Revolution and the Negotiation of Rule in Modern Mexico* (Durham, N.C.: Duke University Press, 1994), especially those of the editors (chaps. 3–23) and Alan Knight (chaps. 24–66). An attempt of my own to deal specifically with the relationship among state building, nation building, and popular political culture in Mexico is embodied in my essay "Conclusion: The State as Vampire— Hegemonic Projects, Public Ritual, and Popular Culture in Mexico, 1600–1990," in *Rituals of Rule, Rituals of Resistance: Public Celebration and Popular Culture in Mexico*, ed. William H. Beezley, Cheryl F. Martin, and William E. French (Wilmington, Del.: Scholarly Resources, 1994), 343–74; and in the same volume, see the fine introductory essay by the editors (xiii–xxxii).

16. There may even be some question raised as to whether the Spanish American "revolutions" were "revolutions" at all. Certainly they were violent, society-wide upheavals that produced basic changes in the form of the state and, what is more at issue in the present context, at least initiated the process of nation building. If the Mexican and other Spanish American independence movements were revolutions of low "revolutionariness," they certainly nonetheless occupy one end of the continuum of revolutionary political phenomena, and their exclusion significantly impoverishes the exercise of model building.

17. One of the most widely influential modern treatments of this theme is Guillermo Bonfil Batalla, *México profundo: Una civilización negada* (Mexico City: Grijalbo, 1987).

18. The term "Indo-America," despite its historically specific political overtones, may be taken more widely to designate those parts of Latin America where a native demographic and cultural presence was most pronounced from pre-Columbian

times, through the colonial period, and into the modern era (as in parts of central and southern Mexico, Central America, the Andean region, and so forth). Apparently dating from the early 1920s, the coinage seems to have been that of the Peruvian thinker and political figure Victor Raul Haya de la Torre, who invoked it in the founding act of his APRA political movement in Mexico in 1924 but in the more restricted sense of an Hispanophobe, proindigenist rechristening of Latin America as a whole; Frederick B. Pike, *The Politics of the Miraculous in Peru: Haya de la Torre and the Spiritualist Tradition* (Lincoln: University of Nebraska Press, 1986), 50–51.

19. This is not to imply that there were no cultural differences among identifiable ethnic groups in Mexico, of which scores, differentiable by language and lifeways—Yaquis, Nahuas, Tarascans, Mixtecs, Zapotecs, Mayas, and so forth—still existed in the late colonial period and still do today. Except in peripheral areas of the colony (such as the far north or Yucatan), however, which for the most part remained inured to the civil struggles of the era, it is highly unlikely that any translocal ethnic solidarities conditioned indigenous responses to the independence conflict in any significant degree; on this point, see, for example, Enrique Florescano, *Memory, Myth, and Time in Mexico: From the Aztecs to Independence* (Austin: University of Texas Press, 1994), esp. chaps. 4 and 5. On indigenous rebellions in the colonial period more generally, see Eric Van Young, "Rural Economy and Society—Colonial: Resistance and Rebellion," in *Encyclopedia of Mexico: History, Society, and Culture*, ed. Michael S. Werner (Chicago: Fitzroy Dearborn, 1997), 1297–1301; and Susan Schroeder, ed., *The "Pax Colonial" and Native Resistance in New Spain* (Lincoln: University of Nebraska Press, 1998).

20. To take but one example of the way the ethnic heterogeneity of Spanish America differentiated it from the other three cases of Atlantic World revolution and nation building, let me cite again the British "jury ideology" discussed by Schwoerer in chapter 1. The legal due process guaranteed to all "freemen" in 1215 by Magna Charta was effectively extended by the mid-fourteenth century to include all men, regardless of social station. Ethnicity or moral condition were not at issue, as they would be in colonial Mexico. Indigenous people in colonial Mexico did have recourse to the colonial legal system (jury trial did not exist for *anyone* in the Spanish realms) and became adept at its use but only as protected subjects of somewhat diminished civil personhood under the tutelage of the king. On the central legal institution for Indians in the Mexican colonial regime, see Woodrow W. Borah, *Justice by Insurance: The General Indian Court of Colonial Mexico and the Legal Aides of the Half-Real* (Berkeley: University of California Press, 1983).

21. John M. Murrin reminds us in chapter 2 that when the American revolutionaries repudiated King George III definitively, no monarchist project was seriously discussed after 1776. For the tensions among mass politics, citizenship, and the question of authority in the early republican period, see Richard A. War-

ren, *Vagrants and Citizens: Politics and the Masses in Mexico City from Colony to Republic* (Wilmington, Del.: Scholarly Resources, 2001).

22. It will be remembered that Napoleon Bonaparte had forced the abdication of both King Charles IV and his son Ferdinand in favor of Joseph Bonaparte in 1808, occupying most of Spain with French troops and thus provoking the Peninsular War (1808–1814), in which British expeditionary and Spanish guerrilla forces fought a long campaign to expel the French. On Hidalgo's political ideas, see Alfonso García Ruiz, *Ideario de Hidalgo* (Mexico City, 1955); on the republicward drift of insurgent political projects during the early years of the insurgency, see Gabriela Soto Laveaga, "Breaking the Silence: Murmurs of a 'National' Identity in the Mexican Insurgent Press, 1810–1813," joint meetings of the Rocky Mountain Conference on Latin American Studies and the Pacific Coast Council on Latin American Studies, San Diego, February 1997; and on creole patriotism, see David A. Brading, *The Origins of Mexican Nationalism* (Cambridge: Cambridge University Press, 1985); Brading, *The First America*; Rodríguez O., *The Independence of Spanish America*; Rodríguez O., ed., *Mexico in the Age of Democratic Revolutions*; and Rodríguez O., "From Royal Subject to Republican Citizen: The Role of the Autonomists in the Independence of Mexico," in *The Independence of Mexico and the Creation of the New Nation*, ed. Jaime E. Rodríguez O. (Los Angeles: UCLA Latin American Center Publications, 1989), 19–43.

23. Hugh M. Hamill Jr., personal communication.

24. For a masterful treatment of one of the most prominent of such royalist pamphleteers, Agustín Pomposo Fernández de San Salvador, see Hugh M. Hamill Jr., "The Rector to the Rescue: Royalist Pamphleteers in the Defense of Mexico, 1808–1821," Sixth Conference of Mexican and United States Historians, Chicago, 1981, and "Royalist Propaganda and 'La porción humilde del pueblo' during Mexican Independence," *The Americas* 36 (1980): 423–44. On the Iberian tradition of Sebastianism and mystical kingship, see Mary Elizabeth Brooks, *A King for Portugal: The Madrigal Conspiracy, 1594–1595* (Madison: University of Wisconsin Press, 1964); Angus McKay, "Ritual, Violence, and Authority in Castile," Bronowski Renaissance Symposium: The Art of Empire—Culture and Authority in the Spanish Empire, 1500–1650, University of California, San Diego, April 1986; and Richard Kagan, *Lucrecia's Dreams: Politics and Prophecy in Sixteenth-Century Spain* (Berkeley: University of California Press, 1990). For anticolonial millenarian protest in general, in which traditions of mystical kingship and naive monarchism are treated in passing, see Michael Adas, *Prophets of Rebellion: Millenarian Protest Movements against the European Colonial Order* (Cambridge: University of Cambridge Press, 1987), and on eighteenth-century Russia, a comparative case offering suggestive parallels with Mexico, see Daniel Fields, *Rebels in the Name of the Tsar* (Boston: Houghton Mifflin, 1989).

25. On politics and ideology in the immediate post-independence period, see Timothy Anna, *The Mexican Empire of Iturbide* (Lincoln: University of Nebraska Press, 1990), and *Forging Mexico, 1821–1835* (Lincoln: University of Nebraska Press, 1998), and the anthology edited by Rodríguez O., *Mexico in the Age of Democratic Revolutions.*

26. For a trenchant analysis of these questions, see Brading, *The Origins of Mexican Nationalism*, 51–52.

27. The former position would be occupied by Brading, for example, and the latter by José Miranda, whose book *Las ideas y las instituciones políticas mexicanas* (Mexico City: Universidad Nacional Autónoma de México, 1978), is glossed by Luis González, *Once ensayos de tema insurgente* (Zamora: Colegio de Michoacán, Gobierno del Estado de Michoacán, 1985), 122.

28. Hamill, "The Rector to the Rescue," 2. On creoles with divided political loyalties, see Virginia Guedea, "Ignacio Adalid, un *equilibrista* novohispano," in Rodríguez O., ed., *Mexico in the Age of Democratic Revolutions*, 71–96. On the other hand, María del Refugio González points out that distinct differences between Mexican conservatives and liberals were late in coalescing; González, "Ilustrados, regalistas y liberales," in Rodríguez O., ed., *The Independence of Mexico*, 247–63.

29. For a pithy discussion of the Constitution of 1814, see Luis González, *Once ensayos*, 109–28. See also Ernesto de la Torre Villar, *La constitución de Apatzingán y los creadores del estado mexicano*, 3 vols. (Mexico City: Universidad Nacional Autónoma de México, 1978), and Torre Villar, *La independencia mexicana*, 3 vols. (Mexico City: Editorial MAPFRE, 1982).

30. As William H. Sewell Jr. makes clear in chapter 3, after 1789 the locus of sovereignty passed from the French monarchy to the (revolutionary) French nation, making of it not only an *affective* but an *effective* community. In Mexico an analogous process produced a truncated outcome: a (partially) *effective* community but little in the way of an *affective* one, and that socially localized to a high degree.

31. Villoro, *El proceso ideológico*, 44–45; Florescano, *Memory, Myth, and Time*, 222.

32. Florescano, *Memory, Myth, and Time*, 226.

33. Sewell writes in chapter 3 that the French nation after 1789 was "imagined as a supreme unit of solidarity, a sphere of universal and ecstatic recognition." Mexican creole leaders tried to build this "ecstatic mutual recognition" around the providential advent to *all* Mexicans, *especially* the most humble, of the Virgin of Guadalupe. The modest indigenous peasant to whom the Virgin revealed herself in 1536, Juan Diego, was canonized by Pope John Paul II in Mexico City in the summer of 2002 despite a wide consensus among historians that there exists no

hard evidence that he actually lived. One factor Sewell does not mention in explaining the consolidation of a widespread French revolutionary nationalism is the effect of a generation of war on Frenchmen, in other words, the creation of nationalist sentiment by compression. In Mexico this would come much later, probably beginning in the mid-nineteenth century at the earliest.

34. Jacques Lafaye, *Quetzalcoatl and Guadalupe: The Formation of Mexican National Consciousness, 1531–1813*, trans. Benjamin Keen (Chicago: University of Chicago Press, 1976).

35. See, for example, Florescano, *Memory, Myth, and Time*, esp. chap. 5, who takes this position; see also Marta Terán, "La Virgen de Guadalupe contra Napoleón Bonaparte: La defensa de la religión en el Obispado de Michoacán entre 1793 y 1810," conference on Historia de los movimientos sociales en Michoacán, siglos XIX–XX, Morelia, Mexico, October 1997.

36. On the role of the Virgin of Guadalupe in the formation of Mexican creole patriotism, see Lafaye, *Quetzalcoatl and Guadalupe*; and on the history of the cult, see Stafford Poole, *Our Lady of Guadalupe: The Origins and Sources of a Mexican National Symbol, 1531–1797* (Tucson: University of Arizona Press, 1995), and David A. Brading, *Mexican Phoenix: Our Lady of Guadalupe: Image and Tradition across Time* (Cambridge: Cambridge University Press, 2001); but see also the rather different and very convincing views of William B. Taylor, "The Virgin of Guadalupe in New Spain: An Inquiry into the Social History of Marian Devotion," *American Ethnologist* 14 (February 1987): 9–33.

37. The number of critical and historical studies of the European literature on the New World from the fifteenth to the nineteenth centuries is large and growing rapidly. Among the most interesting treatments have been Antonello Gerbi, *La disputa del Nuevo Mundo: Historia de una polémica* (1955; 2nd ed., Mexico City: Fondo de Cultura Economica, 1982), still unsurpassed despite its age; Urs Bitterli, *Los "salvajes" y los "civilizados": El encuentro de Europa y Ultramar* (1976; 2nd ed., Mexico City: Fondo de Cultura Economica, 1981); and more recently Anthony Pagden, *European Encounters with the New World* (New Haven, Conn.: Yale University Press, 1993); and Jorge Cañizares-Esguerra, *How to Write the History of the New World: Historiographies, Epistemologies, and Identities in the Eighteenth-Century Atlantic World* (Stanford, Calif.: Stanford University Press, 2001).

38. The English translation of the original Spanish text is my own.

39. A detailed study of the Villagráns is presented in chapter 9 of my book *The Other Rebellion.*

40. Archivo General de la Nación, Mexico (AGN), Criminal, vol. 53, expediente (exp.) 1, fols. 1r–16v, 1810.

41. Instituto Nacional de Antropología e Historia (Mexico), Archivo Histórico, Colección Antigua, vol. 334, exp. 54, fols. 191r–196r, 1812.

ERIC VAN YOUNG

42. It should not be surprising that there were indigenous loyalists ready to defend the colonial regime with their lives since insurgent loyalties could cut through the very center of rural communities and the politics of Indian people were anything but homogeneous; but then, neither were the politics of other groups homogeneous.

43. Rodríguez's cover letter mentions the inclusion of some "seditious papers" sent him by Villagrán that the latter believed would convert the curate into a "true American." These papers were apparently copies of some tracts Viceroy Venegas had ordered burned in Mexico City by the public executioner some time previously and were thus forwarded to the viceregal authorities by the church officials without making copies to remain with Villagrán's letter. Readers will forgive the lengthy transcription of Villagrán's letter since the text conveys not only the substantive ideas of the writer but also the flavor of the discourse.

44. One example of such a letter is that of the rebel *cabecilla* José Salgado to the royalist commander José Celestino Negrete, dated 21 November 1816, characterized by a gentle and conciliatory tone and a reasonableness not to be explained away by the fact that Salgado was seeking a pardon; AGN, Operaciones de Guerra, vol. 151, fols. 403r–404v. See also the letter of the rebel chieftain Isidoro Montes de Oca to the *subdelegado* of Coahuayana, 16 June 1820, in AGN, Operaciones de Guerra, vol. 157, fols. 126r–v, in which Montes de Oca alternately offers to protect the official's personal property if he turns the town over to the rebels and to reduce it to ashes if it is not surrendered and then asks for two bottles of wine to celebrate Mass in the rebels' mountain encampment on the grounds that "war has no connection with the spiritual pact" ("la guerra no tiene conección con el pacto espiritual"). Yet another example is the letter of the *cabecilla* Juan Nepomuceno de San Roman to the royalist commander of San Juan de los Lagos, replying in the most provocative terms to an offer of amnesty, dated April 1816, in AGN, Operaciones de Guerra, vol. 151, fols. 81r–84v.

45. The writer of the letter, interestingly enough, incorrectly identifies the pope of the donation and Treaty of Tordesillas (1494) as Alexander VII rather than Alexander VI.

46. On the fascinating speculation by Mexican colonial thinkers, particularly Sigüenza y Góngora and Mier, on the evangelization of Mexico by St. Thomas the Apostle and his identification with the Mesoamerican deity Quetzalcoatl, see especially Brading, *The First America*; Brading, *Origins of Mexican Nationalism*; and Lafaye, *Quetzalcoatl and Guadalupe*.

47. On forms of religious legitimation in communal identity and politics, see Eric Van Young, "Dreamscape with Figures and Fences: Cultural Contention and Discourse in the Late Colonial Mexican Countryside," in *Le Nouveau Monde–Mondes Nouveaux: L'expérience américaine*, ed. Serge Gruzinski and Nathan

168

Wachtel (Paris: Editions Recherche sur les Civilisations, 1996), 137–59. I have not been able in this chapter to convey much sense of the popular insurrection in New Spain as an agrarian movement—that is, of its agrarian etiologies—though I have treated this topic abundantly elsewhere; see, for example, Eric Van Young, *La crisis del orden colonial: Estructura agraria y rebeliones populares, 1750–1821* (Mexico City: n.p., 1992), and "Agrarian Rebellion and Defense of Community: Meaning and Collective Violence in Late Colonial and Independence-Era Mexico," *Journal of Social History* 27 (winter 1993): 245–69. It is my conviction, in fact, that while there was a good deal of peasant discontent in late colonial Mexico—resulting from population pressure, agricultural commercialization, rural proletarianization, landgrabbing by nonindigenous rural estate owners, stagnant or declining real wages, and so forth—it was not expressed overtly enough to justify characterizing the popular insurgency as primarily an agrarian insurrection. Real and significant as they may have been, agrarian grievances were more a proxy for deeper-lying forms of ethnocultural conflict. For the foregrounding of agrarian grievances as the major motives for popular insurgency, see John Tutino, *From Insurrection to Revolution in Mexico: Social Bases of Agrarian Violence, 1750–1940* (Princeton, N.J.: Princeton University Press, 1986), and Tutino, "Globalizations and Revolutions: Production, Power, and Popular Mobilizations in Mexican History," Conference on "Crises, Reforms, and Revolutions: Mexico's Pasts, Mexico's Present, Mexico's Possibilities," Georgetown University, June 2000.

48. See especially William B. Taylor, *Drinking, Homicide, and Rebellion in Colonial Mexican Villages* (Stanford, Calif.: Stanford University Press, 1979), 113–70; many of the essays in Friedrich Katz, ed., *Riot, Rebellion, and Revolution: Rural Social Conflict in Mexico* (Princeton, N.J.: Princeton University Press, 1988); and Schroeder, *The "Pax Colonial."*

49. AGN, Historia, vol. 411, exp. 14, fols. 84r–116v, 1811; AGN, Infidencias, vol. 17, exps. 7–11, fols. 137r–307r, 1811. The one concrete proposal discussed in the village was the division of privately held land among the Indian householders (*vecinos*) and the setting aside of some goods to support the insurgent forces of Ignacio Allende, Father Hidalgo's sometime lieutenant.

50. AGN, Criminal, vol. 251, exps. 1, 10, 11, respectively, fols. 1r–12v, 309r–319v, and 320r–329v, 1812.

51. The rejection of the Spanish king was in fact rather unusual, as we shall see shortly, since King Ferdinand was more often venerated as a messianic figure. The repudiation of the monarch or even his replacement with an Indian messiah/king did occur occasionally in the more remote reaches of the eastern and western sierras of the country, corresponding to a gradient of acculturation and to the density of Spanish settlement, running from the central parts of the country to the areas less firmly under colonial control.

52. I have dealt with various aspects of popular messianism in a number of articles; see, for example, Eric Van Young, "Millennium on the Northern Marches: The Mad Messiah of Durango and Popular Rebellion in Mexico, 1800–1815," *Comparative Studies in Society and History* 28 (July 1986): 385–413; "Religion and Popular Ideology in Mexico, 1810–1821," in *Indigenous Responses to Western Christianity*, ed. Steve Kaplan (New York: New York University Press, 1995), 144–73; and "Popular Religion and the Politics of Insurgency in Mexico, 1810–1821," in *The Politics of Religion in an Age of Renewal: Studies in Nineteenth-Century Europe and Latin America*, ed. Austen Ivereigh (London: Institute of Latin American Studies, 2000), 74–114.

53. See Sherburne F. Cook and Woodrow W. Borah, *Essays in Population History: Mexico and the Caribbean*, 3 vols. (Berkeley: University of California Press, 1974–1980).

54. The differentiation of these distances is based on reasonable inferences about how people of the time—particularly country dwellers—saw themselves within a given space, in a generally rough geography with primitive means of transport and communication. For a very interesting discussion of these considerations within a European context, see Pierre Goubert, "Local History," *Daedalus* 100 (winter 1971): 113–27.

55. Johann Heinrich von Thünen, *Von Thünen's Isolated State*, ed. P. Hall (London: Pergamon, 1966). Von Thünen's ideas, on which classical location theory in geography and economics was substantially based and out of which central-place theory and regional science subsequently grew, had to do with the determining influence of distance and transport costs on the location of economic production.

56. By *campanilismo* (from the Italian word for a church or bell tower, *campanile*), I mean the tendency of rural villagers to see the world in some sense as coterminous with the view from their church bell towers.

57. Alan Knight, *The Mexican Revolution*, 2 vols. (Cambridge: Cambridge University Press, 1986), 1:559 n. 386.

58. For an extended discussion of the popular insurgency in Mexico in comparison with the French and American revolutions, see chapter 19, "Conclusion: The Other Rebellion in Comparative Perspective," in Van Young, *The Other Rebellion*.

59. The brief comparative discussion that follows is based heavily on the concluding chapter in Van Young, *The Other Rebellion*.

60. The rurality of the Mexican independence movement was in part an outcome of the strategic deployment of the forces arrayed against each other, of course, as well as of the social structure and physical geography of the colony, with many areas of the countryside being heavily Indian in composition. For a discussion of why Mexican cities remained quiet during the 1810–1821 period, for the

most part, see Eric Van Young, "Islands in the Storm: Quiet Cities and Violent Countrysides in the Mexican Independence Era," *Past and Present*, no. 118 (February 1988): 120–56.

61. On France, see Mona Ozouf, *La fête révolutionnaire, 1789–1799* (Paris: Gallimard, 1976).

62. As John M. Murrin points out in chapter 2, the ideas of the Great Awakening served as a sort of social glue on the American side of the Atlantic, but in Mexico religious sensibility became so inextricably entwined with local and ethnic identities that it served more often as an irritant *between* common people and other social groups than as a unifier against the colonial regime; see Van Young, "Dreamscape with Figures and Fences."

CONCLUSION
NATIONS, REVOLUTIONS, AND THE END OF HISTORY

Peter S. Onuf

At a time when the nation-state has been embraced by the peoples of the world as the only legitimate political form, scholars and commentators in the industrial West—where the form originated—have begun to question its viability. In this paradoxical postmodern moment, the world as we have known it, a world of nations loosely connected in a system of states, no longer seems quite so natural or inevitable. The idea of the nation itself, we now recognize, is as much a product of historical contingency and chance as are the histories of particular nations. Scholars are beginning to offer a suggestive array of broad explanations for the emergence of nations and nationalism. Historicizing the process of nation making, they have shown how the founders of new nations "invented traditions" and "imagined communities" in order to mobilize and develop the human resources and industrial potential of modernizing polities.[1]

The nation may be a social construction, but it is one that commands the allegiance and defines the aspirations of most modern people. Constructivists have shown that class, race, and gender are only as "real" as people imagine them to be and so enact them; but as they demystify and denaturalize these powerful abstractions, another, more inclusive and powerful abstraction, "nation," comes to the fore. We are not clearly capable of conceiving of an alternative to the nation, of even imagining a future in which it is not the terminal form.[2] Linked by hyphen to the state and its apparatuses of coercion and control, the nation cannot be so easily dissolved or transcended. Indeed, it is the nation-state, with its more or less effective monopoly of force, that sanctions and enforces the arbitrary and invidious distinctions that constructivists would dispel. Nation-states keep the peace and make war, all in our name. To understand how they do so, we must overcome a reflexive skepticism about nations and nationalism that dates back to the revolutions that led to their original emergence.

Revolutionary patriots of the late eighteenth-century "Age of Democratic Revolutions" were both the inventors of the modern concept of nationhood and its first critics. In asserting that the state is merely epiphenomenal, the instrument of bourgeois class rule, Marx was expressing a revolutionary commonplace. The idea that nation-states do the things they do (enforcing order on their own populations and making war on other peoples) at the behest of privileged, dominant classes was familiar enough to American revolutionaries who sought to purge their New World of Old World corruptions and to French revolutionaries in their efforts to exorcise the incubus of aristocracy. For those who subsequently reflected on revolutionary change, the conclusion was irresistible that real revolutions were marked by the radical transformation of social structure and class relations. In comparison to such profound, structural changes, the specific constitution of a political regime—for instance, the bourgeois nation-state—was inconsequential. After all, Marx famously predicted, the final revolution of class relations would demolish the bourgeoisie and, with its demise, the necessity of any state apparatus at all.

The French Revolution thus gave rise both to the modern idea of the nation-state and to the revolutionary tradition that challenged the nation-state's primacy. The revolutionaries' universalistic pretensions were manifest in their determination to liberate the benighted peoples of Europe and to wage total war against a reactionary "Conspiracy of Kings." Sweeping aside a corrupt old regime, the French sought to purge polities of hierarchy, inequality, and privilege, thus making the way clear for the bourgeoisie's rise to power. But the chief effect of making war was to make enemies and so foster an embattled solidarity. For the French themselves, the Revolution would be remembered as a primal moment of national self-consciousness, of a political people's coming into existence. The massive political and military mobilizations of the Revolution taught the French that they were a people and that the people was sovereign, the ultimate source of legitimate authority.

Popular sovereignty proved to be a protean concept. On the one hand, it is the conceptual foundation of the modern idea of the nation-state. We may say that the very existence of "peoples" is the *result* of successful nation-making projects, but nationalists' success depended on obscuring that circularity by persuading a sufficient number of would-be countrymen that they had always shared a collective identity. This foundational mythology, often the product of the antiquarian researches of alienated provincial intellectuals, was essential to the nationalist appeal. Yet popular sovereignty, precisely because it opens a conceptual space between political society and government, also pointed beyond the nation, to federal or international regimes consisting of republican or socialist states with identical institutions and open borders. Where peoples everywhere governed themselves freely, their differences would progressively give way to widening solidarities; ultimately, they will become a single people. Socialist revolutionaries embraced the teleology of their republican predecessors, inspired by a vision of liberated masses, passing through nationhood on their way to the end of history.

Until recently, scholars have been much more interested in the revolutionary process than in explaining the nationalist appeal. They may either take nations for granted, see nations as anachronistic impediments to progress, or both. Under the aegis of a newly professionalized historiography that sought to distinguish historical study from nationalistic myth-making, historians preferred to focus on underlying forces and deeper structures. Revolutionary history tracked the main lines of their metanarrative: revolutions constituted the epochal moments in the emergence of political modernity, reaching deep into society, bringing all classes into play, and promoting progressive structural realignments. Nationalism became a major scholarly interest during the protracted period of decolonization after World War II, but even then it remained subordinate to revolutionary history. Where the decolonization process met metropolitan resistance, national liberation movements gained moral and material support from the Soviet Union, thus giving new urgency to the study of revolution and counterrevolution.

While scholars and policymakers focused on the preconditions of revolution, anticolonial revolutionaries sought to establish new nation-states. Though prepared to align with similar movements across the world and to identify with the communist struggle against capitalist imperialism, these insurgents were nonetheless nationalists: they paid the ultimate tribute to their erstwhile colonial masters by appropriating the characteristically modern form of Western political society. By linking imperial possessions with national greatness, the colonial powers authorized and exported a revolutionary conception of national self-determination that was then turned against them. But the break generally was less traumatic for decolonizing powers than for the new nations they left in their wake. The connection between worldwide socialist revolution and new nation making in the Third World proved tenuous at best. Rapid decolonization preempted Soviet influence while completing the protracted demolition of complex, extended European (and American) imperial polities and thus finally clearing away the last vestiges of the old regime. A world without empires would be the world of free and independent nations that republican revolutionaries had long ago envisioned.[3]

Thomas Jefferson's notorious letter justifying French revolutionary bloodshed anticipated this nationalist millennium. "Were there but an Adam & an Eve left in every country, & left free," Jefferson told his protégé William Short in early 1793, "it would be better than as it now is."[4] With the belated collapse of European empires, the process initiated by the Revolution neared completion: every nation, sprung from its own Adam and Eve, would have its own country. For celebrants of the emerging "new world order," there was particular satisfaction in being able to call the communist world an "evil empire," thus identifying the professed custodians of the great revolutionary tradition with outmoded forms of imperial rule over "captive nations." The genie of national liberation the Soviets had helped unleash in the Third World provided the ideological impetus for their own destruction. Posing as the enemy of imperialism, the Soviet Union was the last great empire. Its collapse, Francis Fukuyama famously proclaimed, marked "the end of history."[5]

The demise of the Soviet Union actually brought two grand narratives to a close. The revolutionary tradition that the French had initiated and that had promised both the progressive transformation of Western societies and the liberation of oppressed peoples everywhere sputtered to an inglorious and ironic conclusion: captive nations threw off the dead hand of their revolutionary past. But the other, more enduring legacy of the French Revolution, the promise of national self-determination, had finally been fulfilled. History as it had long been understood in the West came to an end with the completion of these two great, interlinked narratives. Was it possible to imagine a political future for the world significantly different from its present state?

Of course, we know that we have not really reached the end of history. In the scholarly community, discussion about our future prospects has focused increasingly on the idea of "nation" itself. Can nationhood really be the culmination, the final term of modern historical development? Skepticism about the durability of the nation form is pervasive, and not just on the constructivist left, where its "reality" is most conspicuously called into question. Tough-minded exponents of power politics, the self-proclaimed "realists" who shaped modern foreign policy, were the first to recognize the artificiality of the "new nations" that emerged in the wake of decolonization, whether liberated from or sponsored by the old imperial powers. These new states exhibited few of the crucial markers of true nationhood that guaranteed liberal democracy and economic development in the Western core. The cruelest implication of this skeptical assessment was that it was simply too late to join the modern world, that "modernization" was a protracted, historical process that could never be fully replicated. Far from being a model for emerging nations, the United States—"the first new nation"—was a standing rebuke to nationalist aspirations everywhere: the authentic nation form, perfected in America, was *not* exportable.

For American exceptionalists, America was the unique domain of liberty and prosperity, the only true nation (with the only truly progressive revolution), or perhaps—given the increasingly atavistic, retrograde connotations of the term—it was no nation at all.[6] The American regime was founded on a distinctively democratic way of life, an elaborate civic infrastructure, and a stable market economy that alone could translate the fictions of popular sovereignty and national self-determination into something approaching reality. Critics who wondered whether the promise of nationhood could ever be fulfilled, even in this most favored nation, only underscored persistent doubts about the unrealistic aspirations of nation makers elsewhere.

Liberal internationalists, like their republican predecessors, might still envisage a world of nations, but theirs was an antinationalist, cosmopolitan fantasy of peaceful states happily submitting to proliferating international regimes. But realists have always known better. The great geopolitical struggles that shaped modern history showed, if nothing else, that all nation-states were not created equal. Great powers—the only nation-states that really counted—would extend their influence and seek advantage as far as they could; notwithstanding their pretensions to equal standing in the international community, the other nations were at best satellites, clients, proxies, or puppets. Nationalism was the characteristic delusion of the modern age, yet another form of false consciousness traceable back to the French Revolution.

The apparent triumph of the nation-state form has thus been accompanied by a pervasive critical skepticism about the very idea of "nation." Ironically, social constructivists on the left are generally more hopeful about the future of "nations" than their realist counterparts on the right. After all, what is constructed can be deconstructed and then reconstructed, a consoling thought for progressives who can no longer cherish revolutionary hopes. Constructivists have followed their critical logic from periphery to center, from new nations to old, demystifying and historicizing the idea of nation everywhere. Yet even as constructivists turn the center's skepticism about the periphery against itself, they also find in the hybrid nation-forms that have emerged in the wake of intercultural encounters some political space within which to enact—or at least imagine—their reconstructive agendas.

How does the kind of historical inquiry undertaken by the authors in this volume contribute to contemporary debates about nationhood, the end of history, and the future of the world? Can a history that eschews the great narratives of revolutionary transformation and nation making— and that reflects contemporary confusion about the prospects of postmodernity—offer any useful signposts? There is no interpretative consensus here about the character of revolutions and of the nations they created. These scholarly disagreements challenge any uncomplicated end-of-history narrative. History has ended only if we understand its trajectory as moving inexorably in this one direction, toward the end of struggles for empire and global domination and the emergence of a world of nations. We would also have to accept that "nation" can be clearly and definitively defined. But different beginnings suggest a range of narratives and therefore different definitions.

Historians offer various accounts of the domain within which the idea of nation and its concomitant institutional forms take root and flourish. Focusing on a long history of constitutional development, with its defining moments in the great crises or "revolutions" of the seventeenth century, scholars have emphasized the precocious emergence of an English (and subsequently a British) national identity.[7] The myth of the "ancient constitution," Lois Schwoerer suggests, provided a legitimating gloss to constitutional innovation, "a disarming way to cloak change in the mantle of tradition."[8] As the trial by jury assumed its more or less modern form in the protracted crisis period culminating in the Glorious Revolution, Whig polemicists gave it an ancient pedigree: "the origins of the jury," they argued, "were contemporaneous with the nation itself."[9] This conception of the "nation" would prove to be protean: later generations of British nationalists would be spared the trouble of "inventing" this mythic, nation-defining tradition. But, as Jack Greene points out, the English revolutions of the seventeenth century "did not facilitate the development of an inclusive idea of the *nation* as the repository of sovereignty."[10] Indeed, the problematic relationship between the "political nation," or civically empowered, ruling elite, and the larger population subject to its rule constituted the major theme of British political history well into the "modern" period. Renegotiating—and reimagining—the relationship between governors and governed, or the "people," also constituted the leading challenge to revolutionaries elsewhere.

In his discussion of insurgent movements in early nineteenth-century Mexico, Eric Van Young warns against conflating the cosmopolitan aspirations of the small creole elite with the communalism of indigenous villages. "For people even to conceive of a state," Van Young argues, and therefore to imagine themselves to be a "nation" in the modern sense, "they are required to share a cognitive map that includes a view of a wider world beyond locality and of the integuments that hold it together."[11] The idea of nation did not rise up spontaneously among historic "peoples," belatedly becoming conscious of themselves, but emanated from the metropolitan cores of European colonizing powers. Only in regions dominated by European settler populations, most notably in the United States, was the fiction of nationhood plausible or compelling.[12] Where European colonies included significant numbers of Indians or enslaved Africans, it was more difficult for creole elites to assert their equality with and independence of their metropolitan counterparts. If in places like Mexico widespread acceptance of the national idea was a top-down phenomenon, gradually filtering down to subordinate strata as they were integrated into a modernizing political economy, in the Atlantic world as a whole the trajectory was from the center outward, from European center to creole periphery.

Yet the nature of that center–periphery dynamic remains controversial. To the extent that scholars emphasize the importance of collective self-consciousness in modern nationalism, they tend to cast creole revolutionaries in the role of political cultural innovators. By exaggerating and idealizing metropolitan virtues (and vices), by abstracting fundamental principles from a notional imperial "constitution," provincial revolutionaries "invent" the very model they are supposedly imitating. This cultural creativity, expressed in the juxtaposition of new world to old, defines modern nationalism, though that modernity has been obscured—for contemporaries and for subsequent commentators—by the continuing hegemony of metropolitan norms. Only with the historiographical turn away from exceptionalist mythologies and the consequent recognition that even "old" nations are recent inventions did the novelty of creole nationalism become conspicuous. As they projected a new conception of nationhood on to the metropolis, first imagining themselves participating in that transcendent identity and then defining themselves against it, creole nationalists initiated a revolutionary, nation-making tradition that would spread from periphery to center.

The idea that the nation is a modern invention, emerging on the creole periphery of the European Atlantic, reinstates the American Revolution at a pivotal juncture of world history. It is hardly surprising that Benedict Anderson's pathbreaking elaboration of this theme in *Imagined Communities* should be so influential among Americanists, who suspected that something important was happening in their part of the world even if the Revolution had failed to overturn the social structures of the revolting colonies or to transform class relations.[13] Yet for many scholars the modernity of the "first new nation" remains suspect.

For those who emphasize the importance of institutional infrastructure to national identity, the retarded development of the federal state calls the precocity of American nationhood into question. According to this view, Alexander Hamilton and his fellow High Federalist centralizers were the great modernists of the founding period: their failure was sealed by the ascendancy of the Jeffersonian Republican opposition in the "Revolution of 1800." Jack Greene thus describes the American Revolution "as a settler revolt" in "direct response to centralizing metropolitan measures that seemed both to challenge settler control over local affairs and to deny settler claims to a British identity." Thomas Jefferson's election "effectively brought to an end whatever nationalizing and centralizing tendencies Federalist leaders had brought to the project of creating a more unitary national state during the 1790s."[14] Americans' primary political loyalties were provincial, to colonies and then states; their attachment to more inclusive, extended polities—empire and union—were correspondingly weak, particularly after 1800.

When focusing on state formation, Greene situates his Americans at two removes from political modernity: in the name of entrenched local rights and privileges, provincial Americans rejected the Hamiltonian nation-making project, the effort of admiring Anglophiles—provincials of another sort—to replicate the institutions of the former metropolis. That Federalists and Republicans alike continued to act within a familiar ideological framework, imported from Britain, revealed the Americans' continuing provincialism—and their underdeveloped sense of a collective, national identity. How could Anglo-Americans, fighting a revolution on behalf of provincial liberties and the rights of Englishmen, develop a distinctive identity? After all, as John Murrin tells us, American independence was *not* the inevitable culmination of colonial history, but rather "a countercyclical event" that "ran against the prevailing integrative tendencies of the century." Before the Revolution, colonists were becoming more British, not American.[15]

Emphasis on American provincialism points to the problematic connection between collective identity and state formation. Whether Americans had a weak (provincial) or strong (national) sense of themselves as a people (or peoples), the revolutionary crisis forced them to think collectively about the array of governmental institutions they would authorize.[16] Popular sovereignty was the premise, state formation its corollary. Recent debate over the relationship between state building and national identity in America has focused primarily on the role of governments in fostering the development of a modern market economy. Joyce Appleby has argued most vigorously that popular loyalty to the new regime depended on circumscribing state power: opposition to Hamiltonian centralism culminated in a nationwide mobilization in support of Jefferson that reaffirmed revolutionary values and sanctioned popular pursuits of happiness.[17] This is not to say that the state withered away as a result of the "Revolution of 1800": the new administration did not dismantle the key institutions of Hamilton's financial system, and state governments would play an increasingly important role in promoting economic development. But Jefferson's election did show that a relatively weak central state could inspire strong popular attachments, that nation-state and nationalism did not necessarily develop in lockstep. Jefferson himself captured this apparently paradoxical state of affairs in his inaugural address. Though it might lack the conventional instruments of state power, the American government was the "strongest . . . on earth," for "it is the only one where every man, at the call of the law, would fly to the standard of the law, and would meet invasions of the public order as his own personal concern."[18]

Jefferson's conception of American identity was predicated on popular military and political mobilization, linking the preservation of the republic to the reenactment of the Revolution in moments of national crisis. This linkage of revolutionary mobilization and nation making may have inspired the French Revolution, as Jefferson liked to think, but French revolutionaries had little use for the Americans' weak, mixed, and decentralized federal regime. Choosing instead to strengthen the tie between nation and state, indeed to fuse the two in what William Sewell Jr. calls the "nation form," the French elaborated "a new framework of institutions, laws, modes of behavior, and cultural assumptions that would henceforth be the hallmarks of a fully constituted nation."[19]

Sewell's vigorous restatement of the conventional view, in which the French Revolution is the first modern revolution and revolutionary France is the first truly modern and therefore "modular" nation-state, accords with Greene's deflationary account of the American Revolution and challenges Anderson's brief for the innovative role of "creole pioneers" in the history of nationalism. Sewell thus raises fundamental questions in the contemporary debate about nations and their future: does the fusion of state power and the collective identity of a mobilized (and mobilizable) people define what we mean by "nation" and/or what later nationalists have understood by the term as they launched their own projects? In other words, do we have to return from provincial periphery to revolutionized center in order to witness the full articulation of a "common revolutionary dynamic" that would subsequently oscillate "back and forth between Europe and the Americas"?[20]

These questions cannot be definitively answered here. Alexis de Tocqueville, for one, was not persuaded that the French Revolution had launched a new historical epoch or that postrevolutionary France was so profoundly different from the old regime, whatever delusionary visions inspired the revolutionaries; it was American democracy that instead constituted a new kind of national society and collective consciousness.[21] The myth of the great revolutionary tradition, the tradition initiated by the French Revolution, is that nations make themselves through revolutionary acts of self-constitution. Surely the myth has been powerfully consequential: every nationalist dreams of national liberation from foreign shackles through revolutionary action. But nation-making revolutions have not always followed the French example; during the Napoleonic era, "counterrevolutionary" resistance to the French Empire was the most powerful spur to nationalist feeling. As Sewell concedes, nationalists everywhere have insisted, contra French revolutionary doctrine, on the ancient origins and historical continuity of nationhood. Doctrinaire revolutionaries elsewhere might follow the French example of unifying the nation in the name of citizen equality by "destroying or delegitimizing . . . intermediate bodies that stood between the individual citizen and the nation as whole" and by suppressing local distinctions through the homogenizing of space.[22] But such projects inevitably failed. Paradoxically, nationalists were more likely to achieve the goals of political modernity—the free movement of men and resources throughout the national domain and the patriotic identification of the masses with their homeland—by celebrating the nation's distinctive character and history, by ostentatiously protecting hearth and home, village and region, from insidious foreign influences.[23] The French Revolution modeled rational and enlightened forms of public administration, reflected in liberal reforms in revolutionary and counterrevolutionary states alike. But I suspect that the Revolution's impact on "the concept of nation" was less transformative than Sewell believes, that instead of embracing the French model, nationalists elsewhere reacted *against* the revolutionaries' homogenizing, universalistic project.

But Sewell is certainly right to set nation making in a broad, historically dynamic Atlantic—and now global—context. The question of which historic nation form was paradigmatic defies easy answers: nationalists have responded to complex, diffuse, and idiosyncratic influences. Better to ask about the process of imitation itself than attempt to fix its origins in a particular place. Why do nationalists find the idea of nationhood so compelling, whatever its sources? In other words, what do they *gain* if their nation-making project is successful? The simple, though often overlooked, answer is that they gain the recognition of other states and membership in the family of nations. Students of nationalism seeking underlying patterns in the distinctive histories of particular nation-states may be looking too deeply, for it is the international system itself that determines the acceptable, recognizable form of the nation, not the "genius" of a particular people—or the logic of industrial capitalism. (Much of the contemporary skepticism about nations focuses on discrepancies between the one-size-fits-all form and the reality of politicoeconomic underdevelopment and dependency.) Nation makers seek to mobilize domestic political support through revolutionary or nationalist ideological appeals, emphasizing the unique historical experience of a particular people (or "imagined community"), but the international community provides their scripts. Even revolutionaries committed to changing the world must, for the time being, pose as legitimate representatives of nations with compelling claims to participate in the international system.

If nations as we now understand them can exist only in a system of nations, if there can be no parts without the whole, then the supposed autonomy and independence of each nation-state must be questioned. To enjoy the benefits of nationhood, every nation must model itself to conform with the customary and legal standards of the international community: the states system dictates the forms of nation-states, not vice versa. Yet it is the modern system's master fiction that nations come first, that nations exist *before* they are recognized by other nations; this, of course, is the same fiction that nationalists invoke when inventing histories for oppressed and subjugated peoples emerging into collective self-consciousness. By the same logic, the artificiality of the international system and the sorry simulacrum of "law" that supposedly governs relations among states is juxtaposed to the solid reality of nation-states capable of enforcing a positive legal order. But we are now beginning to recognize that international regimes are more robust, with a larger measure of legitimacy and effective power than the classic liberal conception of a world of nations would seem to allow.[24]

The history of the international system as a system—and not simply as the arena for diplomacy and war among nation-states—has been too little studied.[25] Historicizing the "modern" states system will show that, even in the heyday of the great powers (and their overseas empires), the customs and conventions that constituted international law had a degree of autonomy and that the system itself was not simply a weak reflection or the sum of its parts. We now recognize the invented and constructed character of nations, which have often proved historically ephemeral and rarely preserve the same forms of government or the same boundaries over long periods of time; we may now be prepared to see that the modern states system is more "real" than we previously suspected and that it has played a key role in determining both the forms and the histories of nations. The nation form is not the telos of all prior historical development—the end of history—but rather the historically contingent function of the operation of the modern international system. Recognizing the historicity of that system draws our attention both to its ultimate demise (in a "postmodern" world) and to pre- or early modern state systems or extended polities, both within what would become the nation-states of Europe and in the complex forms of imperial rule connecting European metropolises with their provincial and colonial peripheries. There is a before, and there will surely be an after, in the history both of the nation-state as a form of political organization and of the modern idea of nation as the ultimate end of political life.

A global perspective shifts our attention away from nation-states as such to the world within which they seek to secure recognition and preserve their independence. It also points to the characteristic and defining paradox of modern nationhood, that particular peoples who define themselves *against* other peoples on historic, cultural, and (sometimes) racial grounds must take on the same form to participate in the international system. This is a powerful, homogenizing force too often neglected in national(ist) historiographies, with their exceptionalist biases. Even when nationalists assert their right to rule in the name of particular peoples, thus privileging and exaggerating difference, they are enacting yet another universalistic imperative of political modernity—the right of national self-determination—first elaborated in the law of nations. In their quest for legitimacy, nationalists identify themselves with the specific moment in historic time when their nations rose up to liberate themselves from the rule of foreigners or class enemies in order to determine their own future destiny. The nationalists' apotheosis of national particularity, their celebration of the people as a kind of family descended from common ancestors, thus stands in juxtaposition to— and is itself a function of—the homogenizing tendencies of the modern system of nation-states. For it is the international system that encourages and sanctions claims to national distinctiveness that in turn provide legitimating myths for nationalist regimes that seek to secure for themselves and their peoples the great benefits, material and psychic, that flow from membership in the family of nations. All nations must be seen as different in order to justify their existence. Yet in the world of nations they must all be recognized as equals.

Reports from the front line of historical scholarship help us imagine possible futures for nations in the coming millennium. The nation form will not necessarily survive in its classic form. But it does not follow that an increasingly interdependent world can or should be governed by international or transnational regimes, however much such regimes have already redefined life on earth. (One effect of the continuing proliferation of international regimes is to offer broad new justifications and support for the nation-states that participate in them: the whole tends to sustain its parts—which is why Delaware will survive the best efforts of enlightened geopoliticians to redraw the American map.) Nor do we know how attenuated the problematic hyphen between nation and state will become. After all, "nations" became linked to "states" only in the modern period; efforts to accommodate cultural differences within traditional unitary or more complex federal states may provide space for distinctive collective identities that do not require the full panoply of sovereign powers that nation-states themselves in fact no longer exercise.

We cannot confidently predict the future of nations or of the national idea. The happy result for historians is the creative confusion that accompanies a major paradigm shift. Today's confusion compels us to reconceive the past, to offer competing accounts of how our predecessors constructed the modern world. Reconstructing these pathways to the present will give us at least a dim sense of where we—as individuals, as nations, as members of the human race—might be headed. History as we have understood it is indeed coming to an end. Confronting the end of this history should spur us toward new histories that recognize the central importance of nations and national identities for modern people but that also recognize the historicity and contingent character of those identities—and therefore the possibility of forging new identities.

Notes

1. The most notable contributions to this rich literature include Ernest Gellner, *Nations and Nationalism* (Ithaca, N.Y.: Cornell University Press, 1983); Benedict Anderson, *Imagined Communities: Reflections on the Origin and Spread of*

Nationalism, rev. ed. (London: Verso, 1991); Eric Hobsbawm and Terence Ranger, eds., *The Invention of Tradition* (Cambridge: Cambridge University Press, 1983); Eric Hobsbawm, *Nations and Nationalism since 1780* (Cambridge: Cambridge University Press, 1990); Gopal Balakrishnan, ed., *Mapping the Nation* (London: Verso, 1996); and Craig Calhoun, *Nationalism* (Minneapolis: University of Minnesota Press, 1997).

2. Thomas J. Biersteker and Cynthia Weber, eds., *State Sovereignty as Social Construct* (Cambridge: Cambridge University Press, 1996).

3. "The Receding Influence of Empires," *New York Times*, December 22, 1999, A30; Michael W. Doyle, *Empires* (Ithaca, N.Y.: Cornell University Press 1986).

4. "Jefferson to William Short, January 3, 1793," in *Thomas Jefferson: Writings*, ed. Merrill D. Peterson (New York: Literary Classics of the United States, 1984), 1004.

5. Francis Fukuyama, *The End of History and the Last Man* (New York: Free Press, 1992).

6. Daniel J. Boorstin, *The Genius of American Politics* (Chicago: University of Chicago Press, 1953); Hannah Arendt, *On Revolution* (New York: Viking Press, 1963); Seymour Martin Lipset, *The First New Nation: The United States in Historical and Comparative Perspective* (New York: Basic Books, 1963); Yehoshua Arieli, *Individualism and Nationalism in American Ideology* (Cambridge, Mass.: Harvard University Press, 1964).

7. Liah Greenfeld, *Nationalism: Five Roads to Modernity* (Cambridge, Mass.: Harvard University Press, 1992), 27–87; Linda Colley, *Britons: Forging the Nation, 1707–1837* (New Haven, Conn.: Yale University Press, 1992).

8. Lois G. Schwoerer, chapter 2 in this volume.

9. This is Schwoerer's paraphrase of Sir John Hawles's *The English-man's Right* (1680), discussed in chapter 2 in this volume.

10. Jack P. Greene, chapter 1 in this volume.

11. Eric Van Young, chapter 4 in this volume, 155.

12. Edmund S. Morgan, *Inventing the People: The Rise of Popular Sovereignty in England and America* (New York: Norton, 1988).

13. Anderson, *Imagined Communities*.

14. Jack P. Greene, chapter 1 in this volume, 19, 20. See also Greene's *Peripheries and Center: Constitutional Development in the Extended Polities of the British Empire and the United States, 1607–1788* (Athens: University of Georgia Press, 1986).

15. John M. Murrin, chapter 2 in this volume, 67. See also Murrin, "A Rood without Walls: The Dilemma of American National Identity," in *Beyond Confederation: Origins of the Constitution and American National Identity*, ed. Richard Beeman, Stephen Botein, and Edward C. Carter II (Chapel Hill: University of North Carolina Press, 1987), 333–48.

16. T. H. Breen, "Ideology and Nationalism on the Eve of the American Revolution: Revisions *Once More* in Need of Revising," *Journal of American History* 84 (June 1997): 13–39; Peter S. Onuf, *Jefferson's Empire: The Language of American Nationhood* (Charlottesville: University Press of Virginia, 2000).

17. Joyce Appleby, *Capitalism and a New Social Order: The Republican Vision of the 1790s* (New York: New York University Press, 1984). See also Appleby, *Inheriting the Revolution: The First Generation of Americans* (Cambridge, Mass.: Belknap Press, 2000), for further discussion of the impact of the Revolution on individual and collective identity.

18. "Jefferson's First Inaugural Address, March 4, 1801," in Peterson, ed., *Thomas Jefferson*, 493.

19. William H. Sewell Jr., chapter 3 in this volume, 97.

20. Sewell, chapter 3 in this volume, 92.

21. Alexis de Tocqueville, *Democracy in America*, trans. Phillips Bradley, 2 vols. (1835 and 1840; reprint, New York: A. A. Knopf, 1945). For a recent restatement of this argument, see Gordon S. Wood, *The Radicalism of the American Revolution* (New York: A. A. Knopf, 1992).

22. Sewell, chapter 3 in this volume, 117.

23. Alon Confino, *The Nation as Local Metaphor: Württemberg, Imperial Germany, and National Identity, 1871–1918* (Chapel Hill: University of North Carolina Press, 1997).

24. Nicholas Greenwood Onuf, *The Republican Legacy in International Thought* (Cambridge: Cambridge University Press, 1998).

25. Peter S. Onuf and Nicholas G. Onuf, *Federal Union, Modern World: The Law of Nations in an Age of Revolutions, 1776–1814* (Madison, Wis.: Madison House, 1993); Daniel Deudney, "Binding Sovereigns: Authorities, Structures, and Geopolitics in Philadelphian Systems," in Biersteker and Weber, *State Sovereignty as Social Construct*, 190–239; Deudney, "The Philadelphian System: Sovereignty, Arms Control and Balance of Power in the American States-Union, circa 1787–1861, *International Organization* 49 (spring 1995): 191–228; David C. Hendrickson, *Peace Pact: The Lost World of the American Founding* (Lawrence: University Press of Kansas, 2003).

INDEX

ABOUT THE CONTRIBUTORS

Jack P. Greene is the Andrew W. Mellon Professor in the Humanities at The Johns Hopkins University. His many publications include *Understanding the American Revolution: Issues and Actors*; *Imperatives, Behaviors, and Identities: Essays in Early American Cultural History*; *Intellectual Construction of America: Exceptionalism and Identity from 1492 to 1800*; and *Peripheries and Center: Constitutional Development in the Extended Polities of the British Empire and the United States, 1607–1788*.

Michael A. Morrison is associate professor of history at Purdue University. He is the author of *Slavery and the American West: The Eclipse of Manifest Destiny and the Coming of the Civil War*. He is editor of *The Human Tradition in Antebellum America* and coeditor (with James Brewer Stewart) of *Race and the Early Republic*. Morrison is also coeditor of the *Journal of the Early Republic*.

John M. Murrin is professor of history at Princeton University and coauthor of *Essays on Liberty and Federalism: The Shaping of U.S. Constitution* and editor of the thirty-four-volume *Outstanding Studies in Early American History*.

Peter S. Onuf is the Thomas Jefferson Memorial Foundation Professor of History at the University of Virginia. His publications include *Statehood and Union: A History of the Northwest Ordinance*; *Jefferson's Empire: The Language of American Nationhood*; and, with Nicholas Onuf, *Federal Union, Modern World: The Law of Nations in the Age of Revolutions, 1776–1814*. He is editor of *Jeffersonian Legacies*.

Lois G. Schwoerer is the Elmer Kayser Professor of History at George Washington University and the author of *"No Standing Armies!" The Anti-standing Army Ideology in Seventeenth-Century England*; *The Declaration of Rights, 1689*; and *Lady Rachel Russell, "One of the Best Women"* and editor of *The Revolution of 1688–90: Changing Perspectives*.

William H. Sewell Jr. is the Max Palevsky Professor of Political Science at the University of Chicago and author of numerous publications, including *Work and Revolution in France: The Language of Labor from the Old Regime to 1848*; *Structure and Mobility: The Men and Women in Marseilles, 1820–1870*; and *A Rhetoric of Bourgeois Revolution: The Abbé Sieyès and What Is the Third Estate?*

Eric Van Young is professor of history at the University of California at San Diego and is affiliated with the Center for U.S.–Mexican Studies. He wrote *Hacienda and the Market in Eighteenth-Century Mexico: The Rural Economy of the Guadalajara Region, 1675–1820*.

Melinda Zook is associate professor of history at Purdue University and author of *Radical Whigs and Conspiratorial Politics in Late Stuart England*.